Cuts and Bruises

Personal Terms 3

FREDERIC RAPHAEL was born in Chicago in 1931 and educated at Charterhouse and St John's College, Cambridge. His novels include *The Glittering Prizes* (1976) and *Coast to Coast* (1998); he has also written short stories and biographies of Somerset Maugham and Byron. Frederic Raphael is a leading screenwriter, whose work includes the Academy Award-winning *Darling* (1965) and *Two For the Road* (1967), and the screenplay for Stanley Kubrik's last film, *Eyes Wide Shut* (2000). The first volume of *Personal Terms* was published by Carcanet in 2001 and the second, *Rough Copy*, in 2004.

D1593915

Also by Frederic Raphael from Carcanet

Frederic Raphael

Cuts and Bruises

Personal Terms 3

CARCANET

First published in Great Britain in 2006 by
Carcanet Press Limited
Alliance House
Cross Street
Manchester M2 7AQ

A CIP catalogue record for this book is available from the British Library
ISBN 1 85754 708 X
978 1 85754 708 5

The publisher acknowledges financial assistance from Arts Council England

Set in Monotype Bembo by XL Publishing Services, Tiverton
Printed and bound in England by SRP Ltd, Exeter

For Beetle

Contents

Introduction

A friend of mine at Cambridge, a pioneer of computer technology, claimed to have begun his PhD thesis with 'As I have said before'. Since this is the third volume of my notebooks, it may sound more hollow than convincing to say again that I never intended to publish them. It is, however, still true. Notebooks are like a huge shadow which lengthens as you go forward, but remains invisible until you look back.

All but one or two of my *cahiers* are written in the spiral-bound squared exercise books of the kind used by French students. They have accumulated, as if written by some stealthy third hand, into a self-generated dossier of my life as a writer. I might have been spying on myself. The disjunctive paragraphs supply a join–up–the–dots portrait of the writer among others. If I am unsparing of those whom I describe, I have been hardly less harsh on F.R.

Since my purpose was to catch and pin ideas and images which might be useful later, I did not strive to be a phrase-maker, still less an entertainer, even of myself. Yet, since they are written in pen, these notes have more of a physical connection with their author than whatever I have typed or, more recently, entered on a word-processor, which is, nevertheless, the compulsive reviser's and rewriter's invention of choice. Holding a pen makes manuscript more like drawing than does the use of mechanical means. You declare yourself more revealingly in handwriting.

Only one criticism of the last volume, *Rough Copy*, stung me when I glanced at it. A reviewer about whose fiction I was less than complimentary some forty years ago, had bided his time, it seemed, to accuse me of 'name-dropping'. In truth, the company of the famous has small appeal for me; and that of the titled or the rich none at all. I remember an occasion when I was in George Steiner's house in Cambridge and he invited me, at short notice, to stay for dinner. Arthur Koestler was coming, as well as 'two Nobels'. Presumably some classy person had failed the Steiners' feast, and disrupted their seating plan, at the last moment. I was, Steiner reminded me, being given the chance to meet 'a *living legend*' (much of Steiner's speech is cursively emphatic): Koestler was on more blacklists than anyone alive. He *dared not* return to (still Communist) Hungary, although *frequently solicited*. The Russians had *never forgiven him* for *Darkness At Noon*.★ I was indeed tempted, but I had promised my wife that I would be home for dinner. I declined to be impressed. 'You are *uxorious*, sir,' George said.

Oh, is it name-dropping to call Steiner George? Or to say that one has been in his house? Come on! Since I am now over seventy years old and will, next year, have been publishing books, writing articles, essays, scripts and plays, for half a century, must I really apologise for having met a number of people whose names are, or have become, widely known? That I include notes about some of them, and have been friendly with a few, hardly turns me into Chips Channon, Cecil Beaton or Alan Clark.

I have, for most of the time, abided by Willie Maugham's advice: if you have to choose between the company of a prominent politician and that of a suburban vet, the chances are that the latter will be more unguarded, and tell you spicier stories, than a cabinet minister.

These notebooks are evidence less of self-importance or social climbing (I have no head for those heights) than of long and emulous addiction to the *Carnets* or *Cahiers* in which French writers, of many persuasions and styles, have encapsulated their private views of life. Logan Pearsall Smith is one of the few English authors who have done the same; and he was a trans-cultural American. Cyril Connolly, who was briefly Pearsall Smith's secretary, did something similar, but more showy (and delicious) in *The Unquiet Grave*, his masterpiece. The quality of a writer is measured more by the attention he gives to his work than by whether or not he 'really means or really feels' what he says: sincerity is not an art-form.

Those who write *cahiers* need by no means be at the centre of things. My most recent purchase in the genre is of the work of Joseph Joubert, who began writing in the last decade of the *ancien régime*.

★ Not a Koestler scholar, I wonder whether it is often remarked that Rubashov, the Old Bolshevik 'hero' of Koestler's novel, bears a Jewish name. It is a mark of Koestler's artfulness that the Inquisitors never (so far as I can remember) taunt Rubashov for being a *zhid*. However brave A.K.'s denunciation of Stalinist paranoia, the fact that Rubashov is neither taunted as a Jew nor physically tortured, as so often happened in fact, suggests that even Koestler could not quite bear to see Soviet Russia for the fascisto-gangster régime it was.

Born in 1754, he lived through the Terror, the Consulate, the Empire and the Restoration of the Bourbons, without much altering his tone of '*innocence mélancholique*' or, it seems, his style of life: his passport of 1822 notes, as a distinguishing mark, that he wore a *perruque* (and that he was more than six feet tall, a useful height for an over-viewer). During all this time, he rarely commented directly on current history, though in 1804 he did allow himself to say of Napoleon, '*Il a tué le duc d'Enghien, mais le duc d'Enghien a tué sa gloire.*' Napoleon had killed the Duke d'Enghien, but the duke had killed Bonaparte's good name. This is neater than Talleyrand's famous 'Pire qu'un crime...'

Provincial *philosophe* and classical scholar, Joubert described himself as '*Platone platonior*': one who out-Platoed Plato. He sustained his succinct prolificity through no less than 205 *cahiers* as well as in many pages of unbound observations. If he was never in the first rank, Sainte-Beuve's *Portrait littéraire* says of him that his work crowned the series of French aphorists which began with La Rochefoucauld, continued with Pascal, La Bruyère, Vauvenargues '*et qui se rejoint, par cent détours, à Montaigne*'.

More recently, Maurice Blanchot pointed out that Joubert did not, like the others, specialise in *bons mots*. Typical of Joubert's austerity is his remark of July 1797: '*La Bible est aux religions ce que l'Iliade est à la poésie*' (The Bible is to religions what the Iliad is to poetry). It is not an *aperçu* of rare quality, but then we get: '... *et [les gens] puisent dans ce livre une sagesse qui n'y est pas*' (and people read into this book a wisdom which is not there). The dry ambiguity matches that of Gibbon's footnote about Apollonius of Tyana: 'Apollonius... was born at about the same times as Jesus Christ. His life (that of the former) is related in so fabulous a manner... that we are at a loss to discover whether he was a sage, an impostor, or a fanatic.'

Joubert's own literary creed was advertised in a programmatic entry of the previous day: '*Ne pas: — définir ce qui est connu: un bavardage. Mettre en question ce qui est en fait: mauvaise foi, ignorance. Rendre abstrait ce qui est palpable: charlatanisme. Et offrir des difficultés qui ne s'offrent pas elles-mêmes ou n'ont qu'une vaine apparence: chicane.*' Which, being translated, comes to: Dont's: define what is already known: windbaggery. Put in question what is actually the case: bad faith, ignorance. Render abstract what is palpable: charlatanry. Create difficulties which are not really there, or have nothing but the empty appearance of problems: quibbling (with a hint of chic perhaps). The list just about covers the sins of the showboating intellectual down the ages, never so keenly paraded as virtues as in today's academic hermeneutics.

As a *philosophe* (and youthful *protégé* of Diderot), Joubert was as keen a reader of Locke and Berkeley as of Descartes, about whose scepticism he was, to say the least, sceptical. Noting that Locke observes 'Maxims do not enlighten', Joubert adds that they may not, but that they guide and direct: '*Elles sauvent aveuglement. C'est le fil dans le labyrinthe, la boussole pendant la nuit*' (They save blindly: the thread in the labyrinth, the compass at night).

Joubert's irony often goes no further than an accurate record of casual remarks. For instance: '*Le mot de Mme de Genlis: "Aux yeux de la religion, il n'y a point de mariages mal assortis"*' (A remark of Mme de Genlis: In the eyes of religion, there is no such thing as unsuitable – or ill-suited – marriages). Does this hint that Joubert was happily or unhappily matched? Or that Mme de Genlis 'believed in' marriage or that she was a libertine wit? The remark stands free; you may make of it what you will, and welcome. In this, Joubert is wittier, and more varied, than E.M. Cioran, a voluble modern epigrammatist who has his glum elegance, but is so resolutely and invariably disillusioned as to smack of smugness.

I have dwelt on Joubert because he is a recent discovery of mine (in an excellent bookshop in Bergerac). I am delighted by his occasional company, but would I have liked him personally? Would he have liked me? What does it matter? An artist's style need in no way match the man himself; a disshevelled, ill-dressed scribbler may be a meticulous grammarian and an obsessive corrector of trifling infelicities. Horace described himself as *Epicuri de grege porcus* (a pig from Epicurus' herd), but his verses were never swinish.

One can perfectly well admire a man's work and detest him personally. Certainly one can think little of someone's work and yet regard him, or her, with affection or even with love. As I edited these pages, I was sometimes shocked, and surprised, by the rigour with which I commented on, for instance, Michael Ayrton, whose company and much of whose work I relished. Yet Michael struck me as he struck me, and there it is, undeniable, on paper. Why should I suppress it, and in whose interest? I still miss Michael and shall never, I hope, forget the day in the Périgord when he and Sarah Raphael, aged fifteen, and I sat side by side sketching the local town, Belvès. Contrary, and surprising, feelings are part of what we are. It is false tact not to acknowledge them.

People may take these *cahiers* as they wish, but in my own view there is no malice in them: nothing is perverted or misrepresented in order to wound. As before, I cannot deny that I have sometimes trimmed, and occasionally – for courtesy's sake – tamed or omitted my raw material. I have tried to keep personal and ephemeral matters in the background: I am not and never wanted to be a diarist. However, since my wife and our children are at the heart of my life, it would be more pretentious than discreet to relegate them to insignificance.

I will, for form's sake, apologise to any who are offended or incensed, but – in the reported words of Pontius Pilate – '*Ho gegrapha, gegrapha*': what I have written, I have written.

I leave Joubert to supply the last *mot*: '*Ecrire, écrire! C'est un talent, c'est un métier et c'est un art. L'exercice en apprend le métier, le goût en fait deviner l'art*' (Scribble, scribble! It's a talent, it's a skill and it's an art. By its exercise the skill is learned; taste gives a clue to its art).

FREDERIC RAPHAEL
2006

1974

Feb. 74. Ralph's in Beverly Hills. A female a little older than a girl, wearing beltless, faded jeans so low on her hipless hips that you saw the crease of her ass and, when she turned, the shadow of her groin; her face veiled by the usual sunglasses, seemingly marooned in a narcissistic nightmare, she drifted up to me and asked, did I know where she would find blue cheese. I looked and there it was. She turned her flat behind and helped herself, as if inviting me to do the same. But her problem was not solved: she wanted *crumbled* blue cheese. Did she want it for a dressing? Right, she told the guy, but she had to be sure it was 'pure'. Had she been dogged previously by impure blue cheese?

The Malibu beach house. A wooden box on a stage of railroad sleepers. You look out of the living room window onto the ocean. Sandpipers race the waves, scampering to avoid wet ankles, then chasing the receding wet for food.

I went with Stanley Donen to a 'bagel-ah'. We had hot Chicago pastrami sandwiches. A young guy runs the place: dark eyes, pageboy haircut, confident grin. 'Where's your friend?' he asked Stanley. 'In London.' 'Yvette go with him?' His wife is more famous along the coast than Stanley is these days.

It was the same with the tennis coach, Forrest Stewart: 'Oh sure,' he said, 'I know Yvette.' He has longish greying hair and his young eyes look at you with venal caution. He charges $20 an hour. The first afternoon he had a canvas harness on his elbow, with straps to keep the arm crooked. It gave the impression that he was playing in pain and needed the money. He recently had a hernia operation and is trying to get back into shape. He played in a tournament on the weekend: four matches in one afternoon. Presumably he got to the final. It was an over-35 event, so despite his skill, he must be a failure. He hits the lines with enviable regularity.

Bill Ballance. We listen to Billo's radio show as we drive to the beach. People call in with stories of their personal grievances, often about ungrateful bosses or cheating spouses. When they tell him a good one, he says, 'You can't beat that with a stick.'

He called one boss about the raise his employee was too frightened to ask for. The boss said, 'Is that Raymond you're talking about?' 'Raymond, that's right. He says you owe him.' 'You tell that cheap bastard he's fired. Tell him not to come in tomorrow.' Raymond interrupted, 'It's OK. It's OK.' 'Forget it,' the boss said, 'far as I'm concerned you're through.' Raymond was devastated. 'Way it goes sometimes,' Billo said.

K. dropped in casually to see Stanley. They were chatting when suddenly he said, 'Of course you know I'm impotent.'

'How do you want your whisky, Ken? Ice?'

She had been in analysis for six years. Her abiding problem was that she could not choose between two men. During one session, she burst out, saying that her analyst knew her better than she knew herself; he must help her decide. He said it was absolutely forbidden by his professional code that he do anything like that. She told him he was a coward and a hypocrite and a moral eunuch and she had no further use for him; she was terminating her analysis forthwith and she would never come back. Five days later she received a letter from him. Since he was no longer her psychiatrist, he was absolved from professional reticence. He could not help her to choose between the two men in her life because he was in love with her himself and had been for five years. He left his wife and children and went to live with her. His wife committed suicide and he then married his ex-patient. He was barred from practising in New York, so they moved out of town.

I wrote a short story called *He'll See You Now* after hearing this (true) story. In 1984, I directed Susan Sarandon in a TV version of it, in the BBC series *Oxbridge Blues*. Susan did it for pennies and won a Best Actress award.

Billy Wilder. He was in Dominick's when we dined there on Tuesday, a thick man with a large greying head, but still snappy enough with a comeback to be tough to pass at the net. Stanley told

us that Billy wanted to make a movie about a Russian scientist who
defects to the West. His wife and child are arrested and tortured.
Then he goes back, because that was exactly what he wanted to
have happen.

Wilder said of 'the Hollywood Ten', the 'unfriendly witnesses'
arraigned by Joe McCarthy, 'Only two of them are talented; the rest
are just unfriendly.'

Stanley told me that he was very frightened at the time of the hear-
ings. People were being blacklisted on a points system, so many for
having contributed to the Abraham Lincoln brigade, so many for
belonging to the Russo-American Friendship society, and so on.
Stanley had 'points in all directions': he had contributed to everything. He escaped because, at the time, he was too unimportant to
be worth sacrificing: 'too skinny for the sharks, and anyway, they
had enough directors.'

I asked if the town was full of ghosts for him.

'No. Truth is, I don't really care about anybody. Not anybody.'
He said it with sly bravado, as if it were a sexual confession. He
added quickly, 'Well, not many people. I care about you. I feel as
if we're really friends, even if we don't see each other very often.'

Stanley has bought a very big property on Stone Canyon, in Bel
Air. The house resembles a wing of a disused airport terminal. You
approach up a sweeping, swept drive, under a huge sycamore; the
wide verge is veiled with ivy. A circular plateau in front of the house
had so many cars parked there that I thought at first that the place
was an apartment building. They belonged to the staff: secretary,
maid, Hickey the chauffeur (who left his wife to come with Stanley
from London), and who all else.

Yvette was writing a script for ABC TV in longhand on a yellow
legal pad in the vastness of the living room. Through wide glass walls
you could see a kidney-shaped pool in the windless patio. Stanley
says he bought the house only because they couldn't put in a tennis
court at Oak Pass, Yvette's house, which we have rented for $1,500
a month. Near where Yvette was working was a model of the new
version of the house. Paramount's design and construction department is charged with the operation.

Stanley also bought the house because, had he not done so, he
would have had to pay a fat slice of tax on the £285,000 he got for
his house in Montpellier Square. Unless he spent the same amount

on a 'primary residence', Uncle Sam would grab it. When he got to Beverly Hills, he found there was a property slump, as a result of the recession. He was shown one house after another by the realtor (Mrs Music, whose boards are all around town). She was delighted to have a customer at all and kept telling him what a bargain he would be getting. Finally, he said, 'Excuse me, but don't you have anything that's overpriced?'

He is going to be fifty in a couple of months and likes to think that he wants to retire. He no longer longs to make movies, but he needs, or likes, to make money. He is surrounding Yvette with a soft prison; he shackles her with generosity. He has her sit on his lap at dinner parties, the envy of staider couples. Plump with happiness, a little pot of pride spills over the top of his diet. Yet his eyes foresee the tragedy which he cannot help imagining, and for which he is building the sets. They never did put in a tennis court.

The fog comes in off the ocean at Malibu, rolling up the sunshine like an old yellow carpet.

Tennis at Carter de Haven's house. A Mexican gardener carries one treelet after another across the terrace. Carter is neat and bearded and has two lessons a week from Forrest Stewart. The latter's life had been ruined by the ponies. He kept the ladies happy around Beverly Hills by telling them how much their game has improved.

In the middle of the tennis game, Carter becomes agitated. 'Excuse me, I see something that disturbs me.' The Philippino houseboy is cleaning the windows with soap and water. Carter signals to him (he is upstairs, inside) and calls, 'Hot water only.' The glass has been specially treated; soap destroys the finish.

The conversation afterwards, with Irwin Winkler, is about grosses. *Zardos* has opened big, but will it hold? By way of courtesy, Carter asks me how *April, June and November* is doing. 'My books don't sell,' I say. 'They're just good.' He greets this with the uncomfortable smile of an atheist confronted by faith.

On the beach. The loud, broadcasting voice of a rather handsome girl, face without make-up, who came and sat on the step of sand marking the limit of where the tractors sweep the foreshore. She was joined by a man in his thirties, dark with deep-set eyes and the kind of beard too blue for television. 'My life has been on the downside for the last six months,' he said, 'and now I think I'm due for the upside. What do you think?'

'Questionable.'

He did not speak again. She thrust her white, unshaven legs in front of her and her monotonous voice told him how she could join the artistic community in San Francisco as easy as anything, only he had introduced a new factor in her life. He looked at her with apprehensive lordliness as if he had taken delivery of something that carried an altogether too heavy tax.

Ray Stark can no longer get the stars to come to the parties in the house he shares with his hated wife, Fran. She is lacquered from the shoulders up and doesn't sway in the strongest winds. I was asked to play tennis at his house. 'It's worth it just to walk through the garden. He has over three million dollars' worth of sculpture in the place.'

'I consider myself a pretty hip guy,' Stark once said to me, in a suite at the Dorchester, when he was trying to get me to write a piece for Miss Streisand ('She's a number one cunt'). He was wearing a yellow sweatshirt and car-salesman's pants. His parties are all black tie affairs. Barbra would come only if he sent a car for her.

The cars drive slowly. One evening there was a squeal of tires and a crash across the valley. Everyone is very polite. They wish you good day. On the morning of our third day a man was found beaten to death a couple of miles away.

Pauline Stone, who was married to Larry Harvey, was at dinner at Carter and Bobbie de Havens'. She has red hair and beautiful green eyes and wears widowed make-up: her grief is a cosmetic which adds interest to her face. She is here to dispose of the contents of Larry's house on Coldwater Canyon. It is priced at $600,000, and has only one bedroom; a high price without Larry in the bed.

Dinner was Chinese, the usual with fried noodles. I helped myself modestly, leaving room for the next course. It was ice cream and then it was coffee time. Bobbie told me that she was most turned on by diamonds. She once had a dealer show her his stock. He opened a flat case and there was a million dollars' worth of stones. Her dark eyes sparkled like zircons as she confessed her rapture. She no longer owns the diamonds she bought: 'Too dangerous.'

Before dinner, Carter's daughter Melinda came in to say hullo. A man had come up to her in the parking lot of a supermarket and 'flashed', right there in broad daylight. 'Yes, I've got one,' he said. She said, 'You won't have if I kick it.' Then she realised that she was being filmed at the same time. As she went out, she promised to be home 'before curfew'. 'Good girl.'

R.G. asked Robin Straw's wife Patty how things went on vacation with her neighbour, songwriter Tommy W., and made it clear what kind of things he meant. She said, 'I don't know what you mean.'

R.G. said, 'Oh come on, darling!'

She assured him that she and Tommy went on long walks together and admired the stars. 'It was purely Platonic.'

R.G. then saw that Tommy had his hand under Patty's skirt and she her hand inside his fly. Which Plato was she thinking of?

Sinatra can fix anything; it is his supreme luxury. Natalie had a make-up man in New York whom she wanted to come and work on the Coast. The California union never allows New York to work out here. She tried everything, and then Sinatra. The make-up man was given an address and an appointment. He was confronted by a well-known Chicago gangster who gave him to understand that this was a one-off concession. He became the only New York make-up man to work on the West Coast, once.

John Schlesinger has a ten-foot-square Japanese bed. His bedroom looks onto the pool where a troop of young men are constantly on parade. 'I call them my puppies, dear,' he told Jimmy Clark.

'What're you going to do? Are you going to stay here?'

He looked very alarmed. His lover, Michael, is a Californian photographer, and an ambitious one. If John goes back to England, how will he keep Michael? John is not faithful to his love: who knows how many of his puppies have been in his basket? Jim thinks he is in great danger: the young men are as vicious as they are handsome. When Ramon Navarro was murdered by a collection of charmers, he was tortured for twenty-four hours first, and castrated, before they finally allowed him to die. They were never caught.

Robert Cohen, at Mo-Town, told us he was at a Beverly Hills party for *Sunday Bloody Sunday*, when 'a guy came up to Schlesinger and said, "That was a film made by a Jew faggot about a Jew faggot and the only people who're going to go see it are other Jew faggots." John turned his back'. Figures.

Lunch at the Brown Derby with Stanley's lawyer, Harold Berkowitz. 'I'm an old, old admirer of yours,' he said to me.

Stanley said, 'I knew about the old, old part.'

A friend of H.B.'s, another lawyer, went to Europe on a 'much-needed' holiday. He no sooner arrived than he had a call in the middle of the night. His second daughter, a student at UCLA had been murdered, 'right here in Beverly Hills, beautiful girl, twenty years old'.

Ray Carpenter. He came to Carter's house to make up a four. Irwin Winkler had shaved his beard, and his smile, and was jet-lagged, but he and Carter took the first set 6–0. Carpenter wore a light-blue tracksuit and played with a metal racket that needed tuning. He was very disagreeable, with the face of a Disney fox, eyes narrowed with calculation, mouth half-open for anything tasty. I won whatever points he did not throw away. He woke up when Carter made a $5 side bet on the second set, and gave us two games lead. We won 6–1.

When Irwin dropped out with a bad ankle, 'Chip' – Carter's twelve-year-old son – came in. Carpenter took him as partner and the bets were replaced. The kid played well and his father went to pieces. They beat us in the first set and lost the second, which Carpenter did not want to play, 7–5. He treated the boy with amiable gruffness, calling him 'Chipper', but grew testy.

Over a Martini, he reminisced about 'the old Beverly Wilshire, where we used to play eight and nine sets a day'. He played with Gonzales and Segura, 'all those people. There was everything: tennis, sex, laughs.' He played a lot with an actor called Mark Stevens. 'Know what he's doing now? He's bought a place in Mallorca and he's teaching tennis. That guy teaching tennis!'

'You know something,' Carter said, 'he's probably happy.'

'He may be, but I'll tell you something: you think I've got bad strokes, you shoulda seen his.'

Stevens was something of a star during the war. 'He was 4-F and just about the only guy under thirty in the place who wasn't a fag. He was a nut, used to walk around Beverly Hills with a German shepherd and a big club. Said he never knew when he might be attacked. Guy ruined his chances by insulting one studio head after the other. "You Jewish cocksucker," he used to shout at them until finally every gate was shut against him.'

Peter Guber at Columbia. About thirty, he has the big office and the two secretaries. As soon as he promised to speak frankly you knew you couldn't trust a word he said. He sat very energetically, constantly altering his posture to emphasise the dexterity of his enthusiasm as he told the beads of his latest purchases. He had paid $200,000 for this book and $300,000 for that. He chided Mardigian – only kidding! – for never sending him any properties.

I said, 'Have you ever consulted your files and checked on all the books your predecessors spent two and three hundred thousand dollars buying?'

He never had, and he was not about to pay much for the suggestion.

David Begelman wandered in during the meeting. I remember him a genial man, plumply available, who was going to do great things for me if I joined CMA. Now he is head of Columbia, but – having recently been in hospital – he looks like a sick prospector, determinedly returning to the scene of the mine. He has been ordered 'complete rest'. There is, it seems, nothing incompatible between that and running the studio. Begelman looks as if he had less lost weight than been robbed of it.

In conversation with my agent, I described Peter Guber, who never sat still, as 'The Electric Jew'. Not long afterwards I was phoned by a New York publisher who wanted to commission a novel with that title. 'Great title.' A fat deal was made for the book and a movie tie-in, but I could never write a word of it. I gave back the advance. My agent said, 'Tell them you did a lot of work on it. You don't have to give it *all* back.' But I did.

Yvette is like one of those easy quotations one keeps forgetting. What *exactly* does she look like? Slim, blonde, light on her feet, she is humble, soft-spoken (in the style of Audrey H.) and constantly smiling. One can enumerate her qualities, as one paraphrases the elusive line, but she still escapes exact definition. Elusiveness is crucial to her style. She does nothing out of the ordinary but her modesty seems too perfectly modulated not to be covering something less harmonious. The house in Oak Pass which she has rented us has the same stringent propriety; it was too perfect, a dream with no subconscious stuffing.

S.D. is reticent about *The Little Prince*, which was recently re-edited. He seems to have quarrelled with all the available personnel, including Lerner of Lerner and Loew, who did not conceal their disappointment with the semi-final result.

S.D.'s Fox picture (*Lucky Lady*) seems likely to go ahead. Warren called when I was with S. down at the Malibu beach-house, next to the Jiffy station where, by the end of February, you were no longer served in a jiffy, or any other way.

'Warren, tell me the truth now, Warren, what do you think?'

I absented myself and walked round the house to where Yvette was reading a Corgi of *The Limits of Love*, which she had bought from John Sandoe in Chelsea. She praised it with such exact enthusiasm that I might have been a potential enemy she was keen to disarm. She is, one feels, a mistress of calculated spontaneity: her advertised desire for S. may be more to do with honouring a deal than with true passion. The publicity of their embraces seems to be his greatest satisfaction. Bob Shapiro says that they 'neck like teenagers' at Hollywood parties. A cynic may wonder if Yvette is adhering loyally to a scenario rather than gratifying an urgent impulse. *A l'époque*, every young actress had to play the nun's part, at least once. Yvette's devotion is hardly devout, but it has the decided docility of the convert.

I picked up the telephone and had composed the first four digits of John's Hollywood Hills number when I thought, 'Why the hell should I want to speak to Schlesinger?'

Stanley says he is fond of me. It's nice of him. Even if he is pulling the wool over my eyes, I have the consolation of knowing that it's the finest cashmere.

On the last day of our stay, Beetle, Stee and I were asked to the beach-house to eat a pot of chili Yvette had cooked. We hesitated, with one-fifth of a tank of gas in the Mercury, but we went. Stanley was on the sandy patch next to the porch and a swimsuited girl was face-down beside him. Her hair was browner than I remembered Yvette's, but hair-colours change like stoplights. The slim body, more athletic than some, could have been Yvette's, but it actually belonged to Yvette's friend Julie Anthony, who reached the quarter finals at Wimbledon last year. She had strong legs and small breasts and greeted us with the keen caution of a celebrity's receptionist. She is 'in school', taking a PhD in psychology at UCLA.

At half past noon, S. offered the chili. Yvette was at the hair-dressers' and running late: she had called, there had been some mess-up about appointments. The newest excuse for unscheduled absence is the energy crisis. Stephen Spielberg was supposed to be there, but maybe he had a hairdresser too. He had told Stanley he had seen *Two for the Road* eight times. S. served the chili, with assistance from Hickey, while Julie Anthony, the good sport, cooked Stee a hamburger. Stanley worried about Yvette.

She arrived in a halo of curls. They did the big kiss. She was *so* sorry, everybody; had they messed her around or what? She put herself out so charmingly for Stee that one only just failed to be charmed. She ran, with a pretty display of her slim hips and rounded rump, down to the sea with him and, with an amazing show of heedlessness, spent her whole hair-do in the first available waves. Failing to notice the implausibility of her action, I needed B.'s later prompting before I could see it as both silly and sinister. Stanley, it seemed, was quicker: the afternoon was charged with unexpressed dismay. What woman spends all morning at the hairdresser, arrives with her hair newly combed (B. says it could all have been done in ten minutes) and goes straight into the sea? Yvette has had many men and no doubt they have been 'generous' as she is to her family ('The generosity of that girl you just would not believe,' Stanley told us).

Harvey Orkin told how old Joe Schenk used to go up to attractive girls and say, 'Here's the deal, if you want to be my girl: a thousand a week, chequing account, etc. Whaddaya say?' Warren is more economical: 'I'm Warren Beatty, the movie star. How would you like to get laid by a movie star? It won't take long.'

Yvette's feelings for Stanley are not incompatible with prudent consideration. In California, women who like money are not in the least disreputable: they are a comfort to those who have only money to offer. To be accessible for money is a kind of generosity: to deny a man because you will not have him except for nothing (a love match indeed) is to remind the ugly of their ugliness and the old of their age.

There are hotels on Sunset where you can hire a waterbed in a mirror-lined room, with closed-circuit porno, for less money, and fewer questions asked, than for an hour's tennis. Prostitution is just another personal service, like murder.

The conviction of Charles Manson, the very fact of his capture, should enable householders to sleep easier, but if Manson is behind bars, his spirit cannot be caged: the most amiable kid could feel like killing you; and what you feel like doing, man, that's your trip, right?

To be surprised is to be *passé*. Stanley can enjoy his suspicions (whatever turns you on), but cannot be seen to *suffer* from them: that would be to break the pact of superficiality to which 'the community' demands allegiance.

Sandy Shapiro (to Bobbie de Haven): 'Beverly Hills is so tacky.' '*Tacky*?' 'It's so tacky.' 'Beverly *Hills*?' 'I think so.'

'How did you like Disneyland? Isn't it wonderful?' We went on a windy morning. The Anaheim streets were out of focus with dust. 'It's the cleanest city you've ever seen,' Bob Shapiro said. It is a bogus town and the wind dispersed its charm. It panders to every vapid fantasy that vapid people will buy in commercially viable numbers. The management's lack of imagination chimes perfectly with its customers'. The 'fun-loving' pirates are watched 'sacking a town' and those who gaze at so harmless a charade see no analogy with Vietnam and Uncle Sam's fun-loving soldiery. To criticise this innocence in solemn terms is to use the methods of the (old) New Criticism to analyse the jingles on a birthday card. Disneyland is the projection of the asexual, pre-Freudian childhood in which old Walt dreamed of lodging the world, and did: he literally cleaned up.

The spotlessness of Disneyland emphasises the dirt it eliminates. It is the triumph of the mechanical and the fraudulent. The Haunted House fails to work as a scary spectacle because it cannot be allowed to remind us of anything genuinely frightening. Ambiguity is forbidden; and a shadow that is not ambiguous cannot give you the chills. The violence works because it is part of the childish mind: war is modern man's second childhood, in which heroin, not candy, keeps you going. Disneyland is a cat-house for juvenile desires.

The Vietnam war reflects the California ethos: the rich man wins and the poor man yields way. 'Why don't the Vietnamese love us?' really means, 'Why don't they bow to wealth the way we do? Why can't they understand how much money we're throwing at them when we bomb the shit out of them?'

Alan Pakula. The russet beard supplies a leonine appearance. You're not sure whether it's because he is a lion or because he's a leper.

5.4.74. In Belize. The first we heard of Karl was in the dining room, when he said loudly, 'If they ever need to give the world an enema, this is where they'll put the tube in.' Karl had blundered into marine survey (he wore a badge with K.R. MARINE SURVEYOR on it) after service in the Royal Canadian Navy. No salvage expert claims to be one. He is employed by a company in NYC. He never sees his boss and does not even know what his salary is; he lives on his expenses and his wife takes care of the rest. He is consciously Jewish and would conform to the stereotype of a Jewish marine surveyor, if such a thing existed (he greeted me as '*Landsman!*'). He is dapper (the upsweep of his moustache maintained by wax specially ordered from France) and, he says, a dedicated coward. He tries to think of, and prevent, the smallest conceivable danger. He is devoted to his wife and children, but above all to his mother.

He and she had a hard time during the war. They lived in a Ukrainian district of Vancouver, BC. Karl was an only child and his father was overseas for five years. The Ukrainians were vigorously anti-Semitic. 'That was when I learnt to handle myself, and that meant staying alive.' Their landlord wanted to evict them (to get a higher rent from a defence worker), but it was illegal to get rid of servicemen's families. He gave them a hard time instead.

Karl's father was a mild man; Karl never heard him raise his voice. When he came home from the war he kissed R.'s mother and then he threw the landlord through a plate-glass window and then he went and changed his clothes and took a bath.

Karl's mother is now a widow. He telephones her once a week: 'I get a hook-up wherever I am, Brazil, New Guinea wherever.' The Canadian at the next table in the restaurant at the Fort St George Hotel called over that he had been to New Guinea. Karl capped all his stories. He told how one time he had been going down a river in a canoe and remarked on the thickness and strength of a liana hanging from a tree they were about to pass under. 'Liana?' said the boatman. 'We don't have lianas.' The man then pulled an elephant gun from under the thwarts and fired. The 'liana' was an anaconda. 'I've seen them twenty-five feet long,' the other Canadian said. 'This one was thirty,' Karl said. 'At least.' The recoil of the elephant gun pushed the canoe twenty feet back upstream.

While he was in New Guinea, Karl treated a native woman's child for a septic ulcer ('He had a hole this big in his leg'). Penicillin was more effective than balls of spiders' webs mixed with mud. The woman gave Karl the amulet which he showed us he was wearing on his wrist. At first he had thought it was a copper bangle. When he got home, he discovered it was 22 carat gold. 'My wife said, "Your arm is worth more than the rest of your body put together." She ought to know.'

At home, he works out every morning with the Early Birds Club from his local temple. Then he swims two miles. Sometimes he doesn't have time to go home at all between jobs; his wife meets him at the airport with a change of clothes and a packet of sandwiches.

He investigates all kinds of losses. One client was being robbed of tons of grain, although there was never any sign of a door or window being forced. Karl found an old map which showed that a disused sewer ran below the building. The thieves had driven upwards through the floor and piped the grain out, through the sewer, into tanker trucks parked several blocks away.

On another case, shipping containers were being robbed even though their seals remained unbroken. Karl asked to go to the plant where they were being manufactured. He realised that some of them were made with special hinges which allowed the doors to be opened the wrong way, using the sealed side as the hinge.

He makes enemies. A longshoreman once asked him what he was going to do about a racket he had uncovered. Karl said, 'If you're stupid enough to ask, you're too stupid to be told.' The man pulled a gun. R. swiped him with a steel bar that happened to be handy. The man lives in an iron lung; it's not easy to shift cargo with a broken back.

The hands that were working for him on the reef where his present problem had been wrecked have gone to the local 'cat-house'. Karl left them to it: 'Me, I figure if you can have *filet mignon* at home, why mess with bought hamburger?'

The skipper of the current wreck won his affection by saying, 'Before we talk, let's have a drink.' His crew were in a bad state until, and even after, the lifeboat arrived. They wanted to get the hell off the ship, which was holed and balanced on the reef. They made a commotion when the lifeboat stood off. Two of the lifeboat crew dived into the terrifying seas and swam to the reefed steamer. 'Got any cigarettes?' they called. The ship's crew was pacified by this act of leisurely cadging; they figured the sea couldn't be that dangerous.

The wreck took place because someone had gone out to the reef and stolen the now valuable mercury on which the marine light floated. Such a thing never happened even during the war when there was an unspoken agreement between the allied and German ships' captains not to interfere with marine lights.

Karl had been in Biafra helping to clear the river at Port Harcourt. There were so many cadavers in the water that it was bright red.

An ichthyologist and Karl were to go down to examine the obsta-
cles. Karl was over the side when the other man flipped him back
in the boat. The water was alive with sharks, over fifteen hundred
of them. Looking through his specialised equipment, the ichthyologist said that he had seen species he had never seen before.

There was no defence to a shark except perhaps to remain quite
still. The shark has very poor vision and is attracted by any distur-
bance in the water. He cannot stop, or he will drown; he must move
constantly forward in order to drive water through his gills. It is false
that he has to turn belly upwards if he wants to eat. He does that
only to twist a joint off a torso. Holt, the Australian Prime Minister
who drowned, was almost certainly attacked by a shark. He had
been spear-fishing and was swimming back with his catch attached
to his waist. A shark was probably alerted because the fish jiggled
and glittered as he swam along. Once one of those things comes in
a line towards you, nothing can make him stop. 'A shark in a feeding
frenzy is the most terrifying thing you can ever hope to see.'

Karl tries to think of everything: 'It's the only way to stay alive.'
Once he was working with an Englishman whom he much respects
on a big job which involved cutting a lot of steel plate. They loaded
cylinders of acetylene in the hold of the supply ship. When the time
came to sail, Karl refused to board. Why? He said that the caps of
acetylene cylinders had a way of working loose sometimes and if
they did the cylinders went off with enough force to blow a hole
in the side of the ship. He would go on board only if they were
stowed on deck. 'To oblige a coward', they moved the cylinders.
Two days out to sea, one of them came unscrewed and went off
like a rocket. If it had been in the hold, it would have sunk the ship.

In Brazil one time, an ocean-going barge had sunk in the main
channel of Bahia harbour. It was deep enough not to interfere with
shipping but the admiral in charge of the harbour insisted on having
it removed. Karl wanted to blow it up, but the admiral refused. The
lifting gear necessary was several thousand miles away and it cost
$8,000 a day to get it there. Karl realised that the wreck had settled
on very soft sand. At four in the morning, he laid charges, quite
small ones, in strategic places on *top* of the aluminium hull. When
the charges were blown, the water of the tideway did not even
blister. The weight of the water was sufficient, as he had calculated,
to return the force of the explosion and drive the wreck *downwards*
into the sandbank with enough impetus to bury it completely.

The next morning, the admiral said, 'When are you going to
move that boat?' Karl said, 'What boat?' The admiral said, 'Don't

play games with me.' 'There is no boat,' Karl said, 'look for your-self.'

The admiral sent for naval divers who went down and reported no sign of a boat in the channel.

Karl's employers were asked to salvage a ship sunk in Bahrain harbour. He had it conveyed to the Sultan's agent that he was a Jew. After some time, he received a message from the Sultan's assistant to go and see him in his hotel suite. The Sultan was pleased, he was told, on this occasion to allow him to undertake the work, despite being a Jew. Karl said he was glad to hear it, but he still couldn't do the job. The Arab told him that he had misunderstood: the diffi-culties had been removed, he could enter Bahrain freely. Karl said that he was not interested in the Sultan's permission and walked out. His boss backed him.

By our last day in Belize, Karl's steamer was off the reef, with a six-inch (?) hole in her bottom which had let in enough water to spoil a third of the cargo. A British army chopper was due to guide her into Belize City harbour through the reef. We saw it taking off as we went to the airport on our way to Guatemala.

Karl loved books and music almost as much, a sour judge might say, as he loved himself. I liked him. He promised to send Stee (who was seven years old) a shark's jaws, but he never did.

'Do you know *everything*?' He thought for a moment and then he said, 'No.'

What Ken McLeish failed to appreciate in my translation of Catullus 3 is the mocking element in C.'s commiseration over the dead 'sparrow'. Surely he was jealous of the endearments Lesbia lavished on the bird. 'Damned sparrow' seems to me a proper phrase here. The rival has been removed; all that remains to vex C. is the evidence of Lesbia's regret.

Two old, academic friends, living some distance apart, have a fierce epistolary quarrel in the public prints (say, the *TLS*). Violent rupture seems certain, but they agree on a final face-to-face, with a neutral audience. The atmosphere is tense when they arrive, but – to the amazement of the witnesses – they no sooner see each other than they burst out laughing and fall into each other's arms. No one else can understand the reason for their change of face: since last seeing each other, they have both grown identical Che Guevara moustaches.

Francis Cairns in *Quality and Pleasure in Latin Poetry*, says of Catullus 31 that it 'reflects the normal responses and conventional utterances of a homecomer'. Colin Macleod comments 'The freshness and humanity of that poem is no more nor less than its appropriateness to its situation.' What useful critical information can be extracted from this? How do the experts account for the use of '*cachinnorum*' and its significant last place in the last line? And why is the same word used in 56 with the strong suggestion that sexual derision is implied by it? There is surely an element of insinuation (a kind of nostalgic *grope* even!) in 31 which makes nonsense of the greetings card reading contributed by Cairns.

The moral tone of Jane Austen's novels is sustained by her attention to what is essential to the English sense of self-respect: money.

A woman begins to have her murderer's dreams.

Hollywood agent (Bob Shapiro) to Ted Kotcheff: 'Lose the tie, Ted. You're creative.'

An angry film director: 'You wouldn't talk to me like that if I had my writers with me.'

Jeremy. He has a Jewish daughter, having married a Jewess after a casually – even charmingly – confessed career of anti-Semitism at Eton. He has been an eager homosexual and declares, 'I still love bums, don't you?'

We drove to London to dine with John Peter and his wife. He is a short, ambitious, russet-haired Hungarian who arrived in England in 1956 and went to Oxford, before becoming a drama critic. When the buzzer was answered, I said, 'Hullo, it's us.' 'Freddie!' Mrs Peter greeted us with such warmth (we hardly knew her) that Beetle and I raised eyebrows at each other. In truth, Mrs P. had taken me for another Freddie, A. (Alfred) O'Shaughnessy, who soon arrived with his wife.

Mrs P. had lit a joss stick as well as lacquering her hair. That, and an aura of spent shampoo, almost effaced the reek of cats. The flat is filled with dusty utility furniture. Wall cupboards are posted at unlikely heights. Beetling volumes of Shaw and Shakespeare are almost at ceiling level. All the ornaments and the peaks of the chair-

backs wear little pointed caps, like witches' hats. The place has an
air of suspended catastrophe: those pendulous cupboards might
come crashing down at any moment.

O'Shaughnessy was a blue-eyed, grey-haired man in pinkish
middle-age. He has made a career in television drama. His wife was
a handsome, large-boned woman with the dangerous dryness of old
gunpowder in a neglected vault. She had been an actress. Twenty
years ago, she was chosen for a production which Jed Harris (about
whom, years later, I wrote an unproduced screenplay for Joel Silver)
intended to direct in London. Three days before her audition, she
had 'carried her little bottle to Harley Street'. She never took the
part. The son presaged by the contents of the bottle was going up
to Cambridge in October.

O'Shaughnessy had wanted to direct films, but had done so only
once. During the shooting, he was asked by an actor if he could go
to an audition with Binkie at three that afternoon. The actor was
due for a close-up, but Freddie lacked the hardness to insist that he
stay on the set. Later the missing close-up proved crucial to the
assembly. 'Freddie' seemed to be regretting – and advertising – that
he was too nice for the movies. He went into television.

He seemed poor casting for an Etonian, but his commoner's
conceit was a side-arm he could put his hand to if things grew lively.
As a drama executive, he has taken extraordinary pains over people
who do not deserve it. Others are always getting credit for his ideas:
only recently someone won an award for a play which Freddie had
written. He claimed that the injustice *amused* him; tongue asserted
what eyes denied. After dinner, and wine, he launched into a catalogue of grievances against the *Sunday Times*, whose legate he took
me to be (and our host indeed was). It was not only going pink at
the edges but also gave space to the likes of Elkan Allen. The literary
pages were filled by failed novelists reviewing books in terms which
nobody with good English soil under his feet could understand.
Wine and food delivered him of all geniality.

For some reason, we began to talk about the concentration camps
and the studied unwillingness of the British (and Americans) to
bomb the railways which led to them. The perfidy of British policy
towards Czechoslovakia in 1938 was not something he was prepared
to concede. 'We weren't ready,' he said. That the Czechs *were* ready
(their army was in excellent order and so were their defensive positions until Munich dismembered them) was something he totally
denied. Anthony Eden – 'forgive me for name-dropping' – had

often been a guest in his father's house and had promised that we
were 'playing for time'.

Mentioning Anthony Eden, I said, was not name-dropping but
turd-dropping: his *états d'âme* had more to do with careerism than
with conscience. When I mentioned that Britain refused to accept
more than a few Jewish children in 1938, he was in a red fury of
politeness at 'a very serious charge indeed'.

'You bet your ass,' I said.

He said that he had seen Woburn Square full of Jewish children
and demanded my evidence. I was able to cite only the title of a
book (*While Six Million Died*).

'*Author?*'

When I could not remember, his face twitched with the rage of
a judge confronting a barrister whose witnesses had failed to show.
Suddenly I recalled the author's last name was Morse.

'First name?'

Engorged with anger, he believed himself reasonable and calm.
He could not credit that British foreign policy was conducted in the
interests, real or supposed, of Britain; he assumed the FO was
governed by principles of abstract rectitude. Britain had been unable
to confront Hitler earlier than 1939 only because the Opposition
had prevented rearmament. I asked if he knew the size of the
Conservative majority in the Commons between 1931 and the
outbreak of war.

He could not accept that the British, by refusing military or diplomatic support, had deterred the French from opposing Hitler's
march into the Rhineland in 1936, when the smallest resistance
would have led to Hitler's withdrawing. He knew nothing, but he
had fought for six years as an officer in the Grenadier Guards. He
did it, he believes, to save the Jews. I wish I had done as much.

A brilliant, but clumsy, dinner-table wit, he always contrived to spill
gravy on his epigrams.

If one says of a writer that there is something inexplicably displeasing
about him, the chances are that he reminds one of oneself. To pick
up, and wrinkle his nose at, his own scent is the hunter's most
disconcerting experience.

Chez Michael Ayrton. We went to collect a couple of his bronzes.
M. was in red felt slippers and supported on stainless steel crutches,
like inverted old-fashioned hat-stands. He has been promised that

he is better, but he doesn't – comic face – *feel* better. He lives on Complan and shots of insulin.

Elisabeth gave us a nice lunch: a cheesy first course, mushrooms and shrimps, which I cannot believe came out as advertised, but was good for all that, and roast duck. Michael sat close to the fire. John Hopkins' new play opens at the National on Thursday. I said, 'Well, as it isn't being directed by Jonathan Miller, there's a chance of the performance not only beginning on Thursday but also ending on it.' Michael said that it was being directed by Pinter. It will probably end on Thursday *week*.

Michael wondered whether Pinter was conscious of what he is getting away with. I said that Harold had learned one essential piece of wisdom: he does not make self-deprecating jokes and he is *never* ironic at his own expense.

Michael is full of jealousies, although he is still, statistically, young and has for years enjoyed not negligible honour in his own country. He said that he left his progressive boarding school abruptly at thirteen and a half (the last time we met, he said fifteen). He had been taken out by his father, Gerald Gould, and apprised of the facts of life on a dutiful, drunken Sunday visit. He found these 'facts' so improbable, never having considered the matter before, that he summoned an amenable co-ed and took her to a barn for a practical essay. They soon decided that Michael must have got some of the instructions wrong and went to summon Moira, an older girl, who came and joined them in the hay where they were later discovered.

When Michael was chucked out, his father laughed and laughed. He never went back to school, but travelled all over Europe. One of his tutors, in Vienna, was an old English lady who had come to Austria as the governess of the Archduke Rudolph. The *doyenne* of the Austrian Communist Party, she was shot by the Germans in the Ringstrasse at the age of eighty-seven for striking a German officer with her umbrella.

Michael was 'very fond' of Jack Davenport, a brilliant man who, at the age of nineteen, was told by Auden that he was better than Auden. He had read everything, knew everybody, had a wonderful wit and tremendous charm. When drunk, he was terrifying. He had been a boxing Blue. Michael once saw him punch a hole in the side of a car which had come too close when he was crossing the street. He said of Malcolm Lowry, 'I don't know which of us will commit suicide first – he because he has now done everything he can ever have hoped to do or I because I have not done anything.'

Davenport gave me a very good review in the *Observer*, when *The Graduate Wife* came out. I read it in the copy which I borrowed from Elaine Steinbeck in 1962, when we were disembarking from the ferry at Mykonos. I suppose that I should have profited from our acquaintance by talking at length with Steinbeck, who was unwell but not unavailable. I funked being intrusive.

A dream last night about Tom Maschler. He had written a remarkable, *enviable* book, so that in my dream I thought 'If this turns out to be a dream, I shall steal the idea.' I began consciously to *hope* that it was a dream. The book was a kind of gazeteer of his 'friends' in the literary world; everyone had a map on which his character was projected. I was Alaska. There were chapters of print too; mine was headed 'And then what? Ah, and what then?' I had the impression of being a cold, probing and uncommunicative personality, at once inquisitive and clenched against revelation. There was an extraordinary beauty and daring in Tom's volume. This morning, when I was reading of Maritain coming to Gide to try and dissuade him from publishing a certain book, I recognised in the former's earnest bad faith the same attitude that I had adopted in my own dream.

In 2005, Tom did write a book, about his long life as a publisher. It made much of the famous names whose careers he had fostered. Critics – having no favours to hope for – ridiculed its witless conceit. Without any public honours, Tom remains *the* literary impressario, especially of fiction, of the 1960s and 70s.

I also dreamed that I was on some kind of a cruise ship, clean and modern like the Swedish liner we saw at the quayside in Bordeaux on Saturday. The ship was moving at some speed. At a certain point, the passengers began to leave the saloon in a dutiful manner. When only two or three of us were left, the steward came up to me and asked if I was not going to attend the service. He did not say so, but I knew that it was Yom Kippur. I said that I was not interested, but at the same time I left the saloon, as if I wanted to. Somehow I went through the other lounge, where the service was being held, and in passing I persuaded myself that I had made my act of association.

Then I found myself on deck. The ship was rushing (as if downhill) through a stone trough of water. I had the impression that the bridge, if not deserted, was badly under-manned. As I looked over the side, the metal hull of the ship, a bulging flank below me, struck the protruding edge of a red stone pier, bounced off and continued its downhill rush. It seemed that she missed total wreck only by a fraction and that the nearness of the disaster had been clear only to me, the apostate on deck. I was amazed at the ignorance of the faithful, their stupidity even, but whereas my nerve was shaken, theirs remained intact.

Film director Victor England: 'They're running one of my old nightmares on TV tonight.'

9.5.74. Philip Norman reviewed *Richard's Things* with welcome intelligence. Contrary to habit, I wrote to thank him. He replied, modestly, 'thank *you*', and asked me to lunch at the Gay Hussar; he had something he would like me to write for the *ST* mag., which he was guest-editing. He was wearing today's London climber's kit: a black button-to-the-chin suit, halfway between Chairman Mao and Little Lord Fauntleroy. Over cherry soup, he unveiled the topic that was meant to excite me: Hughie Green.

I was reminded of how, soon after the publication of *The Limits of Love*, I was summoned to Pinewood by Leslie Parkyn, a nice old thing who believed in the occult. After earnestly congratulating me on the reception of my novel (a full-page rave by Peter Forster in the *Daily Express*!), he proposed that I write a musical film, with sixteen songs, about a Butlin's camp. (It is an odd fact that one of the successes of last year's English films was set in a Butlin's camp in the 1950s.)

'Hughie Green,' I said, as if this were a more demanding poser than I had expected. To remain susceptible to temptation is the fool's idea of eternal youth. I said, finally, that I did not fancy a single piece on H.G., but what if I were to do, say, *five* pieces on aspects of Modern Life (of which H.G. could be one)? He said that if he went back to the office and told them that he had talked me into writing five pieces he would be regarded as a miracle worker. I never heard another word.

Truman Capote to Gore Vidal: 'Gore, I *love* your hairpiece!' Vidal's hair is his own.

12.5.74. The craving for stability, expressed by Cicero in his fantasy of the *concordia ordinum*, is typical of *arrivistes*: those who come to live above their station always want to believe that the roof is good for another year or two yet. A new man who had made his name by prosecuting a corrupt but aristocratic provincial governor (hardly a rare conjunction) might be expected to have scant respect for the *boni*, yet M.T.C doted on them. Did their current qualities recommend them? No, it was their antique language that he coveted: its sonorous style furnished a new man with antique Roman airs.

Had the *optimates* been the men their ancestors were, Cicero's *gravitas* would have been impertinent. As it was, his rhetoric supplied the hot air that filled their void. The man from Arpinum spoke the language of the nobility without quite having their accent. The sincerity with which he sustained their duplicity marked him for an outsider. (Ted Heath bellows his resemblance here, though he lacks Cicero's grandiose eloquence, and wit.)

Catiline was a travesty of the Gracchi: he became a martyr for a radical cause which he never embodied. In executing the Catilinarians, Cicero acted in sincere parody of the *mos maiorum*. After he had sullied his hands doing their dirty work, the *boni* voted him into exile for the illegalities (putting Roman citizens to death without trial) on which they had earlier congratulated him and which now might have cost him his life. Rehearsing a later habit, Caesar amused himself by pleading for clemency.

M.T.C. saw himself as the leading actor in a drama of his own composition. Not without courage, he was not a courageous man; when he put on his breast-plate, it was a rhetorical costume: it spoke for him.

The Giscard–Mitterrand confrontation on TV. We watched the last half hour in the lounge of the Réserve at Pessac, a new hotel so lacking in grace or charm that you wonder whether the good food is not some kind of miscalculation. The debate was tense, but furiously courteous. Both men knew that impatience or petulance would be fatal. Giscard seemed more incisive and less premeditated. He accused Mitterrand of speaking for longer than he; if the point was just, it might have been juster had Giscard not spoken twice as fast as his opponent.

Nettled by Mitterrand's claim to warm feelings, Giscard said, '*Vous n'avez pas le monopole du coeur.*' It was memorably effective, but he said it with a cool head. His poise, and diction, suggested that he was capable of decisive lack of charity, yet Mitterrand seemed more calculating, as if he had always to be careful not to tangle the strings of his alliance or confuse which muscle moved which limb. Uneasy eyes seemed to blink at his composite make-up.

Giscard's purchased aristocracy (the d' came with money) and tart phrases fitted him better. Mitterrand's eloquence was too often cliché; he appealed without being appealing. Giscard was able to hurt him and he never really hurt Giscard. The latter might claim to have a heart, but he could be wounded only in the head. The French never saw him dizzied. As for Mitterrand, Giscard quizzed him disdainfully about his fiscal ideas and made them ridiculous even to those who did not understand why.

The guests in the Réserve relished Giscard's skill. He had clearly won (Mitterrand's mistimed peroration left him anxious for a fade-out). We felt uneasy at being at one with the guests and the natty manager of the hotel. Could one really support what they supported and smile when they smiled? Property makes Tories of us all.

The Times this morning (14.5.74) confirms that Giscard's elegance is preserved by some pretty tough tailors. His meetings are policed by a private army of *Ordre Nouveau* thugs. (Doubtless the Communists too have their muscular charmers.) I am less distressed by the entourage of the candidate of Reason than by my own uneasy hope that he wins. Marx was almost right: wealth, however petty, alters one's consciousness. It may not *determine* it, but it affects one's determination.

The dread of the future in middle age may be a symptom of cowardice; it is hardly proof of stupidity. The young welcome the future because they are eager to come into their inheritance. Politicians of the Left retain their fire not because they carry the flame of righteousness but because they still have the noble prospect of plunder.

3.7.74. I have tried to do too much in too many fields. I relied on my speed, as I did in games: I never learned to play them properly, no doubt through lack of natural aptitude, but I have managed to participate through unguarded expenditure of energy: at least, and perhaps at most, I run and run. I remain too willing to spend myself on any hurdles which anyone sets up for me.

The maze is a safe without a lock. To be at the centre of the maze is the only clever way out.

Illusion: the fork with the single prong. Love, love!

The strait gate is the labyrinth of Christianity.

The collapse of religion also impoverishes secular philosophy. In the elimination of illusion, the scope of truth also contracts. A low church of ideas, without mystery, without charm, without beauty, takes the place of Higher Things. The seven new devils are moving into the exorcised house.

The future is in the storage-jars which, after Daedalus' flight, were discovered to be empty.

Bluebeard. Don Juan as a married man: have you locked the door, dear?

Hypocrisy partakes of something noble. Who is more devoid of human interest than those with nothing to hide?

The miracle of the breast: its flagrant vulnerability and its pure externality. The perfect gift! Vivian C.'s old joke: '*Pourquoi se ressemblent les trains modèles et les seins d'une femme? Tous les deux sont dessinés pour les enfants, mais ce n'est pas les enfants qui jouent avec.*'

Tynan is a gregarious solipsist, forever trying to disprove his own conviction that he is alone in the world.

Aesthetic movements seek to recruit artists into marching in step; which is all that is required for them to abandon art.

In contrivance, every corner has to be turned to perfection. Such is the style of Narcissus. Nabokov is the expatriate who founds a country with one citizen, one language, one crown. Revenge incites him to dandyism; *solus rex*, in his new country he rules out all the banalities from which he had been banished.

One sensed in their presence the relic of some distant and festering regret. Yet they had known each other only a short time. What one took for their past still lay ahead of them.

30.7.74. I have decked my family with – to put it charmlessly – all the things I can think of to keep them quiet, or distantly noisy. Such wilful generosity is close to greed: I want the family to be happy so that I can be free not to be. All domestic concerns, from dripping air conditioners to defective brakes on bicycles, seem to reflect on me. I take them personally, because these things were bought not only to please but also to silence.

At Martin Bamford's midsummer thrash. She had a haggard youth-fulness; her woollen sweater and long skirt had no girlish definition. Her husband has the beard of a corsair without any loot. He is young, but not a boy; although he is almost defiantly *with* his wife, he seems to stand closer to her than she to him.

The men in the wine trade are rarely less than fleshy. A bearded man from Château P. wore a shirt covered with alternately full and empty glasses. One could well believe that he had drained the empty ones himself. They called him Solzhenitsyn, from the shape of his dark beard, but the Medoc is no Gulag and he wore his campaign medals conspicuously low. He had recently been on a trip to the US, where he felt completely *dépaysé*. 'And England?' I asked. 'How do you feel there?' 'England's my home patch,' he said, as if I might not have recognised him for the prize Charlie he was.

The wine market has fallen heavily; those who were bulging with cash last year are now simply bulging. The Dane's husband was an exception: since he was a broker, not a shipper, and had done the right things at the right time, he was safe from the storms which threatened to swamp the trade. He was larger than the other big-shots (who all called each other 'pig') and his eyes were shrewd with a mixture of apprehension and cunning. The present wine glut has created a supplementary level of furtiveness: they are all busy culti-vating the grapes for a new vintage which they hope will be a disaster. The only thing that can rescue the trade is a bad year. A frost in August would be an appalling pleasure. The cost of manpower has risen as the price of wine has slumped; it would be best if all the grapes were collected by a hurricane and swept into the Gironde. In the circumstances, bumper harvests seem certain.

It was a kind of solid dream, this party of vinous Franglais set down in the middle of the Aquitaine countryside. One could imagine a murder there, with no shortage of suspects. The couples were never openly disloyal; marooned in luxury, they had only each other to remind them of who they were supposed to be, and like. The women were lucky and miserable: the men's work kept them late when it did not keep them away. The marriages are bargains and the women are bound to honour them, surveyed as they are by each other's vigilant jealousy. Was I right, I asked the Dane, in thinking of the Medoc as a golf club where there wasn't any golf? I *was*, she said. The French wives had a fuller life than the expatriates, but they had a coldness which, applied to the back of the neck, would staunch a nosebleed in seconds.

Once, after a performance of Ken's translation of an Aristophanes, the producer called for 'Mr McLeish' to come on stage and take a bow. Ken's father, the professor, stood up and said, 'I am Mr McLeish, but it is in fact my son who has done the translation, and here he is.'

The more I see of earth mothers, the less I worship Demeter.

The schoolmaster. He is the grown-up scholarship boy, armed always with a pen. He looks at once for reproaches and for encouragement. He has a sharp tongue but a thin skin and he knows well how to wound himself. He believes that he has a gift for 'pastoral work' among his pupils, but the sheep seem to frighten their shepherd: from time to time, he runs from their bleating.

It is a silly meanness that I have failed to contribute to my old tutor R.L. Howland's retirement present. I keep 'intending to', but never do. He was, God knows, an amiable man. At my interview with him, during the entrance scholarship exams, we talked largely about football. He was an Old Salopian and the Shrewsbury match was the big one of the Charterhouse season. It mattered little that I never played for the school; I was a subtle toady – Dale Carnegie's *How to Make Friends and Influence People* was the only *specific* book that my father ever pressed on me – and I allowed R.L.H. to do most of the talking. He was a keener athlete than intellectual. I have no doubt that I was good value for my scholarship, but the sporting banalities we exchanged fixed me more keenly in his mind than my Latin verses. If Howland helped to get me my scholarship, he did little to make me a scholar. I needed a demanding fanatic and I was faced by a tolerant schoolmaster who wanted no more than that I be a good chap. 'Bede', as colleagues called him, was a man at whom serious scholars might smile and the ambitious scoff, but none could dislike him.

At my first supervision, on Aristotle *Metaphysics Lamda*, he began by telling us to mark those paragraphs which we could safely skip, since no one knew what they meant and hence no Tripos question was ever set on them. It did not occur to him that it was in the unintelligible sections of the book that a scholar might have found his vocation. He exemplified to the novice an idea of academic life so bland that intellectual dedication smacked of excessive enthusiasm. He expected so little that it was difficult to be a disappointment to him. Such men can be remembered with affection but never with gratitude.

I was probably the worst-*primed* scholar at Cambridge. I remained a schoolboy; if I ever seemed more, it was because I had the knack of mimicry. I had the scholarship of a parrot. I met no one at Cambridge who inspired me with a desire to *work*, though plenty who made me want to shine. John Wisdom was inspirational, but he gave one the dangerous confidence that philosophy could be done without bookish diligence: the common analogy of a 'game' led me to believe that it required more enthusiasm than training. I became a passionate philosopher, but never an informed one.

The Ford factory in Bordeaux where they make automatic gearboxes. The boxes are electronically tested after completion. A week after they had had a party of Italian experts check the machinery, all the boxes failed their test. They seemed to be perfectly assembled but they did not work properly. The fault was finally traced to the oil used to lubricate them. It was stored in a huge tank under the shop-floor. Access to it was through manholes. The Italians had worked unsupervised over the weekend and had pissed down the man-holes to save themselves a walk. J. said that they probably thought that they were doing the management a favour by not pissing against the wall.

How banal most directors like a script to be! Is it worth the effort to be ingenious or original? Stanley Donen longed for the finished version of *Two for the Road* to be as I had imagined it but Bogdanovich (or whatever his name is) is most responsible for my wondering whether I can still be bothered. The fate of the Ralegh script, so admired, so applauded, before being shelved *sine die* has not added to my zest. In my condescensions is a kind of lordly fear. What can I make of Don Juan that is new, and that they will want?

Part of Don Juan's pride derives from his sense of being watched, not least by himself. The *galant'uomo* cannot miss an opportunity, even if alone and in disguise; fear that someone will discover his failure requires him to be fearless. The seducer must boast of his conquests as swindlers of their wealth; they would sooner pay tax than be taken for poor. D.J.'s servant is his accountant and becomes precisely that in the modern section where the Don becomes the eponymous owner, compiler, subject of D.J. magazine.

André Gide's *Journals* have been on the windowsill in the lavatory at Lagardelle for years. I had not been able to read more than a paragraph or two at a time. Muggeridge saying he was like a great cathedral in which something has gone wrong with the drains has confirmed my feeling that Gide was rightly shelved in the loo. In a section I read this morning, G. refers to the way in which authors, and subjects, one has spurned in the past come to take their revenge. He is an instance in my case. No writer in the modern canon was less congenial to me, but if he continues to improve, I may have to bring him into the sitting room.

Gide was probably referring to Marcel Proust, whose work he rejected for Gaston Gallimard's *NRF*. Despite Gide's denials (and George Painter's assertions), Proust's beloved housekeeper Céleste Albaret insists that the manuscript was never even opened. It had been tied with a distinctive knot and was returned with it intact. Gide (Céleste's '*Faux Moine*') had dismissed Marcel as a '*dandy mondain*', and could not be bothered to read the fat text. Marcel then paid the costs of its publication, by Bernard Grasset, and had a great success. Gaston Gallimard ate humble pie, and begged to publish later volumes. Proust agreed, but took revenge by receiving Gide, only once, very civilly, in order to hear his recantation.

Gide adopted literature rather than engendered it. He can be imagined, protective and very slightly disgusting, shepherding his small Muse through improving places, patting it on the head and covertly relishing the prospect of its little friends coming to tea. He said few memorable things. His evangelical pederasty seems to have little purpose other than to justify his tastes; one might as well make a moral virtue of garlic butter. What finally wins one's admiration is his determination not to have time for anything except serious work.

However substantial his inheritance (it was probably consider-able, since he regards the mercenary hopes of families as so degrading), one can't imagine him saying, with Paul Valéry, that if he had enough money he would cease to write. He loved the *métier* and fostered young talent, yet those whose lives were changed by Gide more often mocked his meanness than thanked him for his generosity of heart. People prefer the magnanimity of those who remember to stand their round.

There are few sins or crimes which, charmingly enough confessed on the box, would not give one a certain amiable notoriety, except those that touch on the means of avoiding tax. It used to be that the English went to the continent in order to have clandestine sex; now they go to find clandestine banks.

It was in Marmande, a town sporting a boulevard and a rather elegant street in which Sarah was able to transform herself, within a hundred yards, from scruffy child to smart woman, that we saw the definitive headline NIXON OUT. We crossed the Garonne and drove into the Landes, the pine trees crowding to the straight road's edge, the deep-eaved houses promising a winter harshness that the green jungle hid, but only half-hid, behind its back. How can one like the Basque country, for all its wild amplitude? The buildings are too white and lack proportion; they resemble people grown stout shunning the sun. Where else in France would a café insist that one pay before drinking its tea? Beetle had baked a birthday cake for Sarah and we lit its candles as we sat by the road-side and she bent over to blow them out just before the wind did.

He works for Distillers, who have vineyards in the Rioja and have bought another in Champagne. He dislikes the Bordelais; he thinks them stuffy and 'bourgeois'. How does he think of himself? He gloats over the 22 per cent fall in the price of Bordeaux last year. He is sourly fat with the air of one who had drunk too often to his own success and is hungover with self-satisfaction. His wife does not seem to like him very much, but acquiesces in her comfortable bondage. There is a look in her eye of enticing passivity; she will never be responsible for anything she might provoke a man to do. She shook her head when her husband endorsed Enoch Powell; it was as if she were asking, silently, for a separate peace. I suspect that he did not care one way or the other about Powell's racial attitudes.

He believed that the unions should be clobbered because individual 'enterprise' no longer seemed to be sufficient to procure prosperity. He did not altogether wish England well, because he had found a way of living whether it sank or no. His wife feared to contradict him, but tacit dissent gave her a sort of negative identity. With such women, who both submit and differ, infidelity becomes less a passion than a hobby. Her husband is about to go on a long selling trip; she will return to England with the children. How should she dispute his absences when they make time for her to be somebody he doesn't know, and whom she does not yet know either?

The assistant matron. A trousered, bright-eyed lady with an air of combative winsomeness. After revealing that she had a wartime marriage that hadn't worked out ('one of those'), she attacked co-education (hearing that two of our children were at Bedales) and then she defended South Africa. Not the kind of lady to whom one would choose to go for one's Radio Malt.

If Joe were a book, he would be a three-volume novel, cased. He and his fellow holidaymakers were like absentees from the present; they were neither rejoiced by the fall of the Greek colonels nor scandalised by Nixon. They relied on each other; their common lack of sexual charm linked them like participants in a shamelessly chaste orgy. The Bishop of B. was a prize exhibit. He was so well cast, with his powdered chinlessness, that he would have been rejected as too obvious for the part of a vicar in a farce. These unattractive people contrived for themselves a world in which weakness looked strong and narrow-mindedness decisive. Why does one draw a certain comfort from their existence and their unlikely survival? It comes of the same furtive pleasure as that of walking freely in a totalitarian country. The cant says that freedom is indivisible. Nonsense: men are liberated by the sight of others in chains, even when they are made of dough.

Henry de Montherlant. His aloofness is that of the last of a species which had every asset except a good digestion. He is strong and quick and elegant and wily, but he cannot take nourishment. His death is magnificent (like Tolstoy's, writing) but no one is moved by it. The fat are only relieved when the slim have their funerals. H. de M. has no English equivalent; he needs a bullring in which to strut his unsmiling triumphs. When he goes for the kill, he hates the crowd more than the bull. They reward him with trophies, but do not look him in the eye. His skill demeans them; they recognise the scorn in his stride. Gide said, 'It is permissible to kill an angry animal, but to make an animal angry in order to kill it is criminal.' The notion of criminal, how alien that is to everything that Montherlant deemed worthwhile! The man of honour turns no one over to the law except as a gesture of contempt. For him, justice is a matter of vocabulary and timing; never of punishment. The right-eous indignation of the mob, what is it but a platitude up in arms? No hero respects the verdict of anything so ordinary as twelve good men.

There are falsenesses involved in the choice of *any* single and consis-tent style. The snobbery of Proust is more manifest in the grandiose architecture of the mausoleum in which he enshrines his characters than in the genealogies of those to whom he offers privileged places. In similar style, in order to eulogise the Brideshead clan, Evelyn Waugh elevated his prose to the peerage.

The leaders of the working class can no more afford eloquence or wit or culture than Chamberlain or Churchill could afford to drop their aitches or forget their hats. What is absolutely unnecessary is to show them any *respect*, deference or admiration. The changes in English society leave room for an intellectual revolution, for of all the things that Scanlon and Clive Jenkins despise, the intellectual is the greatest. Words are the only means with which to build our privacy and furnish our vacuousness. The use of literature is to create a world elsewhere.

K. is regularly suicidal. Her father, whom she loved, died when she was thirteen. Yet she has considered killing herself since she was ten. She is grand in appearance, walking tall, but not aloof. She is in most respects a commonplace, if majestic, girl. She does not take things too seriously: her acquaintance with death is amiable rather than solemn. A sort of bravado, even insolence, leads her back to death's door. She has no desire for danger or pain. She may kill herself at any moment, but she will not accept a lift from a stranger. Death is a friend she keeps planning to meet. She will perhaps go to find him one day, leaving the heavy envelope of her flesh propped in some convenient place to explain where she has gone.

Promise not to be jealous? One might as well swear not to sneeze.

As things get worse, men's faith in progress becomes more reckless. We begin to look forward to what we dread. Disaster is the cure for miscalculation.

To ask a man for his opinion is like a woman asking for a light: it invites liberties.

Militant patriotism in a civilian: false teeth in a glass.

When you congratulate a man on how young he looks, he immediately thinks of his age.

Those who smile at strangers would as well kill them if so commissioned.

We make a God out of love so that our vices may seem like a deprivation.

There is less difficulty in loving mankind if we do not expect it to be lovable.

When someone says that he is sincerely pleased that something has happened to you, he usually means that he is not interested in having it happen to him.

Those most fervent in their congratulations will later boast of having known you before you were spoiled by success.

The events which touch us most keenly in the lives of the famous are usually the most commonplace. When Homer nods we all nod.

The more abiding our resentment of a critic, the more likely that his criticism was just. Who gives a second thought to a good notice?

Men are keener to use their money to impress the rich than to help the poor.

It is very fine to tell the truth, but what matters is to whom one has the nerve to tell it.

Hypocrisy: a Christian with a change of clothes. But to be free of hypocrisy, how often that means to be free of virtues too!

If mankind were now obliged to live in the Garden of Eden, it would complain of a fall in living standards. When bliss is an eternal condition, it becomes a bore.

The pleasure we take in nature is that of walking in a garden which we need not tend.

No humanist has ever given death an agreeable flavour, hence the number of death-bed conversions. We would sooner be going to Hell than nowhere at all. One may live for pleasure, but it is hard to die for it.

We laugh at those who take the Gospel literally, but how eagerly we ourselves grasp at the slightest fragment of good news!

Love of the crowd? Hatred of self.

If there were no heretics, how should we recognise the faithful? By their zeal to devise a heresy.

No society that welcomes immigrants is respected as much as one that condescends to them.

Spinoza is right: God is synonymous with Nature: He realised every-thing He could think of, the figure in his own carpet.

Truth is the bungalow in which philosophers are still angry not to find a staircase.

I should prefer to pay a man to be good than beg him to be.

Why write aphorisms? To help the mind lose weight.

Ken tells me that Professor Dover of Edinburgh said of our Catullus that it 'shed fresh light in corners that we had always thought well-lit'. Are we flattered? The praise of professors has the gritty sweetness of blood squeezed from a stone.

Maugham. Reading his plays again is like travelling by rail after too much flying: one had forgotten that travel could be so smooth. His dialogue would translate easily into French or Spanish, the languages of Maugham's secret heart. His reaction to the British is like the homosexual's to women. The hated influence of the Rectory made Maugham a moralist without a creed. His plots often turn on the amorality of women; he is appalled by what he admires, their pragmatism. He sees how the female, refusing to be principled, can be the vessel of a compassion which ruptures the bars of cold reason.

What led him to give up writing for the theatre? He gagged on the obligation to please, on having to take more trouble over the sugar than the pill. Yet as a novelist he took much the same pains to be palatable. Contempt for his audience was the first step towards pleasing them, just as his good manners were the measure of his disdain for those he met. Politeness always conceals a dagger.

The medical mode required of Maugham that he regard anything exceptional without surprise. He merely made a note of horrors that might have unnerved a layman (for instance, in the hospital during the opening phase of the Great War). He thought melodrama acceptable as long as one did not get excited about it. His simple style is not *that* simple: it revels in aphorism and *sangfroid*. It speaks of an author insulated from emotion by discounting sentiment while remaining alert to its physical symptoms. The doctor agrees to serve humanity by eschewing human responses; keeping people alive is not much of a life.

Maugham's 'shallowness' was due as much to reluctance to mislead as to want of imagination. He never understood that language is fraught with judgements; lucidity always has a colour. To what degree was his unwillingness to inspire false hope the consequence of his training? Medicine was his visa; as a world traveller, he became the ship's doctor on the Ship of Fools.

All of his characters are types, even if they have unusual histories; eccentric, they are never idiosyncratic. Knowledge of anatomy inclines him to see all men as fundamentally of a piece. Aware of what they have in common, he cannot find distinction credible. He might perceive that the dragon's teeth needed filling, but he would never choose to sow them.

J.B. Priestley's provincial bluffness, dull as boiled potatoes, confronts us from every available niche in this his octogenarian year. J.B.P., who seldom said a witty or a wise thing, was in many ways Maugham's unanointed successor: he too wrote plays, novels and essays; he too took pains to please the common reader. His love of England is a celebration of the parish by one too parochial to go anywhere else. Gruff and whining, Priestley brims with bonhomous rancour. He has embarrassed the British into honouring his longevity as if it were an artistic achievement. If only he had been homosexual, how much more entertaining he might have been obliged to be! It would be impossible to approach life in a Priestleyan style; he is all bluff, inimitable only because there is nothing there to imitate.

The first time we went to the little restaurant we had found it charming. It did not bother us that the *patronne* was a very young middle-aged old woman, with planning permission for senility; she already had the foundation of wrinkles. When we went again, we gave our order hungrily, in French of course, to a plump, pretty waitress we had not seen before. After I had finished, she said, 'I'm English.' She had worked in the restaurant for six weeks and had another two to do. Madame was a slave-driver: she rang the bell if she wanted anyone, and she rang it often. All the help had been hired on the cheap: the tireless old biddy and the Algerian girl with the sketch of a child in her rounding belly. The English girl had the hunched plumpness of discontent. Had she straightened up in the low, timbered room, she might have been handsomely big: nice breasts made up for thick legs. She was due to go to Swansea University at the beginning of October. She served us amiably, but she had introduced an air of truculence. The meal was marred; we shall not go back there.

13.9.74. Yesterday was a day of quiet happiness. I translated Catullus 31, which had eluded me all summer. I am not convinced that mine is the final draft, but I discovered a unity in the poem which others have not. Sirmio and Lagardelle were one across the millennnia; my pleasure at being back here seemed to render the Latin transparent. The day ended with our making love. Should I have had the exquisite pleasure I experienced with the woman with whom I have lived for twenty years as the result of a *coup de foudre*, I should conclude that all marriages were a sham and that only casual sex could occasion such ecstasy.

14.9.74. *In Bluebeard's Castle*. Steiner starts in solemn tones, a judge whose summing up will be verdict and diagnosis. After elaborate lucubrations, he comes to the same conclusion that I advanced, with jejune clarity, in *The Limits of Love*: the Jews were hated not least because they furnished a practical instance of successful dissent. G.S. may add another element – that the Camps were mundane hells, rescued from myth and brought to the near side of Lethe – but my point is restated with an air of important revelation by someone strident in his confidence that novels have nothing more to teach us.

We may see but we are unwilling to punish the evil in clever or personable men. At Nuremburg the upstarts and the vulgarians received the harshest sentences. Speer saved his neck because the British and the Americans recognised in him the kind of managerial operator who was to become the self-effacing *apparatchik* of the post-war world. The hanging of Ribbentrop, which we saw recently on some antique newsreel (a sequence of horrifying callousness), was less the result of R.'s 'crimes' than of his presumption: how dare a champagne salesman pose as a toff and a statesman? Speer saved himself by a kind of penitent impudence. Was T.S. Eliot's 'reticence' any less impudent? He revised his view of Milton, but not of the Jews; he might correct his taste, but not his morals.

The reluctance of the educated and the comfortable to face their own guilt made them willing to load the *ugly* Nazis, such as Streicher and Funk, with all the odium; they preserved the vanity of their own civilised qualities by showing mercy to the sort of people they could bear to have dinner with: Speer, Von Papen, Schacht, von Schirach.

Instead of 'war crimes', it would have been better if the accused had been indicted for criminal offences, such as murder, theft, conspiracy and complicity, which were already on the statute books of their own countries or of those where their crimes were committed. An aura of unfairness still hangs around what seemed like retrospective justice, quite as if the accused could have been expected to know that it was an offence to murder people.

In an old newsreel: images of rows of German prisoners being inspected by those whom they had brutalised. As a man was identified, he was doubled off across the parade ground by a single private soldier. Revulsion was more evident in the zeal with which the squaddies chased their prisoners than in any of the forensic indignation of the lawyers who made their names in the courtroom at Nuremberg. The disgust of the ordinary soldiers spoke more scathingly than any peroration. Their nausea knew exactly what inhumanity was. Mr Eliot went through life exempt from common experience. His fine sensibilities deprived him, in the end, of any capacity for common decency.

16.9.74. The essence of the silent film is the chase; chase and hope. What chase is more appropriate to a movie based on Don Juan than the pursuit of a woman, for instance kidnapped? The American

Eden is the pristine West. Begin there? D.J. pursues and captures the kidnappers of Elvira, only to find himself condemned – by the morality of the New World (and the movies) – to marry her. He goes to Harvard (in a new time frame) and becomes a successful composer of witty lyrics and catchy tunes. He remarries, but E. turns up and continues *his* pursuit.

The Commendatore is reincarnated as the Governor of the State. He comes to unveil a statue and is shot by an assassin (Elvira's unreformed Sicilian brother?) who is concealed in the hollow body of the bronze. Don Juan becomes President of the United States, the white knight of duplicity; the very instance of double standards.

20.9.74. I have resigned from what could have been an enjoyable commission. Don Juan seemed to offer the chance of some light-hearted fantasy. Instead, I wrecked my summer trying to argue a soufflé into rising.

Belize is threatened by a hurricane. What a place in which to be threatened by anything! The ranger at the Mayan site (Altan Huan?) said that last time there was a tidal wave, the spray was carried so far inland that men cupped their hands for the taste of the fresh falling rain and found they had lifted salt to their lips. We were driven to the jungle site by an American called Ted who had been with the Peace Corps. He had returned to marry a local girl who was having a child by another man. He was tall, buck-toothed and wore a sharp moustache. His brother-in-law, Sylvester, was a light-skinned Belizian who had encouraged Ted to stay and drive one of his taxis, though he hoped to become a farmer: there was plenty of land to develop. Ted never disparaged the locals, but his patience seemed to hide a reserve of anger.

When we took a wrong turning, we happened on a couple of his in-laws, sitting on a step. Their brazen indolence mocked his industry; a conspiracy of blood worked silently against him. He was giving himself to these people without any prospect of escape. His commitment to the simple life was a kind of perversion. To choose degradation is a sophisticated act.

29.9.74. The problem with the Arabs is not, as liberals like to imagine, that they are prejudiced against Jews; the problem is that they *hate* them.

Pensées: the littérateur's picaresque.

14.10.74. The curious thing about shields: the enemy is inclined to treat them as *targets* (a target *is* a small shield). The warrior offers a stiff advertisement of himself and his enemy strikes it in spiteful recognition. The shield is as the man would like to be: unflinching, invulnerable, bloodless. Achilles' shield advertised him. By the same token, a warrior such as Hector literally plumes himself with his hirsute helmet. When a conqueror possesses himself of it, he has scalped the other.

As one wonders of an art film, yes, yes, but will there be breasts in it?

17.10.74. Michael Ayrton stayed with us for a week. He arrived later even than prudence advised us to think likely. He stopped the little rented Simca in the lane and immediately declared that his briefcase had been stolen at Bordeaux airport. It contained several books of drawings, texts, traveller's cheques, a bottle of whisky and the slim volume of Michael Frayn's 'philosophy' which (at Claire Tomalin's solicitation) I was to review for the *New Statesman*. The case had been filched in the few seconds during which Michael turned away to take his heavier cases from the carousel. Such speed argues a professional thief, but I went through the motions of calling the airport as if reporting an accidental misprision.

Michael did not brood on the loss, though it included much of the work he had done on Archilochus and drafts of the book jacket for Ken's and my Catullus. We swarmed warmly around our visiting celebrity, but even before he got out of the car I felt the omens inauspicious. Made elderly by his illness, tired by the journey, he had no spare charge of vitality. To catalogue the disappointments seems mean; to ignore them impossible. He was egocentric and yet unable to endure his own company. He left the flat early in the morning, but the heating was kept at full blast all day. He felt the cold even in rooms from which he was absent.

He had, he told us, actually died on the operating table (in Bristol, could it have been?) and he now lacked the confidence in his virility which had always certified his genius. The slump had made his work difficult to sell: the London gallery which had promised him a show was likely to close. The savaging of *The Midas Touch* had wounded him deeply. We guessed before publication that his hopes of best-sellerdom were ludicrous, but the size of the advance and the degree of publicity – a visit from Philip Oakes! – created a confidence merited by everything except the quality of the book. For my part, tact and treachery wore the same face: I declined to review it on the radio. Had I been a painter, I might have done a friend a good turn, but how can I lie about a *book*?

M.'s stay was not a disaster. We laughed a good deal and we talked a very good deal. M. was revealed as fallible (the Phrygians and the Parthians were *not* the same), but he knows his stuff, and other people's. It was not easy to provide him with a book he had not read, though my namesake Max – the Marxist aesthete – supplied one, which I should not have possessed had it not been for our nominal affinity.

Michael has been famous for over thirty years, but all he can think of is that over thirty years ago he was famous. At nineteen he designed Gielgud's *Hamlet*. He was in the RAF at the time and G. kept calling him. When he joined up he had to fill in a form which included a demand for his 'Religion'. He wrote 'Gnostic'. The sergeant asked him what that meant. After M. had tried to explain, the sergeant said, 'We'll say C. of E. then.'

Brian Howard was on the same station and they managed to pinch a stack of 48-hour passes which enabled them to go to London every weekend. M. was finally discharged for 'mental incompetence' and seems to have spent most of the war in theatrical circles. He left them largely, he says, because he was not homosexual. He was propositioned by James Agate in the gents at the Café Royal ('I've got something I should like to show you') and again on the Northern Line: 'Why don't you come back to my place? I've got a pair of Mrs Siddons' nail scissors you might care to see.'

Nothing ever seems to have happened to him except in the company of the renowned. After being expelled from school, he spent the stub of the *entre deux guerres* in Paris and Vienna. He tried to go and fight in the Spanish Civil War, but he was hastily ejected from Barcelona after it was discovered that his mother, Hertha, was on the executive of the Labour Party. She was chairman in 1945. He remembers her being chased by Ernest Bevin one night. He came to their bedroom in a Blackpool hotel (sometime in the late 1920s?).

Michael saw violent action only in Cable Street when the Blackshirts were repelled. He has enough Jewish blood (though his father was not, he says, a Jewish Gould) to alert him to the guilt which exists in Jewish artists, even as Christianised as Epstein, when they make graven images. *His* Jewish blood is, somehow, Zangwill's; one wonders if he would acknowledge it if it were some unknown Itzig's.

Having always mixed with his elders, Michael has the premature age of a precocious boy. Not a few of his contemporaries still dream of one day having the kind of fame M. feels that he has already lost. He envies 'old Henry' his reputation as if Moore were the only other sculptor in England. H.M. has twenty years' seniority over M.A. but that, of course, is why he seems an upstart. M. has never had a homosexual experience – he would not, he says, know what to do – but as the week progressed he reminded me so much of J.R.S. that he prompted in me a kind of *tolerance*. M.'s physical appearance seems quite definite: the brows that hug his own vision, a kind of vigilant meanness, the wart at the base of the nostril, the enclosing beard that makes a nest for the wide, lean jaws. Yet of all things his *nose* seems extraordinarily mutable; at times it was almost inert and flat, but conversation brought tumescence and it seemed then to enclose a central tube which grew inflamed, curved in both axes, so that all the animation, all the warmth, emanated from that unlikely organ.

He is not dull; he is not solemn; and he is not fresh. He makes much of his sexuality; after months of pain and surveillance, he dreams of resurrection. 'Give it six months,' he said to Beetle, embarking on a rehearsal of seduction which he may never have thought to consummate. Rejection did not, however, fail to offend him. I had gone to bed with a migraine and it was obligatory to take advantage. Did he imagine that there was any treachery to me in his overtures? Sex is the measure of his vitality, but he does not take women *seriously*; he would like merely to take them. He has, I suppose, married his mother; he certainly married *a* mother, one who must speak daily to her three daughters, as they to each other, though all are (or have been) married and the oldest is over forty. The telephone bill at Bradfields, even before the latest *hausse*, was over £700 a year.

When a man marries his mother (did not Lady Oxford, the dream Jocasta, most please Byron?), he proves his devotion by boyish infidelities: he shows her his mistresses less to hurt her than to demonstrate how manly she has made him. M. never intended to be faithful; E. did. It was, she told him, the only way to be sure that he wouldn't leave her. Yet she has made him very jealous. After he has had an affair, she flirts outrageously at parties, or did till recently: she is now sixty-four and her looks do not support such a performance.

He says that he has had a lot of women. Yet he is far from confident of his sexual reception. An American woman said to him, after

the event, 'You don't expect me to touch that nasty, dirty thing?'
He laughed, a little, at the story, but what kind of a lover earns such
a remark? (And what kind of woman delivers it?) He was educated,
he says, in pubs; the women were mostly looking after children save
for those (*style* Nina Hamnett) who played men's games. Among
Bohemia's boozers, sex was assimilated to excretion. Tarts and
scrubbers were more frequent sources of pleasure than tender souls.
M. courts a woman with somehow *Irish* prattle.

His only old school is the *Grande Ecole de la Bohémie*. He claims,
like J.W.L., not to regret Cambridge, but he recruits professors (Kirk
is his latest) with grand servility. How good are M.'s Latin and Greek?
Lacking formal schooling, he is wisely modest. However, his feeling
for the world of myth is deep and unfeigned; the past speaks to him
in a language which requires no intermediary. He felt no numinous
presence at Dodona and was startled by our claim to have been
moved by it. It was as if he thought there must have been some
mistake. Quick to compensate for his want of sensation, he paraded
his intelligence and reminded us of the cult of unwashed feet which
had been typical of the priests at the oracle. (I did not remind *him*
that the oracle was based on the whisper of the wind blowing
through sacred oak trees, whose descendants still shade the site.)

Michael lived in Paris and was kept by a rich French girl in the late
1930s. He had a son by her whom he never saw as a baby. Years
later, a smartly suited businessman, with a stiff, flat briefcase, was
sitting in a café where M. went with an old friend. The friend said,
'See that man over there? He's your son.' M. took a look and then
he said, 'I don't think I'll go over.'

The Ayrtons married, he told us, because there was still rationing
and so they were obliged to hand in their books at the village shops.
Though Michael has no time for local company, social uneasiness
was enough to make them put the seal on a relationship neither
wished to solemnise. I suspect that he feels most comfortable in a
triangular relationship (after all, his passion for E. began in one with
his best friend at the Savile). His wish for E. to have lovers was not
merely to justify his having mistresses: he enjoyed the idea of her
being enjoyed by others. Her fidelity was a refusal to join the dance;
by sticking to the rules, she did not, in his eyes, play the game. His
own sexuality is never vindicated by being invested in E. ('This is
too good for Her Grace,' he would say, 'we will take it up to
Piccadilly.') After all these months of attention, her reward will be
to see him well enough to betray her.

He told us of a wartime evening spent in Chelsea with Augustus John and a *copain*, all very drunk. The pal announced that he had to leave and disappeared into a broom cupboard. While he was clattering about, imagining that he was in a narrow street in the blackout, M. felt John's hand moving up his thigh. He removed it tolerantly, exclaiming, 'Come along now, *really*...' John said, 'Sorry, old thing. I thought you were someone else.' M. is sure that he was evicted from theatrical circles because of his innocent but insubordinate heterosexuality. He has the promiscuity of the bargain hunter; he has slept with a great many women for whom he cared little and who themselves cared less.

At the very end of his stay, which had been coloured by what happened at Bordeaux before he ever reached us, there came a call from the British Consulate. M.'s briefcase had been handed in and everything was intact: drawings, traveller's cheques, even his spare teeth. Was he slightly miffed that the thief, if he was one, found nothing worth taking?

This reminds me of Susan Sarandon, who told me, a decade later, of how after her divorce she awaited with anguish the visit of her ex-husband and his new lady who were to choose from among their joint possessions what they wanted in their new house. She could imagine that they would despoil her of all her favourite things. They came and were polite. She invited them to look round the house on their own and waited, anxiously, for them to present their list of requirements. They returned and told her that, after careful thought, they had decided not to take anything. She was insulted. 'There isn't a single thing you want? How could you say that?'

19.11.74. The Greeks are safely through the elections under the (now) whiter than white aegis of Karamanlis. I tried once again to telephone Nikos. Always, before, his number has been engaged or unanswered. This time there was an answer, but it was not he. It was an insurance man, who spoke good English; he said that my friend no longer had that number. Nikos was an outspoken and possibly dangerous man; it is not inconceivable that he could have survived the long years of Papadop, but has fallen victim to the almost anonymous but much more vindictive, because terminal, tyranny of Ioannides. There is particular horror in the possibility of his brutalisation by an insignificant, quickly deposed tyrant. Imagine suffering under men who have no faces and who have not shaved them for a week.

21.11.74. The last of *The Glittering Prizes*. The Yom Kippur war (perhaps a discussion/argument between Barbara, Adam and his brother over going to synagogue); the new house, or playroom, being built; the friend who goes to Israel simply in the line of (jour-nalistic?) duty and gets killed while A. is still dithering with his conscience and his cowardice (could be ANNA's husband, acci-dentally killed on a business trip); the shame and exhilaration in the new house, the 'last' private pleasure dome before closing time in the Gardens of the West: 'We've lived in a golden age and all we've noticed is the glitter.' Death of A.'s father? Rehearsal of empty achievements at the old man's bedside as he lies unconscious, breathing on the respirator. Encounter with an 'Arab' on the tube (turns out to be a charmless Israeli). Not forgetting football: B. stabs the Sunday ball in a fit of exasperation. Return to sources: the Catullus translation. ANNA's (malevolent?) review of Adam's new novel. The moment in one's forties when life begins to flow back-wards and one's life lies behind one. A.'s visit to the Zionist club; a fierce lecture prepared only to be heard by two old ladies. On the way home: witness a furious pub fight, unconnected with Jews or Arabs; sense of being superfluous; calls the police and is thanked by no one. Friends in financial trouble, while he overspends on new house with money from film already abandoned by Mike Clode. Adam's novel, his art, an ignored failure; he is better known for a short appearance on the BBC TV news where he speaks up for Israel (although he has serious secret doubts about his right to do so and about Israeli policies). His brother's two mistresses: Jewish and not. M. Clode's huge new success without him; A.'s sense of rich failure.

Piles? Father's accident? Returns from meeting – hospital? – to find Barbara watching 'interesting' interview with M. Clode. ('He comes across really well.') Desire for Israel as recovered youth and vengeance (for what?): the girls would *have* to accept him. Marriage, the imperfect state, hence its 'adventure'.

In the event, I selected very few of the elements outlined in the menu for the last episode of my BBC series of what were, in 1974, still called 'plays'. Nick Tomalin, with whom I had been at Cambridge, though we were never close friends, had been killed while covering the Yom Kippur war for the *Sunday Times*. He had been reluctant to go, but such was the fame and quality of his article 'Zapping Charlie Cong', which he had written early in the Vietnam War, that he was persuaded to go. He was killed on account of his strong bladder. When the other journalists in the car in which they were travelling on the Golan Heights got out to have a pee, he remained inside. A Syrian heat-seeking missile sought out the warm engine of the vehicle. Nick alone was killed. Harry Evans, then editor of the *Sunday Times*, was stricken with guilt. He later made Tomalin's widow literary editor.

22.11.74. I declined doing another of those radio discussions about The Novel which I was to have done with G. Steiner during the summer, when I had flu. Lamentation and bravado would doubtless be mixed and cooked slowly to a minority taste. My fellow-mourner was to be Marghanita Laski, the woman who is always chosen when the requirements are blue stockings and teeth.

We had returned to the UK so that I could address the Francis Thompson Society on the subject of Maugham and Medicine. I prepared a long, amusing lecture in response to an invitation issued so far in advance, and on paper so badged with distinction, that I was easily seduced. I repented at leisure, but could not bring myself to break my pledge to the earnest Dr Krishnamurti.

Did I suppose myself the recipient of some honour? By the early evening I was sure that I had been gulled, although the meeting had been billed in the *TLS* and was to take place at the National Book League. I went to the London Library in the afternoon, to look out some Wells and R. West (almost adjacent on the shelves). Having arrived at the right stack, I found a man squatting on the floor. He looked up and said, 'Freddie!' The glaucous eyes were like gleaming lanterns at the site of an accident: David Pryce-Jones. He was hunched in a tweed coat and an old book. He is writing a biography of Unity Mitford. He was searching the novels of Henry Williamson for a 10,000-word account of Unity. He had asked H.W. himself in which novel she figured, but 'the old boy is completely gaga and can't remember'. H.W. is president of the F. Thompson Society; I said I would ask him if I saw him, but I didn't see him.

D. showed me some photographs he had of Unity, of Hitler and of Unity's SS lover, deputed to keep her satisfied. D. hates the loftier kind of international, socialite Naziphiles with a fascinated and condescending disdain. I suspect that he has little faith in anyone or anything. 'This country,' he said, with a brilliant shudder, 'is finished. It's collapsing. Don't you feel it? What's going to happen?' He found it most remarkable and most sinister that there was not yet the sign of even the most genteel right-wing movement. (The contingency plans of General Walker are not the stuff of which a backlash is made.) I said, 'The British officer class has already broken and run.' On what evidence? I was thinking of my M.C. stock-broker whose reading of the stock – he reported 'Blood running in the streets' – proves to have been painfully accurate. D.P.-J. and I talked for about an hour, like loud spies at a contrived rendezvous. How similarly aloof we both seemed from all those things – Israel, England, writing, the Nazis – which concerned us most deeply! He even asked me to look around (jokingly, jokingly!) for a university job for him in America (as if I had the smallest idea where to find one or whom to ask).

We talked about the impossibility of reconciling integrity, by which one means art, with patriotism, by which one means social allegiance. Now, certainly, England is a state where no honest man can declare himself dedicated to a single social purpose. When Britain was both rich and powerful, a man might believe himself devoted either to forwarding or to altering her purposes. To read the charts for the mistress of the seas smacked of man's work, but to play the pilot on the round pond of a small fish's world neither satisfies nor deludes. A turn towards a more 'artistic' literature (with its own 'interior' standards and satisfactions) seems likely. The writer must recognise that the available world has, so to say, got away from him: since *all* political programmes are rhetoric, he must now be a hireling, a renegade or an outlaw.

My friendship with P.-J. (singular initials for a literary *revanchard* of the Holocaust) is extremely distant; we know nothing of each other that could be of assistance to the Thought Police. We resemble members of a *réseau* of the international conspiracy of whose exis-tence Julius Streicher was so convinced that, on the eve of his execution he acknowledged that Jewry had proved too strong and offered to become, so to speak, one of us (D. referred me to a book on Nuremburg by a man called Gilbert). What other paranoids resolved their contradictions by volunteering self-abnegation? Where the Inquisition becomes all-powerful it commands its enemies more by the effectiveness of its machinery than by the force of its arguments, or by force itself. The politician, like the believer, will lose his faith not through the refutation of his views but by virtue of the obsolescence of the machine: ideas are not refuted; they rust and become useless, hence meaningless. Any political arrangement that works will have contented adherents (and even contented opponents), but when it collapses, no one can remember what kept them loyal to it.

David and I are alike only in that each might say of the other '*C'est un Juif pas comme les autres*'. (K. McLeish said to me recently, 'You are the least Jewish Jew I know.' He rang up a day later to apologise.) D. and I waited to enter our books at the desk of the London Library. At length, as used to be allowed, I reached for a pad and entered mine myself. I was rebuked by a face full of pimples over the counter. 'Oh forget it,' I said, and left the volumes where they were. P.-J. was amazed. 'Don't you want them?' 'I don't like to be told off,' I said and pushed the PULL door to go into St James's Square. What the hell do I care about Wells and West anyway? I went to the Piccadilly Hotel where Jack Lee (*né* Levy) cut my hair. I waited for an unresentful twenty minutes for my appointment, placated by the pretty breasts and pubic charms of the girls in *Penthouse* and *Mayfair*. I like a barber who knows what I like.

I had finished with Jack Lee by 5.30; two hours before I had to give my lecture. I called B. Glanville who said to come round, but Holland Park was too far to go. He said he had Patricia Highsmith sitting opposite him. I had just read a very poor book of hers, *Ripley Underground*: no plot, no characters, no precision of style or observation. I sent her my dutiful compliments.

No tide of Williephiles was going into the National Book League for my lecture. I sat dolefully in the almost deserted hallway. On a shelf the contenders for the Booker Prize stood on their ends. I read the first dull pages of Kingsley Amis's effort. A man in spectacles, with a functionary's face and a seaman's sweater, came over and said, 'Frederic Raphael?' It was true. 'You've been cancelled,' he said. 'You're crossed out in the book. Why don't you go into the bar and have a drink? Give them my name. I think for the moment you've got an audience of three.'

I don't drink. I don't like bars. I asked for a Dubonnet. The seaman came in with a young man who was, he said, the treasurer of the Francis Thompson Society. 'They're usually here by now,' he said. 'There seems to have been a bit of a muddle.'

'I hope you've got plenty of treasure,' I said, 'because amiable fellow though I am, I am not much amused by all this. If it's a joke, it's not one that I find very jolly. I've come all the way from France for this and it's cost me 1,500 francs.'

There was the usual intake of breath to be heard at any literary occasion when a sum in excess of ten pounds is mentioned. As I was apologising in a crushingly civil way for whacking the only person polite enough to turn up, a short Pakistani, dressed as they all seem to be for Moscow in winter, came hurrying in and shook hands with the treasurer and the seaman. Dr Krishnamurti (it was evidently he) offered me a perfunctory handshake, saying at the same time, 'Has anyone seen Mr Raphael?'

I was eventually persuaded that, whatever the audience, I should give my paper. In fact, there were some twenty or twenty-five people. I had promised them a lecture, I said, and they were going to have one. They seemed to enjoy it, which was rather a disappointment.

Mark Shivas told me that he liked the fifth script of *The Glittering Prizes*. How little I should care for his opinion, were he not where he is! He talked confidently of a March production date and, when I feared conditions, was unconditional about it. We are agreed that I have written three good scripts out of five. Of the other two, I like one he does not and I feel I must prune and sharpen the third, which he likes. What we need is a director. He favours Waris Hussein; I seem to prefer Jim Cellan-Jones, who was at Charterhouse and at Cambridge with me. How cosy that sounds! In fact, I scarcely knew him at St John's (he was a year ahead of me) and at Lockites he was at the very centre of those who, in a few days, destroyed forever any confidence I might ever have had in the basic decency of the British or in the trustworthiness of those I thought my friends. One learns a lot at school, if one is unlucky enough. My case was not *very* cruel (no blood) and though central to my life, it was quite peripheral to that of my persecutors, who soon forgave themselves and forgot all about it. What was said (but never done) to me was a not uncommon reaction to what was going on in Palestine. How did *we* respond to the death of Ghandi? I recall Sinha, our Indian, coming into the dining room long-faced and seeming ridiculous in the parade of his grief.

My zeal to amuse is unsuspected evidence of the lasting damage

inflicted by schoolboy malice. To return comedy for pain is always
to offer the bully an agreeable rate of exchange. When in New York,
I met Robin Jordan, a Lockite who had observed my savaged solitude and done nothing either to worsen or to alleviate it. He claimed
acquaintance when, after *Darling*, I seemed to be famous. The first
thing he said was, 'I'm surprised you're not in a mental home.'

There was floodwater on the main road to Cambridge. Workers
gathered outside a factory to watch cars plough through the unre-
flecting water. When I reached the Ayrtons' lane, under the black
cables of the 'Lynn Chadwicks', as M. calls the pylons, I had no idea
how deep the water was in the dip ahead of me. Already late for
lunch, I left the car on the verge and ran, in my black wellingtons,
towards the house. The water came to within an inch of the tops
of my cold boots. The Ayrtons were in their small conservatory.
Alone, all reconciliations are possible (no other, knowing, eyes
observe one's humbug). If M. had guessed that we had had enough
of him at Lagardelle (surely I betrayed dismay when British Airways
threatened a strike that might keep him with us for another week),
he was loquacious and eager in his greeting. We had soup and cold
duck. M. is working, and worrying: an auction was due the
following week and prices were being monitored 'by all of us'. Some
Moores were to be among the contemporary English work; if 'old
Henry' fell, who would not tumble?
    I saw in Elisabeth (who had, of course, had a holiday from M.,
no less than he from her) the blurred outlines of a beauty which,
twenty-five years ago, must have been inflammatory. When I left,
for the hike back to the car, they loaded me with books: his first,
dedicated to her; his monograph on Pisano (signed by him and
Moore); a translation of the Phaedo and the Apology, with his
portraits of Socrates; and his Verlaine, for which I mean to pay.

A man makes love to a friend's wife, noticing only her beauty. She
finally runs away with him, thinking only that he is an artist whom
she admires, just as he thinks only that she is a beautiful woman.
They have a passionate affair and, as if to prove that their betrayal
of her husband was not a casual thing, they decide to marry. What
will they find to say to each other during the long haul of matri-
mony? They discover, to their surprise and relief, that they have
many common interests (E. turned out to be an archaeologist and
Hellenophile who opened M.'s eyes to the Greek world). However,
the more intellectual respect they have for each other, the greater

their sexual indifference. The marriage survives; their love dies.

Les arbres d'automne se montrent sans chemises,
Car Perséphone, fugace, a bouclé ses valises.

23.11.74. I set off for London and never arrived. The A12 was blocked ahead and also, as I found when I turned back, behind me. I sought Chelmsford by the back roads, became marooned trying to ford a dip in the road, stalled (I tried to accelerate through the flood, instead of going gently), but finally managed to start the engine again and get through. There was a feeling of doom in the black November air. It was a week of bombs and bad news. The weather seemed to be selecting a Noah. I returned to the Wick after six hours of driving, convinced that England was no place to live. This after I had been deprived of the PEN AGM! We watched a dismal *Monty Python*, quite as unfunny as one's own imitations.

A writer of a certain talent, who has led a life of – *mas o menos* – marital fidelity, a bourgeois existence, is asked by a notoriously profligate playboy friend to read the MS of a novel he has written. The writer is apprehensive: what if he has missed all the pleasures, puerilities, of life? Imagine when a great lover tells all! The MS is full of clichés and vulgarities and vanities; its quarrels are undignified squabbles, its only passion is for statistics of conquest: the Lothario has lived a life of repetitive banality. The writer, for all the numerical modesty of his experience, has had a richer, deeper and, in a sense, more varied life. Would it were so.

The ageing Juan begins to count how many shots there are left in his locker.

How is it that amateur writers all tend to be amateur in the same way? Professionalism is, to a marked degree, a matter of editorial expertise. The real writer both sees more and selects *less* than the amateur. He lives in a different world and there is no easy ferry from the common shore to his.

The dread of missing something is the phobia of those who have more rather than less than other men.

16.12.74. We have been in California for a week. The home of greed is nicely furnished. Its face is sunburned and its teeth gleam whitely; one scarcely feels their bite. I go each morning to see Alan Pakula. It is curious how unreliable are the expressions of the bearded. What should identify the face cloaks all kinds of furtive mobility, rather as a theatrical curtain, bulging and swaying with the preparations of amateurs, both conceals and draws attention to the frantic unreadiness behind it. Sir Walter Ralegh, the bearded one, was the incarnation of that 'mutability' to which he drew such scornful attention.

We went to meet Paul and Sarah at LAX. Bernie Cornfeld was one of the first-class passengers who enjoyed the privileges of a world-famous swindler and came off early. He wore a blue yachting cap and a grey polo and a blue blazer. I was struck by the peculiar angle of his head. All out of drawing, it was tilted back, as if flinching from the insults which I, for one, was willing to throw at him. I have never been an investor in IOS, but I felt immediate animosity towards him. There was a twist in the neck so that his jaw was almost, so it seemed, 75 degrees to the side. He had a grey beard which might have been filched from a disgraced general of the Union cavalry; in his eyes a kind of insolent apprehension, as if the whole world was lining up to ask for a dime he had no intention of handing over. One could read almost anything into the terrible yet unchastened face, the swindler-evangelist still humming his own hymns, still cocking one ear for the cops, the other for the heavenly choir.

26.12.74. A Christmas *pas comme les autres* has been and gone. Pakula and I have uncovered the plot that we have been looking for and my journey has, I suppose, proved its necessity. (I now have only the script to write.) LA is a Disneyland for adults; a world without myths and without illusions, except the illusion that such a world can exist and be worth living in. It is a republic of the free, or at least the free-spending. The dollar liberates because there is nothing it cannot buy. If a good time is your idea of a good time, come and get it. Only one thing embarrasses Angelenos: values. The idea that anything might be more worth doing than anything else (unless it makes more money) is unthinkable here. The tedium of freedom – of the *Libertá* which Juan celebrated – is so palpable in its vanity, irksomeness, repetition, that if morals did not exist, someone would have to be commissioned to come up with some.

On Zuma beach. Natalie Wood and Lelia Goldoni, woman to woman, Star to mere star, both once with the same man, discussed having another child as the *bourgeoisie* of the 60s considered having a second car. The beach was too big for the party it contained. That wide sand could have entertained an army. Our brief band of Boxing Day expats made no happy colony. The decline of England is not regretted; it is hardly noticed out here. Nothing that the British export is much wanted, except John Schlesinger and cashmere. There was little conversation. What witticism can thrive in the world of the frisbee? Our Star lay on a blanket while her child played with her husband, who is not its father. She spent most of her time consulting her face in a hand-mirror and looking for trouble. When he asked her what she wanted for Christmas, she replied, 'Yesterday'.

Lelia arrived late. Years ago, when we knew her, she sported a bullfighter's cape and a Cordoban hat and looked undressed without a rose between her teeth. Now she is a short, dumpy mother. She looked at me with chapped modesty. 'Can I ask you something? Have you seen *The Day of the Locust*?' 'I hear it's not exactly the day of the low cost,' I said. She looked at me with a hint of Italian reproach. 'I've seen one day's rushes,' she said, 'and they were sensational!'

Her close-ups were beautiful; the film is a masterpiece. Well, J.R.S. is a master pastrycook: why shouldn't his stuff taste good? I am not of the movies. I am bored by the people; I will take their money, but I cannot take them. What interests them dulls me; I become less and less amusing, even to myself, as the identical days succeed each other. As they looked at their watches for excuses to leave, the beach party made urgent dates to see each other again. How hard they all work to kill the time that is killing them!

A true story. A. and B. were best friends; both were screenwriters, but B. was also a ranking novelist. A. was a gambler and a guileless soul. He was hired to write a screenplay and he and his wife, C., rented a villa in the South of France to do the work in. B. was invited along; he was lonely and he had a novel to finish. At a certain point A. was summoned to London to confer on the pages. The conference was shorter than expected and he caught a plane to Nice without alerting his wife. He arrived at the villa late at night and found B. and C. asleep in the same big bed. He did not wake them. He picked up his bags and walked back into Nice and took a plane back to London. After several more days, C. became anxious; she telephoned A. and asked him when he was coming back. He said, 'Never', and never did. B. and C. got married and had four children together.

I wrote a short story, *Shared Credit*, from the above *fait divers* more than twenty years after hearing about it. I made fiction a little bit sweeter and neater than reality. There is no way of knowing how long an idea will take to germinate. I was once told an anecdote at a party and went home and began *A Double Life*, a novel based on it, the very next day.

George and Joan Axelrod took us to meet Christopher Isherwood. We collected them from their house on Highcrest, at the top of Schuyler, in a section of town that reminds one of the Vale of Health built on a hill: small houses of opulent modesty, lanterns, landscaping, precarious cosiness. The Axelrods once lived very differently. George stepped off the plane from NYC 'straight into Edie Goetz's living room'. (She was the great hostess of the Golden Years; her husband was a power and – being L.B. Mayer's daughter – she was raised to it.)

The Axelrods have spent most of the fortune he earned; they have enough left to live better than 99 per cent of the human race, but their decline humbles them. G. has just been employed for the first time in eighteen years. He has written a thriller (a remake of *The Lady Vanishes*) for a producer who once worked for him. When he delivered it, the producer said, 'I hope it isn't too funny.' It was, so he spent last week 'removing the style and the jokes'. G. is an old pro in the joke game, with the drinker's capacity for brilliant starts and early stops. Cirrhosis of the wits has slowed him, but not made him slow. When Isherwood opened the door he said that he had almost called to cancel, because he had a sore throat. George said, 'Christopher, any cold of yours is a cold of mine.'

Ken Tynan has written a movie ('Brilliant, brilliant,' G. says) devoted to flagellation. He is to direct it himself. G. says that he has half a million dollars in Switzerland from *Oh! Calcutta!* In youth, Ken could convince himself that sexual self-expression was an aspect of the release of the oppressed. Like Byron, he was a spokesman for the mute and a partisan of the rebellious. As he grows older, the sense (and sensuality) of common humanity wanes. He becomes a purchaser of pleasure; he loses interest in dawns he will never see. Ken has wit where Byron had genius (of a kind), but he and the fluke Lord share a form of social schizophrenia. Had Byron not inherited the title, against the odds, would he ever have been liberated into shameless flower? Had K.T. not been the illegitimate son of a baronet, would he have gone to Oxford, flourished, transcended bastardy and taken London triumphantly from behind?

At dinner with Isherwood and Don Bachardy, George gave us a recent instance of T.'s wit: 'If Gar and Ruth Gordon ever get a divorce, who will have custody of the anecdotes?'

A rumour went around not long ago that the Queen was to have a raise in salary. K.T. and a company of rebels planned to march on Buckingham Palace and pee on the railings. When the increase was delayed, or denied, he went and had dinner with the Snowdons instead.

Georgia Brown. Dark eyes, Amazonian helmet of hair, shining cheekbones; a feminist warrior hot for a scythed chariot. Over dinner I paid for, she told us that within twenty years there would not be any money, wealth or property. Wanna bet? Yet she is fierce for success; short, dark and dumpy, in a place where thirty is old, she is forty.

I went with Judy Scott-Fox to the Bel Air Hotel to have lunch with David Lean and his blonde much younger wife, Sandy. Judy said that he was apprehensive lest I find him uneducated; he left school when he was fifteen. I doubt if he fears anything except not getting what he wants. However, I was told now that I hurt his feelings almost ten years ago, in the long introduction I wrote to *Two for the Road*. I never imagined that he would read it. Apparently, he saw the movie on election night and greatly liked it, apart from Albert.

We talked together till 5; it was a sort of audition and audience in one. How ready am I, if selected, to be at Lean's service for the full year he demands? Do I want to be obediently inventive in an office while Big Ears waits for pages? I played those games ten years ago. If working with Lean is an advertisement of eminence, who will care except other screenwriters?

Lean has unexpected loyalties (he loved Pinewood); he knows that Sam Spiegel is a scoundrel, but will not say a word against him, only repeat those others have said: 'Billy Wilder said to Sam, "When you put your head on the pillow at night, doesn't it bother you when you think of the things you have done?'" People say that Billy is terribly cruel (S.D. hesitates to introduce me) but, judging from the originality of the above, his mind is a storeroom with no shortage of antiques.

Lean has the style of an old general, a cinematic Alex who has managed to work with the Yanks and yet remains detached and Old School. He sat on a sofa in the suite, with a mirrored wall behind; I could see him simultaneously front and back. From the back, he was a career officer at GHQ. It needed the flash of his eyes to convince one that he had worked with actors and composed scripts. I asked him about Richardson (Pakula and I had been thinking of him for our movie). 'Ralphie? Ralphie can still do it.'

D.L. has presence but not confidence. He left the wine for Sandy to choose; in the end I chose it: champagne. Why not? They have lived in Rome, this slim old man (he is sixty-seven) and the capable blonde. Now he fears to return. He is famously rich and – he whispered to me – afraid she will be kidnapped. Kidnapping is the only booming industry in Italy. For years, so they say, he lived in a Rolls Royce. He doesn't return much to England and does not like to film there. When he and Sandy are in Africa, they go everywhere by private plane ('It's the only way'). He said he would give me the name of the pilot (British) and I thought 'Perhaps he really does want to work with me.' Does it matter?

Frank Kermode would be incommoded if he could not demonstrate his astuteness by detecting the consistent ideology underpinning D.H.L.'s anti-intellectualism. Maugham had no prescriptive purpose (did his medical training warn him against ideological panaceas?); he preferred the caustic lucidity of French to the parochial conceits of English writers. The Vicar of Whitstable endowed his nephew with an aversion from the religious language which did so much to furnish the dignity of both D.H.L. and T.S.E. Academics who teach these authors find them happily available to scriptural exegesis; they provide texts from which sermons can be tricked. Maugham's language has an embarrassing thinness; his use of cliché (which exasperated Edmund Wilson) can be understood only in the light of the primacy of French in his life: he often mistook a platitude for the *mot juste*. It has been suggested that he settled in Cap Ferrat because Gerald Haxton was *interdit de séjour* in England, but wasn't his reason also sentimental? He belonged in France, he was English; dialogue was his form: it made use of his duplicity.

In the *Sunday Times* literary department. Larry Adler came in, a small man, neat in a shrivelled sort of way. He wore round tortoise-shell spectacles and a blue mackintosh and was carrying an ink-coloured waterproof cap. He looked like a myopic albino prune. His entrance was bright, an audition. He offered the cap, dangling on a single finger, as an enigma. 'Guess who made me a present of this? It's someone you all know.' 'We' were J.W.L., John Peter and John Whitley and Felix Aprahamian, and we couldn't guess. So what was the answer? 'Tony Geraghty!' Who was Tony Geraghty? None of us had any idea. The lameness of the surprise left the conversation limp.

John Peter ambushed me at the entrance to the newsroom. He seemed dispirited, but malice invigorated him: had I heard that Adler had been caught shoplifting and the news had been in the paper the previous week? LA had done some 'amusing' reviews – one on the criminal character of Jebb Stuart Magruder – for Jack Lambert. He now feared that he would be blacklisted (again). The charge against him was scarcely heavy: he had lifted 74p-worth of toffees. A store manager with a sense of humour might have asked him for a tune on his harmonica, but in these moral times a famous man who nicks a bag of toffees must expect the pillory.

1975

8.4.75. Schlesinger's vaunted *Heartbreak House* at the National. A French's acting edition manured with cash. The sets are fine (grotesque without being funny) and the costumes are costly without illuminating the characters they hang on. The actors do all kinds of prodigiously obvious things with their voices and the play is as dull as two Sundays laid end to end.

As for Alan Ayckbourn's *The Norman Conquests*, here's jam without bread. There is laughter, but no *grounds* for laughter; nothing observed, everything contrived. The matter is so thin that it may be recommended for anyone's diet; it will suit fat folk and fat heads. The title depends upon a pun on the protagonist's name; the weariest kind of wit. Norman never conquers anyone, so we have the paradox of disappointment, climactic bathos. On the old Brighton pier, the nudist colony turned out – after you had inserted your penny – to be a colony of ants. Cheating the public is a national tradition: serves you right for having naughty hopes. So Aykbourn gives us lovers who never make love, a conqueror who doesn't conquer, weddings that don't marry people, and children who are born but remain inconceivable: every shallowness in the English repertoire, the dipstick comedy of national pettiness held up as evidence of creative ingenuity. Aykbourn's success is very successful; and that's about all you can say for it.

That Jack Lambert thinks the trilogy a masterpiece is proof only of Jack's long fear of culture. For a man of his drab temper, the very witching hour of night is about half past two on an autumn afternoon. He writes better as a hypocrite than he does with sincerity; he defends Culture nobly and eloquently, in general, but he fears and derides every manifestation of it which does not salute banality or debunk the sublime.

What is wrong with *The Norman Conquests* is just about everything except the *idea*; it is a comedy at which everyone *agrees* to laugh, a two-way mirror in which the audience see actors doing what they themselves do: behave stupidly, emptily, charmlessly. And because those who do these things for them are actors, they nod in condescending recognition and consent to find themselves hilarious. The mediocre feel superior because they have bought tickets to be reminded of their own crassness. That you should have to wait six and a half hours before seeing a cliché silly-ass propose to a cliché minx is about par for the English course. He does so amid shrieks of laughter from those led by the critics to believe that they are people of aesthetic discrimination because they have lasted the course. It used to be that the British believed themselves to be the envy of the world; now their pretensions have shrunk: they believe their *theatre* is the envy of the world. Dream on.

30.5.75. Is there any thrill quite like the read-through of a play? To go to a rehearsal room and find one's characters in attendance is to realise a divine fantasy. (Iris Murdoch says that she envies God designing the heads of his creations; I should prefer to supply the dialogue.) Tom Conti is so perfect an Adam Morris that the battle seems already half won. It was only the one actress whom I knew before who seemed to be trying too hard.

Paul and I went to see them shooting the 'Cresta Run' on Hampstead Heath. Somehow, in those first hours, everything was right: the steep earthen path between old trees was exactly as I imagined. Mark said that we had 'the best cameraman in the BBC' and even the uncertain weather did not dent the serenity of the unit. I could happily spend every day with the actors, but happily I shall not: a writer should write. The director, Waris Hussein, said to me, 'You're as nervous as we are!' 'Yes,' I said, 'but not about the same things.' Will it be good enough? It may. *The Glittering Prizes* make me feel that I may have recovered the wasted years from 1969 onwards, when I wrote screenplays that were not produced and said nothing. Am I a fool to write for TV? There is a pretty arrogance in filling paper cups with better wine than they merit.

7.8.75. In the *Librairie Favalelli* in Sarlat I saw a novel by Hardy Kruger. On the cover was a face at once blondely youthful and maturely crepuscular. I met him a few times almost twenty years ago, when he came to Pinewood to star in *Bachelor of Hearts* (a larky title which, alas, stuck). Tom Wiseman interviewed him for the *Evening Standard*. T. quizzed Hardy severely about his time in the Hitler Youth. Since he was fourteen at the time, and his country was at war, H. was reluctant to be ashamed, but T. kept at him. After a long dialogue, H. conceded that he had subscribed to a criminal ideology and T. was about to leave, when H.'s wife said, 'Mr

Viseman, so far as ze Jews and ze Germans are concerned, vy don't
we simply agree that there were mistakes on both sides?'

Tom's father stayed too long in Vienna, helping others escape (at
a price). He died in a camp. T. and his mother reached England,
where he suffered the intimidations of charitable Jews and the casual
cruelty of the English. His identity was altered, his name and his
language changed. Escaping from charity at an early age, he began
to try and make a living as a journalist. After ten years in England
he was both fluent and caustic enough to sell his work. After my
ten easy years in England, I was a Cambridge scholar, but could I
have made my way in Fleet St without the assistance of my father
and the sub-editing of Guy Ramsey? My course has been spruce
with hurdles of a height everyone knew I could (or should) clear. I
hated the Germans, but no branches had been ripped from my family
tree. In fact I feared English more than German anti-Semitism. I
was a stranger in a far from strange land; I shared its prejudices,
except where they hurt me: my father called homosexuals 'pansies'
and so, at times, did I. Hardy K. was mooted as a leading actor for
Bachelor of Hearts weeks after the first drafts had been written. I took
the idea as a joke, but such absurdities occurred every day in the
crazy world of the movies. My disdain for the milieu made me an
accessory to its follies.

10.8.75. How well, and how charmlessly, John Lehmann's obituary
of Cyril Connolly displays the smugness of a certain kind of *littérateur*! What short story writer could put himself in a less favourable
light than J.L. manages to shine on himself? He has the arrogance
without charm of the Kingsmen to be seen at Cambridge At Homes,
when courteous prigs took Sunday tea sitting in rows of chairs, like
so many Narcissi with an indoor pool before them. J.L. thinks that
Cyril deserved an old age of luxurious ease more than Maugham
(the usual butt). It may be that in a universe of heavenly *bourses*, C.
might warrant generous subsidy, but if 'deserve' means anything in
a mundane sense, why should Connolly's idleness merit the dividends of Maugham's industry?

11.8.75. *After Babel* seemed an impressive, charged book on first
reading, but the abiding effect is of erudite shallowness. Donald
Davie's review becomes less spiteful and more convincing. The
display of critical reading with which *After Babel* begins turns out to
be the best number in it. And, on reconsideration, what large brilliance is to be found even there? Steiner's work has a Babelish

structure itself: beginning with a grandiose design and a splendid ground-plan, it ends in reduplication. Synoptic summaries are piled on bibliographic catalogues until one senses that the builder, as so often with tower blocks, is adding another storey because it is easier – once proportion has been abandoned – to go on, and on, rather than to conclude. One critic protested at the difficulty of G.S.'s 'arguments', but it was more the long words than the subtlety of the prose which made reading a lumpy process.

Steiner cannot understand how language is used by those who are at home in it. He can speak with instructive erudition, but he does not belong to the society in which he is so ostentatiously at home. He rents, as well as rends, a culture. What man at his ease would need to be so cultivated? He is like a guest who gives you *such* a good time that you end up taking very long walks to avoid another dose of his suffocating thoughtfulness. How impressive is his list of elegant engagements and yet how monotonously high-minded he affects to remain! His emblematic examples are all – with the exception of Noël Coward – taken from life's great set books: his thesis, you feel, will finally be handed up to Yahweh for judgement, after which he will be chosen as God's right-hand Prize Fellow. One can see him as a sublime version of that handsome, egregious interpreter who accompanies the top Russian gangsters: indispensably impotent, he will stand between Lucifer and the Godhead at their summits, the translator *par excellence*, obsequiously storing the secrets which he will leak, with a sly smirk, to a few chosen angels after the last trump.

My father has no more hope. He is a derelict from whom more and more is taken every day. Like those roadside wrecks which, at first, appear little different from what can be repaired and made road-worthy again, he seemed at first so much less bad than he might have been that it was possible to believe that he would return to mobility. Then, with the slow suddenness of so many declines, the irreparable became evident: there was no remedy for the depreda-tions which cripple and humiliate him. The worms of ruin never cease their cruel drilling. His mind fights with wit the mindless decay that saps it. He can scarcely walk? Soon he will not walk at all. He is obsessed by his bladder? Soon he will be unable to control it. He forgets things? Soon he will have forgotten everything. There are no consolations for a man so accurately disconsolate.

My father had been seriously injured in a road accident in 1970, when he was thrown through the windscreen after the driver ignored a Stop sign. My father was in the passenger seat and had not put on his seat belt; he feared that it might imply that he lacked faith in his friend's driving. He belonged to a generation of men for whom courtesy formalised respect. He was in a coma for two weeks. He had struck his head on the road and never fully recovered his speed of thought and movement. He had, however, retrieved a certain mental and physical competence, but then he fell and broke his hip, after which he degenerated. He bore his misfortunes with stoicism, but not without anguish.

12.9.75. I am pettily tortured by financial anxiety. The fear is anaes-thetised by the offers which keep coming in. Auditions are my drug. On Saturday last, at the Dorchester I set out to impress Martin Scorsese, whose *Alice Doesn't Live Here any More* won Ellen Burstyn an Oscar this year. He did not impress me. He is small and – despite the black T-shirt and the weightlifter's shoulders and a big-buckled belt – asthmatic and nervous. When he draws himself up to his full height, a dwarf would not be dwarfed. They want to do a movie of *Haunted Summer*, a novel about Byron and Shelley at Lake Geneva so bad that it could hardly fail to be taken seriously by the company. I spoke at length about his lordship and P.B.S., quite as if I had something to prove. The female examiner – S.W. – carried her shapeless, pronouncedly nippled breasts slung as low as a legion-naire's water bottles.

The Dorchester still had the shakes after the Hilton bomb, which had gone off twenty-four hours earlier. A pink doorman – Mr Pickwick doubling as Buttons – examined my briefcase, briefly. Outside, a wedding party in 50s costumes – the women in hats like French *patisserie*, the men ho-hoing under grey toppers – stood and gushed like figures in a rococo fountain. Now and again a horse in a hat would come through the lobby. Two children, a page and a maid of honour, played tag. The page was rolled over the check-ered floor by the little darling; the staff ignored them like royalty.

London was at peaceful war with a brutal enemy whose griev-ance aggrieved it. The innocent guests of the Dorchester – who could possibly have a serious quarrel with *them*? – had been pitched into the street by three false alarms. Unless a bomb went off soon, there was going to be trouble.

13.9.75. The Summerskills who are they but the insensitive invaders, no worse than the Dorians, who descended on our quiet Aegean bay and served notice that the lotus would henceforth be available in Libby's tins? We hated their coming and the ostentation of their staying (they built a large house right in our eyeline) and now, I suppose, we should regret their leaving. They are very friendly and obliging: their man looks after *Kapa*, Sarah's donkey, and their presence – more continuous than ours – deters those who might colonise our house.

Mimi is a stately lady, at least sixty, with enough money to live elegantly but not, it seems, enough to buy a good set of teeth. Her sons are all tall and broad and, we are promised, handsome. Their names and achievements are paraded whenever we meet her. I dropped a brick years ago when I passed a scathing remark about a fat girl on the beach who turned out to be one of Mimi's daughters. I pretended that I had been talking about someone else and my explanation was immediately accepted; M. has no intention of being offended by a celebrity. She has the American faith that money and success can never have bad breath.

Mimi was first, unhappily, and for a long time, married to an amateur tennis champion. She is aware of the short time left in which to enjoy John and the life that she now finds so amiable. Both have grown children and it is now their turn to be childish; they plant flowers and play houses. Late love gives them a smutty innocence; they are much possessed by nakedness, their own and the young tourists'. John scans the beach with Japanese binoculars. He can spot a naked body almost anywhere in the bay. When all else fails, he turns his gaze on our terrace, where we do not disappoint him. He and Mimi are always being discovered while in the nude, fortunately never by us. They talk much of the *Kama Sutra* and give you to understand that they are up to having sex on a swing. John too was married before and, in his new-found conjugality, he gleams like a happy prisoner who no longer looks at the gate or asks the time.

'Our' beach is no longer ours. People come in by the crowded bus from the village. When we first came to the island there was no wheeled traffic because there were no roads. Now the far end of the beach, where the bus halts, is mined with rusty tins and expended bottles. There are warnings, in English, against camping and nudism, so the kids take their clothes off and pitch their tents. The girls bare their breasts without hesitation. Many lie completely naked, or with dresses hitched up under their chins, like rolled blinds, bushes burning brightly in the sun. Their nakedness wears expressions of, it appears, deliberate nullity. They lie like spent shells along the path indented by the donkeys and ourselves. The Greeks seem not to react to the nakedness. It is not as novel as today's young girls may think. The bay harboured a nudist colony before we even came to the island; its huts were already derelict when we bought Flora's *spiti*. If there is no evidence that outrage closed the colony, Mimi and John say that it is *male* nudity that scandalises the Greeks. The innocence of their daughters is, we are promised, sacred to them. The sight of two naked men playing paddle-ball offends against all morality. There have been cases of Greeks descending from their mules and physically assaulting the 'indecent'. One man was badly injured, another deported.

The *phylakos* employed by Jean-Marie Drot was particularly livid about the nudity on the public beach, though his employer, the Rabelais of the Cyclades, entertains his mistresses stitchless without exciting any resignations from his overpaid staff.

What appals people now is the shamelessness with which the poor and unprivileged assume the manners and morals of the comfortable. They have not come to Greece; they have come to have fun. A hippie said to me, 'Hey, man, what island is this?' They rejoice in being no one in particular in no particular place.

As for the islanders, what kind of Hellenes are they? Many of them are descended from refugee Albanians. If some are indeed outraged by the new morality, it is only those with virgins to market. The majority remain calm and collect as much money as the kids bring with them. They are beginning to relish the prosperity of which the affluent *xenoi* are already tired. What does either side care that the island has lost its magic? Here no Polyphemus threatens, no Circe bestialises; she makes dresses to measure and he roasts his sheep for cash. If Procrustes were a hotelier today, he would make your bed any length you wanted; it's your drachs he'd be after.

The islanders are as often robbed as robbing. The kids eat in the *tavernas* and run before they have to pay the bill. Yorgios D. is now of the *troisième age* (I remember him, *podokys*, dancing all night) and cannot scamper down the rocks and across the beach in pursuit of those who break his bread, eat Irini's *keftethes* and then beat it. Yorgios has become rich enough, all the same, to winter in Oregon, where he has a daughter.

One of Mimi's adult sons lives away down the coast when he is on the island. He and some friends have built three houses which they let to the rich and romantic. His partners are his older brother, who sells Asian 'art' to New Yorkers, and Bill Bradley, an American basketball player who makes over $100,000 a year and stands six foot seven. He stood that tall in the boat which took us from Drakos' pier to the harbour on the last day of our stay. He is bearded and confident and overpays the boatmen. The Summerskills are paupers in his wake. 'Bill is what they call a superstar,' their son Robert told me.

I said, 'You're going to intimidate me in a minute. Don't tell me he can spell too.'

Bradley, standing below me in the well of the boat, asked me what I had written, as if I were up for a job writing basketball games. He is big and nice and boring. He is spoken of as a future candidate for the presidency of the United States.

Mimi's daughter, Helen, a young American lecturer in Classics, was arrested last winter after incautiously signing for a package of books at the *tachydromeion*. They were discovered to have been hollowed out and filled with hash. Her signature on the unopened package rendered her technically guilty of drug-trafficking. She was arrested and put on a boat to Crete in the company of two murderers. One of them attempted to rape her on the boat. She spent the rest of the journey hugging a policeman. People from our island travelled to Crete to give evidence in her favour, but not Yorgios, who had built the Summerskills' house. Someone said that it was, after all, not his problem; true, but Y.'s hotel had been built out of materials most of which had supposedly gone into the Summerskill *spiti*. Thanks to the testimony of the islanders, Helen was acquitted.

Y.'s failure to put himself out for his benefactress was not untypical. He is a charming bully with a sailor's neatness and a pirate's morals. He drove his pretty daughter to go and live in the States. How they chased and worked her when she was a child! Sarah always thought that her name was 'Gregora' (the Greek for 'quickly') because her father said it to her so often.

Hellenes, Hellenes! Why did I weep with joy at the Colonels' eviction? How white a knight is Karamanlis? In Athens, on the Sunday of our return from the island, I was alone in the afternoon streets. The Parthenon museum had put paid to the children's appetite for culture; and the National Museum on top of it to Beetle's. While they slept, I walked around under a sky muttering with jovial threats. What does a country do when it has shrugged off a tyranny? It shrugs again. The banality of bricks and marble saves the face of a city.

The idea of a third Greek novel recurred; the ghosts of the characters ran at me like memories set in the future. Why was I somehow diminished by the restitution to the Greeks of the clumsy freedom which they enjoy once again? I thought of the naked girls on the island beach, the curled gift of their cunts to the landscape. One dreams of a world without repression or hypocrisy and when it presents itself, what does it remedy?

Love, like liberty, seems brightest in a sombre world. I imagined a passion which seemed (was) based on a common ambition for humane values – justice, honour, etc. – and which begins, mysteriously, to disintegrate as those very values are redeemed. Think of Vassili, with his hooded ambiguity and protracted London exile. Imagine him returning, a modern Odysseus, greeted with the joy his steadfastness deserves. His long rectitude has served as an example, an encouragement to those in darkness that a candle was still burning somewhere. But soon his unblemished character seems a reproach to those – some his close friends – who agreed to make the best of life in a tyranny and elected – as though cynicism was a kind of resistance – to profit from it.

Ordinary people will find almost anything ordinary and accustom themselves to it. The intellectual has a furtive yearning for repressive states, in which he is alone and his enemies are omnipotent. Such a state makes him feel *right*. The cowardice of those whose concern is solely *sauver les meubles* gives his simplest act the allure of fortitude. His freedom remains that he thinks freely, whatever anyone else says or does. Reticent eloquence sustains him in the silence of fear. No one can guess with what disdain he defers to what he cannot, for the present, change. He is tortured, but he does not lose his unspeaking voice. Only with the coming of the dawn does night fall on him. The people who long suspected him of courage are reminded of their cowardice. The hero stands out, tiresomely, against their shame. Those who have done well – because they could do nothing else – out of the fallen regime now advocate amnesty; those who have not are tired of the subject, and of politics. The shrillness of 'extremists' on the left causes such alarm among the ordinary people that they soon forget the arrogance of the tyranny and remember only its warnings. The threat of Communism is exaggerated (since the democratic right has a huge majority), but it is enough to cause a rueful nostalgia for the 'safety' which the military dictatorship guaranteed.

People grow impatient, even vindictive, towards the apostles of democracy. Reaction against the Colonels *strengthened* the left when they were in power, but who will control it now that they have gone? The indignation of 'respectable' Athenians at the new, loud liberties has something of the outrage of the peasants whose daughters' virginities are threatened by the tassels of the volley-ball players.

Think not only of the bad conscience of the compromisers at Vassili's return, virtue in person, but also of *his* dismay, rage even, at his countrymen's mundane use of the freedom which they have not fought to regain. Could V.'s condition be revealed in some kind of perversity – let's say – becoming *once again* a feature of his sexual behaviour with a mistress (not necessarily one who was with him in exile)?

In actual fact, Vassili's wife was not in London with him. She was refused an exit visa by the Colonels. He spoke of her 'imprisonment' with a kind of amused rage. He had got away from her. Her maltreatment by the Junta, though painful to him, gave him – one can guess – a kind of satisfaction. It promised that they took him seriously; it lent political glamour to his monkish isolation. Both a martyr and a man who martyrised another, he inflicted his principles, and their consequence, on his wife. She had to care for and feed the children whom he was magnificently unable to help (I gave him money when Nikos told me that he needed it).

The Colonels imagined, if they were capable of imagination, that they were hurting him, but in fact they lent him the mantle of an arrogance he could scarcely have worn otherwise. If they had been cruelly enlightened, they would have sent his wife and children after him to England. He would then have had to deal with daily domestic problems instead of enjoying the penurious luxury of plotting and pamphleting.

Meanwhile, his friend Nikos was one of the few who did not compromise with the Junta. He had been an airline pilot until he was landed with a wife, Evdoxia, and one, two, three, four children. He had to come down to earth as an Athenian shopkeeper. He despised the Colonels with an outspokenness which terrified E. She favoured discretion. His loud public remarks were, for instance, meant to be overheard by other diners in Athenian restaurants. He dared them to agree, or disagree, with him. Once a man who seemed dangerously well-dressed paid his bill just when E. was afraid that he was going to have him arrested. Nikos punished his wife for her timidity by the aggressive shamelessness of his behaviour; she shivered to see that he enjoyed causing fear in her. What began in him as a genuinely brave gesture turned into righteous sadism.

When the Junta was overthrown, Nikos decided no longer to

work in the shop. He abandoned the servility which had made him, in his own eyes, a coward and in hers a bully. As Vassili returned to *his* wife, Nikos left his.

The exile learns, and is sustained by, the affectations – not always unworthy – of the society that gives him refuge. Yet he is diminished by not suffering from the faults of the country he has been forced to leave. He sees his native land as the healthy see the sick, with divorced pity; he suffers for it, but not with it. In London, Vassili takes a drab Greek mistress whose place might later be taken by a more beautiful woman who, at first, resented the sexual use he had made of her dull 'sister'. The second woman would be more political and more alien. Part of the exile's pain lies in the pleasures he finds elsewhere.

Did Philoctetes exaggerate his limp? How bad was his foot? Who chooses to go to war? Take the damn bow; leave me my wound! The exile suffers, but not *much*: he has avoided brutal confrontation with the secret police. He has denounced international cowardice, but he has not wet himself in front of bullies. (The fate of Ben Bella in Algeria, cheered but not loved, and soon unloaded, makes the point.) Those who welcome the exile home come to accuse him of not knowing what it was like to be subject to tyrants. The tortured dislike their leadership being assumed by some one who shared their ideals, but still has his fingernails. As for collaborators, they resent being judged by a man never tempted, by profitable prospects, to compromise. It becomes a petty pleasure to make the returning hero feel out of touch. In Katzanzakis' version of the myth, Odysseus did not stay for long in the Ithaka he had recaptured. Perhaps his dog bit him.

Vassili's disillusionment is compounded of a bad conscience (he was never tortured) and violent ambition (like Lenin, he knows what should be done). He is greeted with more enthusiasm by his family than he can spare for them. Is it for a return to banality and to the hope of preferment that he sacrificed the cold years? He is applauded and fêted when he returns to his office in the newspaper but the disdain which is visited on *Madame la Directrice*, when *she* comes back from her comfortable travels, does not fail to splash on him.

The welcoming Penelope lacks the shamelessness of that prosaic Calypso who shared his bed in London. (He 'chose' a plain, politically energetic, mistress for fear that he might come to like it *here*.) As for his *gambros*, Nikos has been imprisoned by his family, whom he has threatened, during the Colonels' tyranny, with his rebellious candour. Vassili can admire the able wife who gave his friend his children and created the successful business which made an outspoken coward of him.

A possible incident: during the tyranny, Nikos gives a foreigner an icon which he particularly values to take to A., in London, so that he may live on the proceeds. Evdoxia's indignation makes Nikos realise how much he envies the man who has escaped domesticity. The grounded skipper dreams of the clouds. At the end of the novel, both men see that wholehearted friendship is now beyond them. Everything is politics? Politics are never *quite* everything. The dancers and their dance are separated. Cf. the linguaphone: ' "*Chorevete?*" "*Ochi, gyerasa akoma*".'

17.9.75. How different men are without their wives! How garrulous and how lost! When Michael stayed with us last year he was sick, and we were soonish sick of him. We laughed, but were we amused? We talked, but was there a conversation? The threat of an air strike had filled us with comic dismay: he might be with us indefinitely. When his car refused to start, on the last morning, I pushed him on his way. A year later he was much fitter, and there was also E. She dignifies him like a pedestal. *Chez eux*, she comes forward with his price list like a French wife. She may not be greedy, but she does like money. They live still in the warm shadow of their treachery to Nigel. 'You would have liked him,' Michael tells me, 'and he would've liked you; you would've amused him.' No doubt as Michael did.

Nigel called Michael 'the Praetorian Guard'; meaning, perhaps, that he made and unmade the emperor and that it was from among those whom they trusted that Caesars could look for treachery. Does E. compensate for her bad conscience – which is not *that* bad – with egregious concern with her daughters' welfare? Did she have some score to settle with Nigel? She told us that when she first met Michael, at the Etoile in Charlotte St, she was contemplating an affair with a homosexual doctor. Was her passion for M. a premeditated *coup de foudre*?

We awaited them with apprehension and saw them off with regret. Michael liked Sarah's work and said so. Like Malraux, he believes that art is made by attention more to art than to life. He has ingested his external world and carries in his own musculature a sufficient idea (he insists) of how others must be. His notion of art is very high-minded. Must this preclude commercial calculation? We have been good patrons; is that why we are cherished? A sheltered life makes one suspect treachery everywhere.

Michael and I spent a morning on the Catullus, dreaming of images and decoration. We had an exhilarating time; I have always felt that the best friendships are of *working* friends. Yet have I ever for long felt affection for my collaborators? I cannot abide being an underling, which is what equality always involves. If I am eventually an assassin of those with whom I was once keen to be associated, they are seldom hurt when ditched. I am so tactfully lethal that, had I been his assassin, I should have tried to do Trotsky in with a *tooth*-pick.

Michael has had bad experiences with P. Hall, for whom he designed a *Cymbeline*, only to find that somebody else had been commissioned simultaneously. Guess who won. P.H. must have remarkable qualities, since no one has a good word to say for him. Everyone seems to say that he is not a good *film* director, but I – and George Axelrod – rather admired *Perfect Friday*. P.H. has refurnished almost every aspect of his life but he cannot conceal the net curtains of his gentility. Michael is not suburban; he lacks the optimism. With more charisma than P.H., he is not as charming: he *frowns* when he says 'Cheese'.

He showed me the scripts for the series he is planning for the BBC on mirrors; they are erudite and illuminating, but he sees only himself in them, never the self that others will see, and may find affected or conceited. I fear for him; criticism will make him even more vulnerable and impel him to put even stronger locks on the draught-proofed hideout from which he tries to get wind of the outside world.

The R.W.s. She still looks chic and attractive, if you are attracted to chic of that kind. He is a loud little man of surprising refinement. He shouts and he is vulgar, but he can shout sound sense and his vulgarity is offset by the decency he cannot shake off. He has better taste than his tastes suggest.

18.9.75. Yesterday in Sarlat I had a moment of utter, incredulous and genuine horror. B. had flu, so Stee and I went alone to do some shopping in the wet. It was a modest joy to be with so self-possessed and so ungreedy a small boy. He wants what he wants, but he wants nothing more. Patient and helpful, without being cowed or characterless, he is very lovable. We did all our *courses* – bank, baker,

crèmerie, etc. – and then went to the sports shop and bought him the
new tennis racket which I had offered him for going back to school.
He bought a new shirt too. We were in excellent spirits. Then I
remembered (for the third time) that I had to buy a birthday card
for my mother: sixty-five! We crossed the raised *place* where the
Saturday fair is held, and went down the steps, across the glistening
road, to the *librairie*. It was crowded with people fulfilling their
requirements for the *rentrée*. Birthday cards had been relegated to
the back room. I went through, uncertain whether S. was coming
with me or preferred to stay among the scholars. I had no doubt
that he had come with me into the shop, but when I had waited
my turn and paid for my mother's card, I turned and could not see
him. He was not in the shop. There was a toy shop next door where
he had pointed out some plastic footballs hanging in a net. Could
he have gone back to examine them? He was not there; I went back
to check in the *librairie*. Had they seen a small boy? Oh – with a
smile – they had seen many small boys. I did not smile.

There was no crowd in the street, no accident. It began to rain
dull drops. People stood in small groups either under the shop
awnings or – some Africans – in the open. I ran to the car, trying
to make out of a huddle of coats in the locked front the figure of
my son, Houdini Jr. I ran back to the bookshop, which had been
transformed into a narrow hell of the wrong people. I ran, shouting
his name, to the *crèmerie* and to the other bookshop, to the sports
shop, and back to the car. My shouts neither alarmed nor interested
anyone. I was never in a nightmare before. I saw a policeman waving
his arms and blowing his whistle. He was running after a Peugeot
van which he thumped with his palm, bang, gotcha! The van
stopped, aslant the street, but no one seemed to notice or care. The
gendarme leaned on the driver's sill. I waited in vain for him to re-
emerge. All he wanted was a chat. Where *was* Stee? How long since
he disappeared? Ten minutes? Five? Twenty? How could I ask for
help when I did not quite know what I feared? Did I think S. had
been kidnapped? Could he have been forced into a car, or gulled
into one, under the eyes of these damned Frenchmen with their
provincial garrulity (they were *still* talking in the damp street as I
galloped back through them)? Was there some dark plot in which
the Africans played a watchful part? Fear, hatred, prejudice, dread,
what man under fatuous pressure does not know them? What would
I not have done to restore things to banality! All the mature fancies
of the novelist were banished, except melodrama. I thought of
suicide because it was inconceivable that the loss of my son could

ever be forgiven or forgotten. I was so ashamed. I did not pray, perhaps because I never thought of it. I kept thinking that there had to be some simple solution; what dramatist seriously imagines himself at the centre of a drama? How long did the petty agony last? I was desperate; my son had disappeared. What did he look like? What was he wearing? I could think only that he was carrying a plastic bag with a tennis racket in it. How long before I returned yet again to the *librairie* and saw his little face, aged with terror and babyish with tears? He was standing near the *romans policiers*. His fear dissolved into relief, his voice quavery with tears (wasn't mine?), I seemed unable to hear him. I imagined that he said that he had wanted to pee and immediately dreamed up some ugly experience in the public jakes, but he had not said that at all. He had missed me in the shop and had gone racing all over the strange town, finding places where I might have been (he went as far as the bank) before returning, I do not know how, to the *librairie*. I never have felt such relief, such joy. How glad we were to see each other! Catullus and Sirmio!

A telegram from Peter Green, in response to my question of whether he had received the Catullus I sent him: PEDICABO VOS ATQUE IRRUMABO SEQUITUR EPISTULA SPURCISSIMA AFFECTIONATE GREETINGS PETER. What fun to be in the old boy net! Later I had a letter from Michael, in longhand (proving authenticity), effusive over my Catullan prolegomena.

The best notices are the enthusiasm of friends, but there is nothing to beat the money of strangers.

24.9.75. The last wilful cynicism (anything to salt a platitude) was punished by a weekend in Paris at the behest of the currently most successful director in the world. Stephen Spielberg is twenty-six or twenty-seven and his film, *Jaws*, has in a few months become the biggest grossing movie of all time. More than one in six of all Americans have already seen it, more – one may be sure – than have received Holy Communion in the same period. When I first met S.S., a couple of years ago, he had just made *Duel*. I had seen some excellent clips and met him in 'Laddie's' office at Fox. I felt rather generous at agreeing to work with the young feller on such small scrappy evidence. He was modest, confident and an admirer of *Two for the Road* (he drove a little green Mercedes 280SL in tribute). In the casual style of the Coast, the deal – such as it was – was struck

that he would direct *Roses, Roses*. S. has given no formal commitment to do the picture, but Fox feel that it has done something
rather clever in yoking so hot a director, however tenuously, to the
Raphael project.

S. has come to Europe to promote *Jaws*, ending at the San
Sebastian Festival, where *Two for the Road* won the golden conch,
or whatever it's called, in 1967, I think it was. S. is accompanied by
his editor, a stout middle-aged lady called Verna Fields, who was
Bogdanovich's editor up to and including *Daisy Miller*. I met her in
the viewing theatre on the Paramount lot when they screened the
picture for me. The shared credit, which Peter had filched, was still
on the screen. It might have been endurable, had the director made
a masterpiece. He had made a stinker. I was disappointed, but not
surprised. Afterwards V.F. said, 'Peter says, will you come up to the
office?' 'No.' 'You're not coming up?' 'No.' It was the first time
that I ever saw a Hollywood movie in which the star, the clumsy
Cybill Shepherd, actually fluffed a line on camera and it had to stay
in the final cut because there was no cover for her.

Now Miss Fields was in Paris and we were asked to dine with
her and some French friends. B. decided, rightly, that it was too late
for Stee to be out, so she and he elected to remain at the Plaza-
Athénée, with room service and TV. *Quite* rightly. It was an evening
of tedium. We took a limo to the Left Bank and, for a moment, I
thought we were going to Allard. It is not what it was, but the place
we went to never will be. It was like a *fin de siècle* brothel; if it had
been, they would have served the girls tepid. Present were Stephen,
the Fields woman, Jerry Lewis (a publicity man of worldwide
responsibilities without a word of any language but English), José
Whoever, a blonde *Française* who was there to pay the bill, and
Robert Henrico, the bearded French director of *Le Vieux Fusil*, a
hit which S.S. admires.

I wore my one-size-fits-all-occasions suit and tie, appropriate for
someone undergoing torture by luxury (it has never appealed to me
as much as comfort). What a scandal and what a relief to be so bored
by what money can buy! The horror of the occasion was that I was
pinned; and a pinned piece, the chess books rightly tell you, is a
paralysed piece. I hate to be a leaf in someone else's calendar.
Stephen is charmingly sozzled with good fortune, but manages to
keep his head ('My name isn't Peter,' he said). He talked unaffect-
edly to Henrico about his movie, but José had to interpret every
word; there was no flow or spontaneity.

Henrico had been a young success and then an unaccountable

failure, reviled by critics, deserted by the public. The new film has restored him to favour, and to a conceit which can show all the arrogance which failure made furtive; he was *very* full of himself and had no room for anyone else. Around the eyes, above the rusty bucaneer's beard, are the smile lines of the hurt fighter who has winced and tried to hide his pain with a victor's humour. He is an ex-sufferer one would be unwise to trust: an intellectual in appearance, an opportunist by vocation. We did not leave the restaurant till after midnight, even though we had had nothing edible to eat. Miss Fields appeared to be your standard fat, black-trousered tourist, with her diamanté spectacles on their safety-chain, but she was smart enough to observe that the restaurant was like a French restaurant somewhere that wasn't French. She speaks fairly fluent French in a grating American accent. She cut all Peter Bogdanovich's hits and dodged *At Long Last Love*; she did *Jaws* instead, only because the deal came through first. She will probably get an Oscar instead of a wooden spoon.

Spielberg is a young man so unformed that his face changes – like a postcard one tilts to procure smiles and grimaces – as one watches it; he is beyond, unless he is this side of, description. Success attempts to make his features correspond to his new office (as wonderboy), but the conviction of his own importance is regularly replaced by eager uncertainty, a bewilderment at his own fate which makes endearing the realisation that he can have anything he wants. 'You need a hooker,' a girl said to him in California the other week, as she might have said, 'You need a holiday.' She could even propose the very one he required, a very nice, bright girl, eager to meet him. 'Only you'll have to pay me.' She enumerated this other girl's 'erogenous zones' (part of the attraction of a hooker is the fantasy that she can be sufficiently excited to forget her bill and her calling). S., the procuress promised, would not regret the experience. Was he grateful? 'I was in-sul-ted,' he said, giving the same weight to each syllable. Was he also warned of what success could now and would forever be able to buy him?

A young director becomes suddenly, hugely successful. 'It hasn't changed him,' people say. He is living with a girl it *does* change: she realises how much his new wealth has corrupted her expectations of him. It is a matter of moral survival to be quit of him. Only her friend, the hooker, could be happy with what his success now makes her feel when she is with him.

It seems that Peter Bogdanovich has been abandoned by Ms Shepherd. By putting her in *Daisy Miller* (after Orson had said that she 'born to play the part'), P.B. damaged his own career, perhaps fatally. What better reason for a tough, ambitious babe to dump a man than the knowledge that he has done everything he can for her?

Calculation yielded to sentiment when P. decided to do *Daisy Miller*; it was never going to be any kind of a movie, once he had rejected my early suggestion to extend it through time, so that Daisy wound up as a drug-victim, dead on a beach outside today's Rome. He decided to make it exactly as it stood; he crammed James's words into Cybill's mouth like fish into a letterbox. He chose humility at exactly the wrong moment; when he might have done anything he pleased, he did what pleased *her* and Orson. (Cibylla, Cibylla, *ti thelis*?!) Of course P. did not want *failure*, but perhaps he thought that he deserved it, after walking out on his wife and children. Spielberg told me that he had gone to one of those terrible screenings (of Peter's latest movie) at which, as the lights go up, 800 specially invited guests reach for their lies.

These movie guys are very young. How are they to live up to the Midas expectations of backers and agents and admirers? After the triumphs, do they sometimes crave a return to mere success? Yet how tempting for them to find a cold, conceited, mercenary bitch to satisfy; knowing her not to be satisfied with satisfaction, what better way to spend inexhaustible fortune? And how delicious to be free of families, duties and simple pleasures (how exacting *they* can be!) and, above all, free of a woman who asks nothing of you. Committed to the service of a heartless trophy, the success can tell himself that he *needs* to be a greedy bastard. Such a man may well choose his guiding star from the cover of a fashion magazine: he is a piggish Pygmalion who saves time, and chiselling, by breathing life into the *prêt-à-porter*.

Hotel ashtrays: incitements to steal what you would be appalled to be given.

25.9.75. On Le Capitole going to Paris. B., Stee and I had at our table for lunch a Frenchman who carried much of his middle-aged weight below the plimsoll line. He wore black-rimmed glasses and a ginger moustache cut in a narrow bar whose linear exactitude proved that he never had to shave in a hurry. He inquired of my citizenship, occupation and tax situation. He was complacently Giscardien: Mitterrand would soon follow Robert Fabre (of the *Radicaux de Gauche*) on a fawning visit to the Elysée/Canossa.

My neighbour was born in Algeria, where he lived till he was thirty. At forty-three, he was – dear God! – younger than I, a PDG who said of himself '*Le bon dieu m'a donné de l'intelligence.*' He had never made so much money as since coming to France, but he still resents de Gaulle's 'treachery', his cry of '*Algérie algérienne*' which sold the pass. All that was needed was to *say* that France would stay. There would always have been minor incidents – '*un petit coup de grenade*' – but the mass of Arabs would have stayed 'loyal'. When it seemed that the French were going to depart, the Arabs deserted. *Normal*! They had to make peace with their imminent masters.

Why had de Gaulle ratted? The usual: he had had a poor reception in North Africa in 1943 ('*C'était un inconnu*') and all the cheers had been for Pétain or Giraud. Giscard, I was promised, would certainly rehabilitate Pétain during his *septennat*. The Marshal had stayed in France (those who stayed were the '*vrais résistants*'), while de Gaulle fled. De Gaulle had never *intended* to rally the Free French but elected to do so as a hastily heroic afterthought.

Years of sincere prejudice had settled, like youthful cataracts, on my neighbour's vision of French politics. He believed, as if in a sovereign panacea, in a differential of five: a *cadre* should not earn more than five times the wages of a *main-d'oeuvre*; a Président Directeur-Générale not more than five times a *cadre*. Such a policy, officially declared, would prove to the work force ('*les moins doués*') that they were not being exploited.

Alexandra Stewart was in the next compartment. Louis (Malle), whose child she has had, was (deservedly) the cat with the *crème fraîche* when *Lacombe Lucien* came out, but is cast down by the reception of *Black Moon*. They are leaving for California. A. came with a baggage train which included a surly nanny and Louis' child by his German lady. His child by Alexandra remains in the Lot, with another nanny. Louis is an intelligent man trapped in the honey of fame and fortune. His face is asymmetrical, like the surface of a planet with uneven planes of forces. He seems to wish that some other fate had befallen him, though he can do precisely as he likes; freedom is too demanding an obligation.

The twenty-year-old peasant who played Lucien Lacombe bought a fast car with his wages and killed himself and three companions by hitting a tree at 220 kilometres an hour. I can believe that, in comparable circumstances, John S. – for instance – would 'not give a damn, dear'. The mortality of others increases his vanity and is a happy economy at Christmas. When a director has done with someone, he often wishes him dead: if the other has contributed to a success, he threatens the director's credit; if he has been recruited to a failure, he deserves extinction, lest he remind the *auteur* of what he wishes he had never done.

Louis was distressed by the young peasant's death. He had not been a virgin in films, but his sudden fame made it hard for him to stay down on the farm (he was the youngest and favourite child of eleven), although he loved country life. Some on the left said that *Lacombe Lucien* was an apology for fascism; others that the actor had been underpaid, though he clearly got enough to die on. Those who were killed with him had been picked up, here and there, for a midnight spin. Has this damaged Louis' standing in the area where he lives, *en baron*, in his family's *château*, Le Coual?

Paul and I went over there to the shooting of *Black Moon* last autumn. They were shooting a scene – not in the final cut – in which naked children, between five and eight years old, rooted under the table, jostling a pig, some turkeys and other domestic animals, in the search for scraps. I found the *ambience* disturbing on account of the zeal with which the hairless children prostituted themselves. Parents had competed to sell their offspring. One father – a photographer from Villefranche-de-la-Rouergue – had the smugness of a man who had brought a plump animal to a seller's market. The servility with which the kids stripped gave the farm-house kitchen the close air of the children's brothel in Durrell's *Justine*. One could imagine the pretty boys and girls acquiring a taste for this petted life; worse, one could *imagine* acquiring a taste for them and their casual, unquestioning nakedness.

The parent of one of the child whores turned the pages of a script, from back to front, with the uneasy reverence of a Gentile trying to find the place in a Hebrew prayer book. The scene they were shooting lacked drama: nothing *happened* except that the children tried to rival the pig without ever making Louis's point, whatever it was supposed to be. Joe d'Alessandro went through his blanched motions with professional compliance and Ms Harrison clutched a hot-water bottle against her gripes and performed with pregnant pallor.

This morning on the radio, she was said to be the daughter of a mother with four children all by different fathers and to have four brothers, all by different mothers. She was blonde and bland and beautiful with the fragile toughness so often displayed by the walking wounded from marital wars. Joe d'A. was pale too, but that was part of his persona (one does not expect Pierrot to have rosy cheeks); his plastic, unblinking eyes gazed in mesmerised unworldliness at some far from clean memory. His cynicism was a function of his stance and his fixed voltage. He was one of the machines Warhol dreamed of being: he could neither function otherwise nor change station. If he were cut, you would not expect him to bleed but to exude some extra-terrestrial ichor. He was unlike any other actor: indifferent to any notion of art or career, he was neither charming nor surly. One would not be surprised to find that he was switched off at night, like a piece of office equipment, and covered with a plastic hood. Did he have feelings? Did he care whether he had done something well or badly? You could not think of anything it might be appropriate (still less *welcome*) to say to him.

My agent Judy Scott-Fox's family sports judges and senior civil servants; her uncle greets foreign dignitaries on behalf of the Foreign Office. He recently welcomed President Mobutu and showed him into a suite inadequate to the vanity of a successful murderer. The President stalked out and returned to the scene of his crimes, where he receives his due.

Judy is a stately lady with an uptilted nose and blue eyes; she might have served as the figurehead for a Thames barge. Old world courtesies are easy to observe with such women: if she took off her clothes, one would turn one's back *immediately*. She became my agent, after I dumped 'Ziggy', less because I wanted work than because I missed the gossip, which – like flattery – she constantly supplied. When she introduced us to Alan Pakula, I never guessed that they were having an affair; he was a successful director/producer, elegant and apparently sure of himself. What would such a man be doing in bed with all that? When I became aware of their relationship and then impatient at A.P.'s failure to pay what was due on delivery of the first draft, Judy told me to try 'not to be paranoid for once'. I did not find this a seductive line. She then said that A.P. wanted me to 'do him a favour' and come out to LA and confer with him on the changes, to work for 'a few weeks' and *then* to deliver the alterations, upon which he would authorise the payment for completion of the first draft. I was, she soothed, of *course* going to get two first-class fares. The more diplomatic she was, the angrier I became, first with A.P. (from whom I have not heard a word during the three months since I sent him the script) and then with her. Yet it did not occur to me that I had decided to sack her until the next morning, when I told her second i/c, who – relief and surprise! – told me that I was '100 per cent right' to do so; it was a start.

24.10.75. We arrived in LA on Monday afternoon, but A.P. – being in 'post' (production) – could not find me a spare minute until Saturday; this at the end of the week when, after I had agreed to his terms, he was to have worked with me. Meanwhile, we did everything; and the usual nothing. I love Hollywood rather as T.E. Lawrence must have loved the RAF: it takes one's identity away. The burden of moral and literary solemnity is lifted; no one speaks that kind of language out there. When Hollywood tells me (as did the lady who 'reads for' Freddie Fields) that it admires my fiction, I am embarrassed: I have not come for praise but for deals. If we could not trust the locals to be fools, would one come so far to see them? Were their judgements accurate, would they pay the fare? Every time I am solicited, I am the whore who quotes a brazen price for charms she knows that only fools would choose to pay for; she also knows that if she didn't ask a lot for them, they wouldn't.

Those who run the studios are kings for a day. Fox was once dominated by a real Boss, with credits for credentials, but Darryl is now publicly regarded as senile. His son has just made twenty million dollars from *Jaws* (so has D.B.). Darryl fired them both in a Herodian attempt to stay on the throne. Now Fox has brought in Alan Ladd Jr., a young man of enough dull and taciturn mediocrity to bring hope to every mother of two short planks. Gareth arranged for us to go to San Francisco and to visit San Quentin. I suppose that he is vice-president in charge of turning things down (it is 'Laddie' who will get the gratitude for what is green-lit).

Gareth is at least now 'comfortable', rather than anguished: he has an income and a bigger car to put in the slot with his name stencilled in it than the stick-shifted Ford in which I saw him, *in extremis*, on Rodeo Drive not so many trips ago. He has a big office and Dick Zanuck's old secretary and he has triumphed over the anti-British odds. He is at last in the lifeboat, so who can be surprised that he is tempted to be too busy for Georgia, who looms like a Jewish iceberg? Now that he has married her, he is well on the way to getting rid of her.

After the *troika* of 'Laddie', Jay Kantor and Gareth had displaced Frank Yablons at Fox, the displaced potentate put it about that if you called the studio and asked for an ass-hole, 'three guys rush to pick up the phone'.

How handsome Arabs are since they have become rich and powerful!

George Axelrod. His poverty is not in figures but in expectations. He has a play, *Souvenir*, opening this week in LA, with Deborah K. She was the star of *An Affair to Remember* (the remake with Cary, which he insisted be shot, by the same director, frame-for-frame like the Boyer–Irene Dunne version). Someone wanted me to script a remake of the remake (thanks a lot). When I called the Axelrods, a strange voice answered. 'Who is this?' I said. 'This is Peter Viertel, the new butler.' 'This is F.R.,' I said, 'the old writer.' Peter is older; he is collaborating with George on the play. He is married to Deborah; I met him when she was interested in doing *Richard's Things*. She went cold with abrupt silence, though I later heard that she continued to speak of it as 'the one thing I want to do'.

   G. and P.V.'s play is said to be so bad that it may close before it opens. It cost $250,000 to mount, but 'Swifty' says that if they have to cancel out they'll have to cancel out. I saw him, a little old gnome like a 'Where-are-they-now?' version of Mr Magoo, at La Scala on Monday. He was lunching on a telephone as red as a tomato. When he had finished his conversation, he walked up and down the restaurant as if it were a plane with a buffet, helping himself to fruit from the decorative display. He is as bald as a whore's proposition; ready to be wheeled, he still deals. When my host, Bob Shapiro, said, 'Hullo, Irving', his voice positively *curtsied* to the old bastard.

George and Joan Axelrod saw a lot of my producer/director when they were all in London. A.P. was very miserable after his divorce from Hope Lange. He used to come to their house in Chester Square and mope. When J. asked 'Hopie' what was so wrong with being married to Alan, she said, 'It wasn't *that* terrible. I just kept falling asleep all the time.' 'Hopie' was known to have had an affair with Sinatra. Joan was curious to know what it had been like in bed with him. 'Push and squirt', Hopie told her.

Pakula read Mordecai Richler's new novel at G. and J.'s urgent suggestion, presumably with the idea that George produce, A.P. direct and Mordecai write the script. A.P. acquired the rights to *St Urbain's Horseman* and the Axelrods were immediately spared both his tears and his presence.

Some time later, A.P. saw Joan at a party. 'Joanie, darling, what a long time since we saw each other!' 'As far as I'm concerned, Alan, let's keep it that way.' 'Why? What's the matter? What am I supposed to have done?' 'Let's just keep it that way, it's fine by me.' Pakula could see nothing wrong in having backed a horseman on someone else's unacknowledged tip: what are a producer's friends for except to steal ideas from?

When he saw the 'gag reel' which Dustin (and Roy Scheider and John) had made while shooting *Marathon Man*, in which Dustin mimicked Bob's twitchy diction, Bob Evans said, 'I don't mind being ridiculed, but why does it have to be by a dwarf?'

27.10.75. We left LA for San Francisco along Route 101 in a huge, white four-door Ford LTD. It was like driving in an endless suburbia. As darkness came down, we saw nothing but the uniformly lettered signs announcing the various turn-offs. We stopped in the dusk at a coffee-shop in Gaviota which still has a manual telephone exchange. I had an urgent message to call Bob Shapiro and imagined some dramatic, unwanted, irresistible zillion-dollar offer. His secretary said that he had had a tennis game in which I could've played if I'd gotten the message sooner.

We left it late to eat and found ourselves at the peak of hunger with never a restaurant, not even a McDonald's, in sight. The unaltered lettering of the highway signs promised that we were still in touch with thin reality, if these luminous places were real. At last we found a Denny's (the *worst*) in a small town and realised, after eating some of the food, how tired we were. We made the Laurel Inn, a few miles short of Salinas – The Lettuce Capital of the World – and took the last and (so the two Maltese clerks assured us) best room before they turned out the VACANCY sign: king-sized bed on a carpeted dais; thick blue-green shag floor; screened fireplace with gas logs; shackled TV; magazines on every table; shampoo; shower cap: $30. The double tiers of rooms hooped the parking lot, but the construction was solid enough for us not to hear the departing cars which left us, at 7 a.m., pretty well alone in the place.

In the Dining Inn for breakfast, I sat at the counter next to a big woman with hair recently decurled into hollow sausages on her head. She wore no make-up and a cigarette. She was due in court in Salinas later in the morning as a witness in a murder trial. A boy of twenty-three had killed the county sheriff by blowing half his head off with a shotgun. The sheriff was a man of thirty-nine with a wife and two kids, 'One of the best men you'd ever want to know.' The witness knew him well; he died in a house she owned. He was the kind, he found a kid drunk or anything like that, he'd drive him home in his own car and then go round in the morning and have a talk with him. Nothing was too much trouble and he goes and gets half his head blown off by some kid with a shotgun who thinks he's going to kill himself a cop. What kind of a kid? A stranger, a hippy: long hair. Didn't belong in the district, he'd been hanging around some time, but he didn't *belong*. I said that the gun laws were crazy (explaining why we didn't have as many shootings in England). She shot me a .22 glance: 'I've got five guns in my house right now. What's more, you'll find more guns in this motel right now than you ever saw in your life.' The place was filling up with cops come to town for the trial.

I told her that I was on my way to San Quentin. 'They've got the hard cases in there,' she said, 'two- and three-time losers. I reckon they should put them in that gas-chamber. They should be tougher with them,' the lady said, scoffing her French toast. 'They give 'em too easy a time.' She was a nurse (a *male* nurse, I almost wrote). She was down from the mountains to see a hippy get what I daresay he deserved.

'It's the mother I'm sorry for,' the waitress said, 'that's who I'm sorry for. Terrible for her. Is she here? Because it's terrible for her.'

'Meantime he's laughing, shows no more concern… but, yes, I'm sorry for her. Can you imagine what that woman is going through right now?'

There was sympathy, and relish, in her beefy voice. She is not the kind of witness anyone would care to have give evidence against him: she wore navy blue trousers and a blue sweater and she meant business. There hadn't been too much in the papers about the case, because the DA was determined not to have the verdict set aside on the grounds of prejudicial publicity. The lady was going to do what she could to see that boy got what he deserved, but next time she saw a murder committed, she was going to look the other way. She didn't mean to be a witness to anything ever again.

28.10.75. San Francisco proves that the movies show you every-thing, and nothing else. It looks exactly like it looks, but nothing *is* as it looks. The trolley-cars do go steeply up the steep streets and on each narrow plateau (where cross-streets form a shelf) the oper-ator yanks on his lever to re-engage or tighten the long cable to which the car is tethered. But who sees the fault-line which runs, wilfully unacknowledged, beneath the humps? The city is angular with its unnatural nature; the hills seem so much steeper than the steepest camera angle that they amount to paved cliffs. You cannot hurry, though local drivers continue to howl their haste. The cramping propinquity is both comforting and claustrophobic. Boas of cloud scarf the thin throats of sky between the tall buildings. Reaching upwards, the city seems at once ambitious and compressed by its blue lid.

Our Nob Hill hotel was a huge, ochrous-yellow pile. The view of the bay was a peek between the skyscrapers (one a pyramid tapering to a top storey with a single cute window in it). The LTD, once parked in a neighbouring garage, took twenty minutes to recover. *Jesus!* Imagine if we had been spending our own money!

I drove to San Quentin in sunshine bandaged by swathes of fog that unravelled autumn by the yard. Now the bay sparkled all the way out to Alcatraz and then the car lights were fuzzed and out of focus in the muzzle of the fog that covered the Golden Gate Bridge (no toll going north) and gave a Warner Brothers chill to the ominous drive. I turned off for San Rafael along a bumpy road that slid left, easy as the descent to Avernus.

One of the first jobs of bread-winning drudgery I ever had to do was rewriting the memoirs of a man who had been a secret agent in Belgium during the war. His manuscript was full of clichés. He had a Pooterish genius for observing the wrong detail and failing to see what were the most interesting parts of his story. He described how, in Paris in 1942, he had had to leave a 'safe' house in a hurry, without money or luggage, knowing only that he had to go to a certain address in Lyon for help in reaching safety in Spain. His typescript explained how he went to the *Gare de Lyon*, passed 'unnoticed' onto the platform and 'somehow' managed to slip under the train and hang face down under it.

The next chapter began 'When I got off the train at Lyon'. He did not quite understand why I was disappointed that he had not gone into detail about the hazards and alarms of the six-hour trip hanging with his face a foot from the ballast between the sleepers.

After walking over the Pyrenees in winter, wearing a pair of espadrilles because his shoes were worn out, he lost several toes. Eventually, however, he reached Madrid and was given an audience by the British ambassador, Lord Templewood, once the appeaser Sir Samuel Hoare. The ambassador looked at the lame and unprepossessing secret agent and said, 'You know, I sometimes think you people are more trouble than you're worth.'

Jacques Doneux's manuscript and my notebooks sometimes have something in common. My visit to San Quentin is no better annotated than J.D.'s railway journey to Lyon. Part of the reason for it was that I was about to write a movie script, *Roses, Roses...* which drew on what I learnt from my six or seven hours in the Big House. Stephen Spielberg had agreed to direct, more or less (which is always less, if the director has a success meanwhile).

At first sight, San Quentin was not as intimidating as one expects. The prison is pale yellow and might be a provincial college. You drive up to the gate into a big yard and join a line of cars, all of them with the trunks sprung open. Whoever you are, you are required to have the trunk ready for inspection before they will let you in. I was met by a guard who had been assigned to show me round by the PR people. He was a middle-aged black man with a calm style and seemed on good terms with the inmates, and with himself.

There was an unfenced rose bed in the middle of the main yard. It was neither protected nor vandalised. How come? It was the *violon d'Ingres* of a psychopath who would kill anyone who messed with his roses. My guide took me to a cell-block and introduced me to a painter, whose cell was full of sticky canvases. The main problem of my plot was that I did not know what the MacGuffin was, what 'treasure' it was so important for the authorities to trace that they were willing to allow a man to seem to escape in order to lead them to it. When I suggested some kind of a drugs stash, heads shook around the cell where a number of convict-executives had gathered for my inquisition. Drugs were already dated as a plot-driving device.

One of those who turned up to participate was a black man, in wrap-around shades, tall as a basketball star and cooler than the cooler he was in. He wore prison clothes but they seemed to have been tailor-made for him. My cell-mates told me how someone had escaped from the prison not long before under the garbage truck which he helped to load for many weeks.

They neither joked nor lamented. If they were three-time losers, they took it better than I do a double-fault. When we left the painter, the tall black inmate came with us. His name was Heysbert. My guide told me that the painter, who was a lifer, was a drug addict. I wondered how he managed to get drugs in jail. The guard and Heysbert laughed and laughed.

H. said he had an appointment, so he would say goodbye. He dismissed us rather than the other way round. He told me that he would be out of jail before the date I was hoping to do the movie and that he would be glad to be in it. I asked how I would contact him, so he gave me his day and night telephone numbers. I was Britishly amazed that a man in jail would already have day and night numbers on the outside. When he had shaken hands and moved away, the guard told me that Heysbert was one of the big pushers in the joint. In civil life he was a successful pimp who had gone too far with one of his girls. Man, he was probably every bit as rich as I was.

The guard neither sympathised with the inmates nor judged them. Many of them, he said, had had little chance in life. The jail was divided into three camps: Hispanics, blacks and whites. They none of them trusted the others and not always each other. Often, as now, the place could seem so calm that you could not imagine trouble. It never came slowly; it erupted and when it did men could kill each other just for belonging to the wrong group.

On the way to the gas chamber, we passed a black man and a white man playing tennis on a stretch of tarmac with a net across it. The balls were not new. In the death chamber, there was a thick glass panel between the viewing chamber, where selected guests and officials could watch a strapped man, on the other side of the glass, choke to death in a big armchair. The prevailing colour was institutional green. It was, as the football commentators say, clinical. There was nothing to *feel* in such a place. You registered that it was there and what could happen in it, but there the imagination seized up and would go no further.

31.10.75. In Marty Scorsese's cutting room, I bumped into Spielberg, wearing a new pair of glasses with an elaborate bridge over the nose. 'I saw your film,' I said, referring to *Jaws* (which I had not seen when we dined in Paris). In fact, I had seen it on the Jumbo and looked but did not listen. Stephen was pale, as if the shock of success had terrified him; he was bleached by fortune. 'Did you like it?' 'Not as much as *Sugarland Express*,' I said. He nodded gloomily. 'But don't worry,' I said, 'I haven't lost faith in you.'

Marty – the nicest thing under five foot four I have met in a while – told me that until he made '*Alice*' – which I liked much less than *Mean Streets* – he had always found it difficult to talk to women. We chatted in the annexe to the cutting room about Byron and Shelley. The next morning he came to breakfast at the Beverly Wilshire; my (Fox's) treat.

I first met Alan Pakula when he was living in London. He had just made *Klute* and seemed both modest and artistically ambitious. He had been a producer before he was a director and was elated to have combined both offices so successfully (he had won Jane Fonda an Oscar for *Klute*). Carefully handsome, with that trim red beard, Pakula had been to Yale and passed for an intellectual. He was liter-ally ambidexterous; he could write with either hand. His character was similarly double; he was as warmly friendly one day as he was distant the next.

When he married his second wife, he returned to live in Beverly Hills. They had a big house in North Linden Drive where, on our preceding trip, I went for conferences about the script of *Hullo, Angel!* He had celebrated his new status by constructing a viewing theatre-cum-office in the back garden (Herbert Ross did the same thing). A rectangular building without windows, light came from a clerestory aperture running narrowly round the whole room. The office and its new furniture was at one end; at the other was a dais with a huge *armoire*, in which the movie screen was concealed. There was something Yaley about A.P. which insisted that he was now emancipated from the Jewishness that his name did not deny. When I saw the tasteful room, with its unadorned white walls and the closed ark on its dais, I could not help saying, 'Alan! You've built yourself a synagogue!'

His affable slyness waited for the writer to supply the detail of a story which he would later claim to have 'developed', if not devised. It is part of the ritual humiliation of writers (for which they are paid) that they are obliged to run things past the director/producer; one must get used to the strip-search of one's inventiveness. Directors are like chefs who take credit for the number of tins they open without anyone guessing their dependence on them.

A.P. had an educated courtesy and very clean socks. It was his habit to go unshod indoors; his stockinged feet soft-pedalled the impression that his office was a place of worship. Ed Henry, our supervising executive at Universal, was known as Dr No; he had famously negative habits. I never met him and acted as though he did not exist. I imagined, with wilful naïveté, that A.P.'s reputation would get our picture made.

When I sent the first draft, Alan was shooting another movie and I heard nothing for months. Since I rely on the movies to pay the bills (art is something else), I became anxious at the delay. By the time I agreed to meet A.P. again before Dr No got his chance to spike us, I was not destitute, nor without prospects of other work (*Roses, Roses...* for instance), but I had honoured my deal and I wanted to be paid. During the whole week of our stay, A.P. was in the cutting room. His current movie took understandable priority. However, we had flown to California in order for me to see him and clear that payment.

I had arranged the visit to San Quentin late in the week, in the expectation that I should have concluded with A.P. before we went. Instead, he agreed to see me on the Saturday afternoon, before we flew home on the Sunday. This meant our getting up at 5 a.m. to drive back to LA from San Francisco. When we arrived at the Beverly Wilshire, there was a message that Alan was delayed at the studio and could not see me that day. If I was to see him at all, we had to delay our return to Europe. Having dreaded the meeting, I was humiliated by its postponement. I called A.P. and said that he wanted to cancel an appointment which I had driven 500 miles to honour. I was going home the next day whatever happened. He arranged to see me at his house at the previously agreed hour.

The place seemed deliberately emptied. Neither his wife nor her many children were there. No servant opened the door. There was A.P., in white socks. I was not appeased by an offer of tea. I had assumed that he would declare that I was indispensable to him, whereupon I would consent to be wooed back into availability.

His living room was expensively furnished. Unlike his office, it had handsome engravings on the wall. The Yale magazine had to be on the coffee table. He had money and, second time around, he had also married it. The books announced a thinking – not to say calculating – man. We tried to talk about the script, but I was too angry, and choked, not to become sarcastic. Eventually, I said, 'I've delivered the script and I want the money I'm owed. The second draft is time enough for fiddling.'

When he said he wanted just a little work done before Dr No axed us, I heard myself say, 'Alan, you don't seem to realise. I don't work in the movies for fun. If I want to write for nothing, I can try epic poetry.' I looked round the impeccable room with all its proofs of success and I said, 'Unlike some people, I don't have a rich wife.'

His face became congested with blood that was not usually in evidence. He said, 'I think you'd better get out of here.'

He was a neat, unmuscular man who would not want any trouble. I said, 'How are you going to work that?'

After he had agreed to turn the script in and get me my money, I left the house. I never spoke to him again. Dr No took care of that.

I was not proud of my remarks and suffered the usual feeling of failure when our project was aborted. I was relieved when I read Bill Goldman's account of working with Alan, on *All the President's Men*. Duplicity seems to have been his trademark. He wanted to be a serious film-maker, as his subjects suggested, but he turned everything into solemn, often mildly erotic pap, except for *Klute* which had a good original script. He was a good enough producer to procure backing for the kind of commercially noble films with which rich men imagine it is creditable (and profitable) to be associated: *Coming Home*, *Sophie's Choice*, etc. He played safe with dangerous subjects; his movies too wore clean socks. I wished him neither good nor harm. He died flukishly while driving on the East Coast. A car or truck ahead of him kicked up a steel bar from the roadway. It smashed through his windscreen and hit Alan in the head. I was formally sorry when I heard of it, and as unmoved as one can be by the unfortunate death of a two-faced stranger.

6.11.75. What do reviews matter? Byron pissed on Keats for being a cry-baby, but had he forgiven *Scotch Reviewers*? Maugham claimed that he never read his notices, but the title *The Mixture as Before* alluded defiantly to a recent, scornful review.

The horror of civil war is that the two sides are able to understand each other perfectly.

In the Périgord. The divisions between those who resisted and those who did not; between the smugglers and the *sérieux*. Madame S.

told us how they had two sittings during the war: one for the Parisian blackmarketeers, with their suitcases, and another for the 'Fridolins'. They will still point out which wood was a nest of *Résistants* and which hotel was the headquarters of the Milice. Betrayal, as adultery proves, is a kind of liberation. No longer to be faithful, is that not freedom itself? The Liberation, *par contre*, is seen by the cowardly or '*les réacs*' as a kind of betrayal, a perversion of what it was perfectly sensible to think respectable – Pétain and the right – by those ('Free French' and Anglo-Saxons) who turned the Marshal into a scapegoat and his supporters into villains. Some Frenchmen were more humiliated by being liberated than by being defeated.

Chaban-Delmas, the sad charmer, corroded by his own bonhomie, speaks of 1945 as a second chance, something he never expected to enjoy. What has his post-war afterlife been but a kind of mundane heaven, salvation in advance of judgement? No fear equal to the fear of torture has complicated the political career of *charmant* Delmas; he had already looked death in the face, and worse than death. The same is true of Robert Maxwell, whose impudence derives, like Polanski's, from having already been in the pit. Can we expect a man who has known what the Nazis could do to fear the finger-wagging of the Board of Trade?

The United Nations' General Assembly has voted that Zionism is a form of racism. And of what is the United Nations' General Assembly a form?

Zionism is said, by French (and Frenched) intellectuals, to be disreputable *surtout* because it cannot be 'universalised'; that is the best argument for it that I have yet to hear.

The consistency of the autobiographer is the measure of his art; his inconsistency that of his honesty.

Who can believe himself an artist if people refuse to misunderstand him?

It used to be that people affected to be tolerant when they were full of prejudice; now they are ashamed of their tolerance and claim to have more passions than they feel. They 'hate' what they mildly dislike and hold to be 'totally unacceptable' what they find it easy to live with. The Communists say that Frenchmen are not '*à son aise*' in today's society; that – rather than injustice – is their warrant for '*une société nouvelle*'. Workers of the World, Unite: you have nothing to lose but your uneasiness. *Bon dieu!*

Jim Ferman's appointment as the Secretary of the Board of British Film Censors is one of the small comic twists of our generation. That he is an American and a Jew (careful now!) makes him an unlikely choice to be the moral guardian of (post-)Christian England. Yet, as he told me, the more he examined the requirements for the job, the more uniquely qualified he seemed to be. 'Though I say so myself' is a phrase which the *Observer*'s bitchy columnist found too frequently on his lips. The white teeth also offended her (are brown more patriotic?). The comedy of the appointment lies not in Jim's self-righteousness but in the skill with which he censors himself. Having known him for twenty years, I cannot claim really to know him at all. If he has a guilty secret, perhaps it is that he has led a blameless life; in modern England, that is something to keep quiet about.

Monica has become steadily more left-wing. In the 60s, she was a doomwatcher who, like the Bea Lillie character, had come to be insulted (or horrified) and was not going home until she was. She awaited the self-destruction of the human race with I-told-you-so impatience. She loved her children but, in view of the risks of pollution from gamma rays and pesticides, it was with reluctance that she allowed food to pass their lips.

In the 1970s, she has become more political; she persuaded Camden Council to put a compulsory purchase order on the block of rent-controlled flats where she and Jim happened to live, thus enabling it to become the first tenants' co-operative in London. Energy and leadership have triumphed over grasping landlords and governmental apathy. She has the drive inherited from a mother whose bigotry she detests. She has moved, in twenty-five years, from being a flagrant Bohemian at Cambridge (with a *pink* bicycle) to becoming a vessel of righteousness. Since she caught Jim – with both hands, like a good slip catcher – she has become as dateless as Marmite.

At Cambridge, Jim was a glamorous American graduate student, with a zippy MG already. When he wrote a musical *Zuleika Dobson*, after Max, he seemed destined for West End success. When *Zuleika* bombed, he crash-landed on Television Centre and became a busy director. He did good work, but seldom remained within budget. Even during the years when he could be afforded, his perfectionism built up a slow silt of ill-will; a *moral* spendthrift seldom wins many friends in management.

When budgets got tighter, and belts followed suit, Jim's phone stopped ringing. He kept his zippy little car and they had the rent-controlled flat, but things were not easy. He turned to public service and made unpaid films about drug abuse. They ceased to visit us in the country. Living in the real world, they now scorned the false-ness of the movies and the theatre.

I took no pleasure in Jim's eclipse and am relieved at his resur-rection. Goodness how enthusiastic he is about being the Censor! 'Full of *beans*,' as Vincente Minnelli used to say, he debates the issues with urgent candour: what he really *must* do is to keep the film industry on the right side of the law. He *can* attempt to ease it away from violence and from other disreputable ways of garnering ducats, but such artful high-mindedness is a luxury. If he allows the Board to be caught bending the law, he cannot survive.

Jim's heart, although rather small, is in the right place: slightly to the left. He and Monica have a long and serious relationship with the *Manchester Guardian*; they share views on all the issues. We have never had the illusion of being *intimate* with them; the atmosphere at their table is that of a nice Hampstead (Swiss Cottage) debating society: something is always not being said.

Monica is one of the liberated middle-class women on whose lips the four-letter cosmetics do *not* appear; she is up to date, but she is not modern. Her passion for underdoggedness cannot quite conceal the fact that inside her is a conservative lady, hatted and gloved and willing to shake the law till its wig falls off, not for the sake of the Revolution but in order to make people *wake up – AT ONCE!*

Jim has something in common with me: the resident alien, the Jew, the New Yorker, the urge both to please and to moralise. The metic is always likely to be hot for Reason; he cultivates the quiet voice of good sense and humane sensibility. It is neither in his inter-ests nor in his unnatural nature to stir up the surlier depths of human emotion; he risks eviction if chthonic passions are aroused. Oh that middle ground, how he does love it!

My sense of affinity with Jim never amounted to a true friend-ship, although we visited back and forth, *en famille*, for several years. I continued to *seem* friendly, and so did he until the 1970s. In the early 1960s, he had directed one of my 'plays', as we used to call TV dramas, taken from my novel *The Trouble with England* (the trouble was the weather, of course). We were abroad at the time, but I was promised by Stella Richman, then a power (and my generous patron) at ATV, that it had gone very well. A year or so later, I was walking towards Bumpus bookshop when I saw

Ian Bannen, who had taken a leading part in my script, walking towards me. As we met, I introduced myself and thanked him for his performance in my 'play'. He looked puzzled; he did not know that he had been in any play of mine. I mentioned the title. He looked even more puzzled: 'Jim Ferman wrote that,' he said. 'He told us he did.'

Unusually for me, I had not been at rehearsal. Nor had I seen the final version, but Jim had certainly *not* written the script. When I told him the story, another American in London, a painter friend of mine, said that if I did not face Jim with what Bannen had said our friendship was doomed. I said nothing; and it was.

The breach was caused not by my festering resentment of his taking credit for my play, but by money. When things began to go less than famously in his career, I was conscious that I was a lot more fortunate than he. One Christmas I sent him a cheque for a sum I could easily afford. His first response was, he said, to be offended, but then – he told me in a letter – he decided that he would keep the money in a special account and would draw on it only if he absolutely had to. In this way, it would earn interest which he would insist on my accepting. I do not know if he ever had to draw on the special account, nor do I know what it is now worth. He never sent me back the money and we hardly ever spoke again.

Was the *foreignness* of so many sophists an aspect of their businesslike attitude to teaching and of Plato's animosity? Too clever by half; their intellectual credentials made them shine with an alien sheen. The *arriviste* alien finds its *almost* standard instance, in Christian circumstances, in the Jew. The Jew is so outstanding an instance of the class of outsiders that he almost stands outside *it*: in the eyes both of the Orthodox and of his Nazi enemies, the Jew is the very case of the man who can never be assimilated, who will never resemble anything except himself. He is also the product of a religion in which law is more important than 'belief' (seldom a feature of ancient religion). Such a man will take easily to societies in which law prevails and is likely to be an enthusiast for Reason and its social correlative, due process.

Reasonable men find it particularly awkward to justify the systematic paramountcy of the Word over muscle. Why is it always right to argue and never to fight? Why must the strong man be constrained, but not the rhetorician? As Sorel and the German romantics (Hermann Goering among them) embarrassingly pointed out, such axioms impose verbal privilege, an artificial empire of the lettered. But then their denial leads to mob rule.

There is bound to be a tendency to prudence on the part of the metic. His reasonable posture, however evangelically therapeutic and impersonal (the mark of a certain philosophical style, cf. Isaiah Berlin), assumes – more or less presumptuously – that he shares common ground with the *autochthones*; it even *insists* that he does. A pastor who cannot be a master, he is determined to see all social and dogmatic crises in a reasonable light. He becomes selfless not least because his self is what puts him at risk; he will be a leveller – reason knows no privilege, as logic knows no surprises – because to be equal with others is as high as it is safe to aspire (*Jew Süss* is the awful warning against undue aspiration, though the Rothschilds suggest that the exceptional can ignore it). No insincerity is involved in being rational, but a certain partiality (in favour of the impartial!) cannot be denied.

Ken McLeish told me that he did not find *The Story of O.* erotically stimulating. Is he a man of rare propriety or incapable of responding to the written word? Or did the fact that I *asked* him about it alter his consciousness of the book? I tried to breach the privacy of his response and so dissipated the fantasy.

The notion that the *threat* of inflicting or receiving pain should play no part in 'normal' sexual practice is a kind of vegetarian idealism. Nakedness offers the body to caresses and caresses verge on, play at, violence as well as tenderness. The couple – and the pleasure they take in each other – embraces mutual assault: they abandon the standards of other people wilfully, and greedily, and judge each other by what each finds exciting. Why argue the point? A man wholly impervious to the eroticism of *The Story of O.* limits his sexual desires to what seems consciously (i.e. publicly) desirable: he castrates his subconscious.

There can be no truthful account of a sexual experience; this does not entail that nothing can ever be said about sex, only that what is said is not sex: something is always *not* said.

My father, unsteady on his feet now: 'I don't find it easy to stay on the straight and narrow.'

'I always thought it was overrated,' I said.

13.11.75. The supreme achievement in fiction would be to write a book which conveyed with utter conviction the exact opposite of one's true sentiments. A clever Jesus would be the author of *Mein Kampf*. Sincerity is the thumbprint of the amateur.

If one could achieve a totality of disjunctive elements, one would have created a work of truly modern literature. How does one multiply three oranges by five elephants? Force of character.

No man whose peace of mind depends on other people's good faith can hope to sleep well.

If you want the respect of other people, cease hoping that they will understand you.

The perfect sentence? One against which there can be no appeal.

One imagines death as an incalculable horror, but I await my father's as though it were a petty dividend. I am scandalised by my lack of feeling, but the truth is that he died for me five years ago, when he had his accident. One recalls George Moore's 'Oh, I can't go through all that again!' And yet there are other reasons for squeamish callousness: he never allowed himself to be fallible. Something died in him when he became respectable. He let go of life and now we wait for it to let go of him.

14.11.75. Penelope Gilliatt was a late addition to the company *chez* Hilary. I met her once before, in 1969, when she was living in Mike Nichols' huge apartment on Central Park West. Jo Janni had an appointment with her and I went up to her place in the narrow private penthouse elevator. I waited in a little lobby, refusing drink and playing sullen second fiddle. A rather gaudily hennaed girl with a big grin, part schoolgirl leer, part deformity, she had the smugness of a smart party who has begun a new career at the top. She had hooked Janni and Schlesinger for her movie and there was no sense in telling her that she was the fish, not they. Apparently confident, secretly doubtful, I was hoping to direct *Guilt* in the near future, which was soon adjourned *sine die* (Jo and I were on our way to California, my first trip to the then slump-stricken capital of the movies). I was jealous of the sparkling little adventuress who had usurped the role with John and Jo which I both had and had not enjoyed. She was very well-connected; she had made all the best beds.

At the Rubinsteins', I awaited her arrival with vengeful polite-ness. Since being a star with the *Observer* and, more recently, the *New Yorker*, she had had a fall. For whatever reason, medical or neurotic, she had been caught in an act of plagiarism so manifest that deadline panic alone could explain it. She was a burnt-out case whose career had nowhere left to go. She had boasted, loudly enough to excite John's repeated displeasure, of how she had created *Sunday Bloody Sunday*, an achievement more immortal in John's view than in mine.

Penelope had just 'skied in' from New York and, boy, was her backbone tired. She was a bent little old lady with a sack of invis-ible male slung over her shoulder, memories like lead. The dyed red hair was dry as tinder, the large eyes blind, almost, with the pain that slowed her speech to a deathbed crawl. She reminded me of Adrienne Corri in *Chrome Yellow*. She came down from Oxford in 1955, which made her – *pauvre vieillarde* – younger than I am.

She read Greats and rather grandly disclosed her knowledge of Greek, at least until I disclosed mine. She had a tendency to flatter, the mark of vanity on its uppers. She told me what excellent work I had done on *Far from the Madding Crowd* (not knowing how sick I was of being congratulated on a paste-up job). She had written a fan letter to J.R.S. about it, long before she thought of working with him. How long before? Twenty minutes, I daresay. Oh my God, could she home in on the famous! I would not have shared her life, even in order to know her friends. She is not merely in a poor shape; she is bombed out of all recognition. No restoration grant, no number of king's men will ever put this one together again. How could there be anything left in her creative wallet except very small change indeed?

Yet there she is, at the centre of things as well as beside herself; six months of the year are still spent at the *New Yorker* by this Persephone who has lost her spring, the other six doing the writing. In her sagging white suit and her bulging strap-over shoes she seemed the very stuff of Jean Rhys's imagination. She must, I suppose, still find men, but the thought of the persecuted flesh under those expensive wrinkled clothes is not seductive. If she is a free woman, it is not surprising that so many of her sex choose bondage. This defiant little clown did tell one funny story, or a story that would have been funny if someone else had told it. Her electricity bill came in from Con Edison and it was $30,000; a computer joke, no doubt. She called the company and was promised they would look into it. A new bill arrived: $75,000. When she complained again, another investigation was promised and another bill arrived: $130,000. It turned out, finally, that her bill was for the electrical consumption of the entire block. She called the company and asked to speak to the president. She was referred to the vice-president in charge of customer relations, Mr Greenberg. The secretary asked her to specify her grievance. P. insisted on speaking to Mr G. Mr G. had 'stepped out'. When would he step in again? The secretary could not say. P. said she would wait. And the secretary burst into tears.

A likely story, but (she *promised*) true: there was no Mr Greenberg. He puts the con in Con Edison; P. said that the company employs no Jews in high executive positions; Mr Greenberg is a computer. The story ended with P.G. taking the secretary who couldn't take it any more out to lunch. Vulgar imagination might put them to bed together after the pastrami, but a lighter touch would taxi them to the Bronx Zoo to look at the people. P.G. is like that sole survivor of the Sicilian Expedition, reeling home with a tale of disaster and announcing the collapse of all her fine hopes with such an air of relief-to-be-back that one cannot believe that anything *that* terrible can have happened. On the other hand, why is she rather more than half dead?

15.11.75. Imagine a series of mythic revisions in the brazen tradition of Picasso's *Las Meniñas*: critical rewritings of (modern) fiction but without the criticism. The 'true' story of *Daisy Miller* might encompass the making of the (or, at least, *a*) film of H.J.'s story: a vision of the myth extended through a whole century. A succession of fresh-as-Daisies come to Europe and encounter the going treatment of young American girls on the sexual/social make. The hopes of Cybill Shepherd, practising tap-dancing in the Connaught bathroom, how do they differ from Daisy's own? There was innocence in her knowing dedication, a belief that comely brass could not fail to get her where she wanted. Similar playfulness could make a dry comment on Maugham's *Rain*; or contrive a happy ending for *Death/(life) in Venice*; antibiotics cure Philoctetes, whose bow is inaccurate without his wound; *A Farewell to Arms* ends with a successful Caesarian which leaves Papa's hero with a baby and domestic life instead of an immortal *donnée*. Such revisions could discover what is implicit, in a subversive sense, in the 'myths' themselves.

16.11.75. THE REUNION. After many years of absence abroad, a man is invited to Cambridge for a feast. His academic career was cut short by a scandal – an accusation, let's say, of plagiarism or imposture – which resulted in eviction from his Fellowship (or in its abortion). Perhaps he was tactless, on the eve of his election, in refuting an authority high in the college: a premature display of trenchant scholarship which, had the authority been from another college, might have been greeted with applause. It would be neat if the derided pundit had a daughter who was in love with him. She might even be the one who furnished details of her father's scholarly delinquencies. The latter could resemble our friend George S. in having denied her a place, as an adolescent, at his dining table because she failed to do him credit in conversation with other intellectuals whom he greeted with such obsequiousness that her stomach was turned.

The exile has known that he was in the right. His certainty has made him a prisoner fettered and rubbed sore by his own innocence. He has waited for the moment when the college would summon him, like an academic Dreyfus, to resume the Fellowship (perhaps the Mastership) of which he was unjustly deprived. The card which bids him to the reunion is, in truth, a routine invitation sent to all men (and now women) who matriculated in certain years. Famous for the accuracy of his readings, he has misread a circular for a reprieve. He is asked, as is normal, what rooms he would like and by whose side he would prefer to be seated.

He has a long, disturbing journey back to the place whose dust he so long ago shook from his shoes. The train is full of unfamiliarly *modern* faces; the air thickens his lungs. In their modern dress, local realities do not fit his memory of them. He reaches the college, however, and when he enters Hall, the applause seems to signal – as it were in some witty Morse – that the academic world is ready to return to him his broken sword (or snapped pen) and restore him to the place he deserved when young. When the Master greets him and escorts him to his place, the exile's belief in the honour of scholarship is at last vindicated. The tears which blind his eyes are for the refutation of the bitter misanthropy that humiliation has perfected in him.

In fact, his place at the reunion is empty. Those on each side of where he should be seated speak to each other through his ghost. When the porter goes to his rooms in the morning, he finds the old man, in his gown and dressed for dinner, dead on the floor of the gyp room, perhaps with the 'eternal flame' of the gas-ring lit like a gasping halo (the porter will be sure to turn it off). The prospect of his vindication has been more than the old scholar can bear. He might have lived for many alien years with his bitterness for company. Reprieve has killed him.

Suppose, alternatively, that the old 'scholar' is indeed the opportunistic villain which his college accused him of being. The story then takes place in the little French town where an invitation – possibly not intended for him – is delivered to the *pauvre type* who adds a few francs to his pension by translating brochures and local guidebooks or by serving as an English-speaking lecturer in the underground caves where the 'prehistoric' paintings are as gaudy as they are doubtfully genuine (modern experts suspect that the Abbé Breuil had a hand in painting at least some of the Dordogne cave-paintings which he made his reputation by authenticating). The old man's pension dates from his days as a drab provincial schoolmaster, but he gives it the allure of something rarer: the fruit of working for the secret service, ours or theirs or both.

A brilliant student, on the verge of academic distinction, is accused – justly or unjustly – of stealing his ideas or falsifying his data and commits suicide. In the moment of kicking away the chair, he imagines, or lives through, a long life of humiliation and/or remorse, culminating in a feast in his honour. His accusers are fed with humble pie and he hears of his appointment as extraordinary professor. It seems that he has had second thoughts, but then a college porter reports that he has found the hanged body of a young man. The author of the story is first saluted for the ingenuity of his tale and then accused, as he is about to receive an award, of having plagiarised Ambrose Bierce.

A young and ambitious writer goes to call, in a *visite d'hommage*, on an old novelist who lives alone in a palatial hotel in a distant place (cf. V.N. at the Montreux Palace). Excited by admiring avarice, the young man puts the great man to sleep with his prolonged deference and, as if in final tribute, steals his talent. The following morning, the young man is found dead in his single bedroom. He has died of old age.

17.11.75.

Here is the earthquake
And the fall of stones.
Here are storage jars,

Empty, and the clanking statue
Pitched in the sand. Here.
The sentinel failed and fell.
Fled is Daedalus
Once petalled in bronze.
Daedalus gulped down
The blue throat of the sky.
And Icarus?
Alive, stammering
In the empty air.
Break in the stone,
Flaw in the heart.
Minos' kettle is on for tea.
D. gone; I. live.
Michael dead,
The crafty one, the sly,
Those fingers still
That drew life
On the mirror of art.
The Cretans? Blank
With loss. I. lands,
Clears customs, safe.
D. flew too near the moon:
In its mirror
Caught his death
Like a common cold.
Life is witless,
Ploughed *boustrophedon*.

18.11.75. Death weighs like a press on a flower; we are flat. Words
need thought, correction, form; grief is thoughtless and takes no
direction. All formal mourning smacks of ritual, and of oppor-
tunism; one does not want to write well, but to weep. Ink tears are
for clowns and professionals. Here is loss, loss and nothing but loss.
If there are compensations, we will not think of them yet. Selfishness
comes into your feelings, doesn't it? Should we care without caring,
or without being ourselves? He is, as they say, taken from us. You
loved him in part because he was your *famous* friend. A bit; *il n'était
pas tellement connu*. It was pleasant to be reassured that his praise
(rather than his affection) had some public warrant. It was entertaining to hear the famous – Dylan, Gloomy George (Orwell), John,
old Henry – enumerated in his stories, but I loved him because we

drew strength from each other and remained fuller than before. You loved him because he had become frail and needed you. Possibly; I was able to meet his need, and hence needed it. I grieve for a friend with whom I could make things. I grieve as one hand might for the other, that will never shape something together with it, the third something which celebrates its makers. It is only three years that we have known him. 'It's the end of everything,' Elisabeth said on the telephone.

We hung up Africa like the saddle of a dead charger. We will not ride out. We had such plans: Catullus, the Cretans, the Greek plays; we had such plans. We sat down by the pool that August day in the sun and there was such ease of communication; we talked like angels. All things seemed possible; few were. I have never hated death more or feared it less than in the last twenty-four hours. Can good come of this? Can one rig fresh sails from mournful crêpe? I doubt it. We have lost him and that is all there is to it. There are dedications, tearful libations which promise and hope and fear, fear failure, hope for excellence, promise Art. The moment comes when the possibility of a caesura in this mad rush for whatever it is for which one is scrambling so crazily comes like a cruel reprieve.

There are those who will find what I say about Michael Ayrton mawkish or embarrassing. To me, after thirty years, it is also surprising. The surprise is double: I did not know that I was *so* devastated by his sudden death, from a heart attack (the result of a failure to diagnose his strain of diabetes, despite the many symptoms which should have sounded an easy alarm). And I am surprised that I spoke so disparagingly of him in the same notebook in which I wrote his elegy. The living are not depicted from the same palette of words which describe the dead.

20.11.75. Pain wears off more slowly than pleasure; the world is a history of anguish, not of joy. There can be no true pain/ pleasure axis; they are the oil and water of the emotions. Neither eliminates the other; they do not mix, still less dilute, or sweeten. We fear death as we fear love: because it is charged with emotion, because mourning is love in black. We have a horror of purely spiritual passions as official Victorians did of physical ones. It is modern to conceal the poverty of our emotional convictions; we attempt to escape the cycles which have ennnobled mankind, and enslaved it.

By being sensible, not sensitive, we think to dodge mortality. In avoiding it, we are always unprepared, exiled to a cold moon.

Death comes like a terrorist, to whom one says, 'What do you want? What do you hope to achieve?' And he replies, 'Nothing.' Death makes no demands and accepts no ransom; it is our only absolute: death is death.

Michael had known many great figures, not least but not only because his father had been editor of the *Observer* and his mother prominent in the Labour Party. *Et pourtant*, he had been the youngest person ever to be on *The Brains Trust*, at a time when that programme was a certificate of intellectual eminence (as long as you exempt Commander Campbell, who was the resident plain man). His first broadcast put him in the ring with Bertrand Russell. The last question was 'How would you define truth?' Asked first, Michael tried to be mature and philosophical in a way which he thought would recommend him to Russell. Russell's answer, for which there was not much time left, was 'Truth is what the police require you to tell.'

When, aged eight, I was sent away to prep school, my parents sweetened my agony by giving me a 'Compendium of Games', a box containing chess, and draughts and other diversions. Perhaps they hoped that I should be more popular for the choice of pleasures I could offer. In the event, rougher, tougher boys pillaged my compendium almost as soon as I opened it; I incurred the odium of ostentation without having anything to show for it. Michael was, in a way, a compendium of celebrities, but he could not be robbed of the brilliant party that went on in his head and which died with him.

21.11.75. Michael is to be buried today. Have we chickened out, or have we been tactful? The funeral is said to be 'private, no flowers', but are we not part of his privacy? I have written the difficult letter to Elisabeth; I have promised my friendship, but she will have more pain than consolation in seeing us. We confirm what every famous artist's woman is likely to think: it was only because of *him* that we knew her. Elisabeth and Prue and Justine, they are the Trojan women, Hector gone.

I have been reading Iris's *The Black Prince*. Was ever high intelligence so subservient to the low English disease, frivolity? No novelist thinks better than I.M.; yet she writes like everyone else. No, not quite: she can conjure a scene from a few traditional props – a church, the names of plants, the colours of the sky – like a penurious mother making a wonderful theatre out of a few scraps of vivid paper, some twigs and an old carton. She reaches into that old workbox and comes out with brilliant new things. The trouble with her secrets is that their ingenuity is a kind of cynicism: who wants to find that what art conceals is just a clever twist? Reading a novel, if ever I wish that I had thought of its ending, its 'solution', as if to a clue in a crossword, it ceases to interest me.

What disconcerts the novice in art is its coldness, the severity of its distinctions, its resistance to convertibility to something nicer. The attempt to humanise art is always a way of doing it down; it makes what should daunt the common citizen dependent on his criticism, his pleasure, his needs.

Art and intelligence are untransferable assets. A man may drive through the poorest quarters of a city in a Rolls Royce and be admired for his ostentation. What can be destroyed or appropriated never enrages people as much as what they can never have.

The charge of *superbia* that drove Coriolanus into exile is nothing compared to the fury which expels the mind too clever for its time. To equate excellence with arrogance is the kind of definition that will make Philistia the world-state.

Let's not sanctify Michael with whitewash. He was an old-style Bohemian, rescued from just this side of alcoholism, sheltered in a belated monogamy against which he chafed like a madman in a cell padded with nettles. He was once six feet one and we never knew him over five feet something: spondylitis. He had been a dangerous sexual pirate; it was comfortable to have him in tow dismasted. With full powers, as Nigel discovered, he was a menacing marauder. He still felt rejuvenating guilt about Nigel; what is more cocky than victorious remorse?

The Daedalus whom Michael revered and whose mask he usurped was, to a degree, a slave; a contriver of ingenuities, a man commissioned to be artful no less than original. The separation of art and state preceded that of art and religion: every time an ancient craftsman made something of his own fancy, he seceded furtively, from the common view. Modern landscape begins with what is seen through the windows of pious works; the background of a Holy

Family or a Crucifixion is, to begin with, incidental. When the camera pushes focus, the secular becomes central and evicts the religious *dramatis personae* from the frame. In the same involuntary way, abstraction begins wth naturalism.

Plato's suspicion of the artist lies in his knowledge that the better the artist the more dangerous his subversion of what he may seem to be endorsing; the philosopher knows, better than the insurance man, what underwriting involves.

Simon Raven proves that it is still possible to write entertaining fiction by being an honest advocate of one's own prejudices. Only a classical education can lend panache to shamelessness.

Michael Frayn. One senses a lack of *sérieux*. Everything is trimmed for the sake of a mild *divertissement*: if he appropriated the plot of *The Man Who Came to Dinner*, it would become *The Man Who Stayed for a Light Lunch*.

The first news of a death
Stammers as a storm
Scissors the far horizon;
Fuse of unheard thunder,
Primes the powder
Of perished certainties.

What fish the flyer saw.
What shallows in the deep.
Island and monster;
Undertow of jealous eyes;
Muscled swimmers,
Striped sergeants
In aquatic regiment.
What fish the flyer.

High heaven drowned him
In its blue;
Ecstasy of wings.
Enterprising mirrors.
Perished Perseus;
Wreath of snakes.
See their hissing?

Done Trojan horse
Drenched to a shack
Of wet wood.
Peasants forage
Heroic billets;
Curse what will not catch.

Floozy moon,
Canted on her smile,
Lolls on the toppled tower.
Phengari, phengari.

4.12.75. The thrill of completion was voided by Beetle's sudden rage at the last of *The Glittering Prizes*. I never saw it coming. Vanity is a poor oracle. After a mild nightmare of a return to the UK (fog, cancelled flight, enforced overnight at Orly), I went at once to the bliss of rehearsal. Then, on Saturday, B. came to the studio with Sarah, whose naïveté made it difficult for her to accept that anything she was seeing was not based on fact. How could I argue, once the passionate storm broke (on Sunday), that I had had no intention of identifying Barbara with B.? Complacency had been fuelled by the admiration and devotion of those involved with the plays. After my long, smooth flight to the stars, I was shot down in abrupt, abject humiliation. B. proves her independence, her very existence, by her implacable indignation. The word is exact: the sense of being used unworthily arms her scorn and her rage. I was so unbalanced by the sudden assault that I actually fell to my knees. My intentions were as irrelevant as Buddhism; my protestations of innocence were charged with guilt. What good was it to say that Miss Kellerman's pretty performance lacked the charm and depth which I had always read into the character of *my* Barbara?

I wished that all my eloquence could be silenced and that we could be as we were last week – last week! – when our happiness seemed so serene, our unity unbreachable. I responded only with entreaty and excuses. I failed to play the part of the artist who cannot abandon his Muse. I did not deny the relationship, but I offered to renounce my fidelity to it with unloverly speed. I had brought the plays to B. in the style of a gift: look what you made me do. I proved myself to her with them (as the Freudian child is said to deliver his faeces) and she was saying only that they stank.

She took *A Double Life* as an insult, when I thought that she would see it simply as a comedy of married life, of marriages much more like the P.s' or the Q.s' than ours. Oh, I had plucked a few familiar leaves from our family tree, for the sake of verisimilitude, but the secret garden was unbreached.

I may have cringed, but there remains a part of me that is proof against all reproach: I will be an artist, whatever I promise and whatever it means. Oh, I am also ineluctably married to B. My relief at recovering her is always so immeasurable that it is almost (*almost*) worth the risk of losing her in order to experience the joy of having her again, but there is nothing deliberate here; it is a joy I should gladly forego. B.'s fury is as lacerating as her tears are inconsolable; I should not, and do not, willingly incur either.

Love and marriage; what is more complex, or more simple? The whole notation of my private life clusters here, just as my social being does about the contingency of Jewishness. The freedom of my writing, when it is free, proves art to be *my* anima figure. What the married man proves by his infidelity, the married *artist* proves by allegiance to a crafty Muse.

Treason is the assertion of a man's right to hang separately.

5.12.75. A letter from George Steiner, supposedly about Michael but in reality almost all about G. He laments keenly enough, but in terms of self-pity and self-inflation, at once comic, endearing and nauseating. In the *ST* office, someone compared George to a torrent which at first flows deep between clenched banks; one trembles to think of the profound majesty of the eventual river. And at first sight the estuary too is magnificent; one can scarcely see from this side to that. The disappointment is that the water is now only ankle-deep; one may wade clear across it without wetting one's knees. The someone was me.

The large first edition of *After Babel* has sold out. Announcing hardly disagreeable news, G. contrives an air of grievance. England is unwelcoming to him. Did he expect a ticker-tape parade? What are the great qualities that the English refuse to honour? The book, he says, 'has changed *nothing*' (with G. emphasis is *always* being added). Was his *magnum opus* intended as an advertisement, a brochure, a prospectus? To what high office does he dream, Reith-like, of being appointed? F. Kermode speaks of *After Babel*'s 'awesome stature' (G. has spoken similarly of Kermode). Well, the stature of any book which heaps Ossa on Pelion, and more or less keeps its balance, is likely to be imposing. G.'s true purpose ought to be instruction rather than self-advancement. His visions are noble; his ambitions vulgar.

Nigel Balchin called Michael 'the Praetorian guard'. M. was puzzled, as the clever are by the obvious (a straight line is the most baffling maze). The truth was simple: only the Praetorians had the power to make and to break emperors. The trusted insider is the likeliest traitor.

A curiosity of marriage: desire becomes an option not a command.

They say that Jack Lambert is soon to retire. The mood in his office was glum, resentful, suspicious, as it often is in centres of small power. John Peter, pouter pigeon in new feathers, showed me the invitation he had received to join the Critics' Circle. Well worth crawling all the way from Hungary for. They were all off to the Garrick for lunch. Jack conferred on me the dignity of *almost* asking me to join them. 'It's all right,' I said, after chauffeuring them to the corner of King Street, 'I'm off to see my Thesps.' Stanislavsky's second home is better than any club.

E. will not go back to Bradfields, ever. 'That was Michael's house.' E. confessed to me that she tried to kill herself but 'That didn't work, so we shall have to try something else.' She and Prue are going to live near Bristol. I wanted to promise support and affection, but I knew I was saying a guarded goodbye.

The mutability of M.'s face (what did he really look like?) reflected the many-chambered recesses and resources of his mental museum. It contained riches that were not always his, but he paced the world like a kingly curator, owning what was common and holding the key to what was secret. He seemed sedentary, but he had been everywhere; the catacombs, the serried stacks, musty caches, dusty attics. Europe was his library; he could always find the required text. One could imagine Daedalus as the author of Europe, postulating the whole labyrinth of Christian and post-Christian art as an example of how men can furnish even the most unlikely myth. Recurrence is a mark of the mythical; what recurs does not die. Art as for-instance is disencumbered of the perishable. Daedalus escapes time by refusing to serve his; jail-breaker, he solicits and declines service with *temporal* powers.

8.12.75. Myth is compatible with philosophy, but not with science; it is spared contingency. Myth may date, but cannot be dated.

Plato's myths as instances of the Necessary: preconditions. The rules of his game are either absolute or arbitrary, or both: he aimed to root the arbitrary in the Absolute. The Platonic myth is to morality as the axiom is to Euclid. Should we speak of his world as an elaborated tautology? We could have a go.

Myth is the source of language: one cannot go further back. Myth *can* have no authentication. It does not explain the past, it furnishes it. Those who forget the past are obliged to live it again? Better: those who remember the mythical have confidence that *it* will live forever. The promise of the future? That it is locked into – made meaningful by – the past. Messianic myths – Marxism, Christianity, etc. – require a past that is *so*; and a future that therefore will be.

The only useful criticism of myth is narrative; discordant, parasitic, satirical; myth can be barnacled with variants until it loses its seductive form. It is then seen as fat and fatuous, as jeering Lucian saw Pheidias' Zeus, which had filled generation after generation with pious awe.

Motive is irrelevant in art, and in religion. Monreale was built to put out an archbishop's eye. So what?

Shaping language and shaping man, the Tweedledum of nominalism and the Tweedledee of Realism fight eternally on this ground.

Passing certain frontiers, one seems to experience *at once* a remarkable change of temperature, as if Spain, for instance, were *really* another country, as Belgium can never be. When you sign your way through the customs house of the quotidian, you accept subjection to the empire of death. You bite the pomegranate. The greedy concession which Persephone made, in a red mouthful, confirmed her choice: to be eternally free and eternally enslaved.

Bell Rock and Royal Sovereign, the boom of the mourning bell and the clangour of independence. Only the fixed bell can swing. Between such poles did Daedalus – does Daedalus? – fly. Knossos was his grand hotel (like the Palace, Montreux) where the artist may put everything on the bill, where he meets no other guests and whence, on his little balcony, he may look out at mountains spread with the fresh napery of snow, a landscape barred like a prisoner's prospects. (Cf. Nabokov's chimpanzee who, encouraged to express itself with paper and pencil, first drew the bars of its cage.) The escape of Daedalus was an escape from being given everything he wanted, provided he stayed put. There is always something missing in arrangements where everything is provided.

9.12.75. Come dust and do your work. Decent people have so much to hide.

She is not a dull girl; she is a dull actress. She relies on her looks for fear that her intellect is less pretty. Coming from a clever but provincial family, she has little faith in her own worth, despite her beauty. She is its servant, bowing to its requirements (be nice, be clean, be famous), but she wears her looks like a dress: forever wondering if they look all right on her. And, in truth, they do not quite hang straight. The bend of her back reminds me of Hilary, who also hung her head, as if ducking the burden of beauty. Such a girl is loaded with her charms like a donkey; unless she has brains or a brave recklessness, she is as joyless as porcelain. The dread of autumn, when the leaves of youth will fall, fills her with apprehension, the enemy of an actor's inventiveness.

To see imagination inhabit an actor (and working overtime) one has only to watch Conti; his performance is lustrous with acquisitive observation. He will steal your slightest gesture if he can use it. An actor!

'Fucking actresses,' Tom said, after a scene with E. He had been worrying about it throughout the early stages of rehearsal. He telephoned her privily so that the three of us could meet and go through it without the director, with whom E. had had an abortive romance. We made some progress, but I was not happy that we had what we needed or all that E. was capable of giving us. However, I had only a couple of days. Before they were to do the scene in the bar, I had a moment with E. and told her how the scene had originated in a kind of improvisation on the typewriter (as if most of them had not!) and – reaching for some means to inspire – that it was a kind of 'audition piece', a short story almost, which required neither motivation (damn motivation to hell, by the way) nor antecedents. That did the trick, she told me afterwards. She did the scene almost exactly as she usually did it, from the point of view of movements and even (if it showed) motivation. What was new was the *voice*, a voice now raw with alcohol, calmly strident, a voice that spoke, Kingsley might say, as the floor of the parrot's cage would, if it had a tongue. The effect was shocking, almost embarrassing, and it gave Tom's performance a sort of appalled tenderness which seemed to me to have been absent before. Admiration was dosed with relief and even with a measure of irritation. She might have let us hear about this a little sooner!

Afterwards E. was pink with pleasure at the surprise she had given us, slightly ashamed too (that we had to be so surprised), but gently triumphant. 'Now,' she said, 'you won't have to knock radio any more, will you?' It was true: her performance owed everything to how she *sounded*. Television pretends to be a visual medium, but what comes first, and remains longest, is what you *hear*. Even in films, I have always felt that if a line was *said* right it would look right; and if not, not.

E. drives an old Morris Minor with a canvas roof. When I saw her across the carpark she made a shrugging face, indicated her car, and said, 'Just like me, isn't it?' She was the character, not herself. E. is a lovely, but not beautiful, girl who seems already to be preparing for a lonely old age. She goes to LCC evening classes and has learnt to make lace. She can cope with as many as eighty bobbins at a time. Recently, she made some black lace in class. The other ladies, mostly elderly, thought it rather fast of her.

Noel Stock's *Ezra Pound*. On the face of it, a responsible piece of academic seriousness: one hears the flip of cross-referenced index cards and the whirr of ticketed tapes. The early life is as interesting as most early lives and the early struggles as warming as early struggles often are. Yet one grows conscious of the thin matter on which the floor of the narrative rests; the joists reach only *just* to the centre of the structure on which, as riskily as a dancer in an old Venetian *palazzo*, Stock reposes his weight. The anecdotes which serve to humanise young Ez amount to an amiable portrait of the emergent spirit, but much of the evidence of his amiability comes from the subject's own accounts. What sounds like reconstruction is a cross between hagiography and narcissism.

Almost all the serious turns in Pound's life – those areas where one wants to go slowly – are briskly described, with the corners cut. His marriage, the rupture with England, the collapse of his coherence, his inability to correspond and yet his *cacoethes scribendi epistolas*, all these things are handled with cursory meticulousness (*metus* = fear). Stock flinches from any speculation which might explain P.'s petulant fall from promise into paranoid megalomania. His sexuality appears vigorous (his language boasts it) but why did he marry and then so quickly renege on marriage?

Stock treats P.'s 'ideas' with remarkable solemnity. Yet most of them (most of *it*, one might say) lack credibility or sense. What got into him? What got into pretty well *all* of them? How *could* they have 'believed' what they advocated, Lewis, Eliot, Pound, and the rest of them?

P.'s generosity seems his only agreeable quality, but it was financial rather than magnanimous. He lacked all reason, yet he wanted to argue. He believed in definitions (from which everything else followed) just as Christians believe in miracles, because they prove what cannot otherwise be true. What the *hell* was he playing at? One inclines to the banal: he was a silly old poet bearded for prophecy. Stock allows Pound's view that 'Hitler was a martyr' to stand without the mildest of ironic demurrals.

P.'s value remains as a gadfly, an ideogram of the man of letters. A gadfly, however, is a good fly only when a herd needs to be piqued out of its complacency; there is no sense in, or use for, a swarm of gadflies. Why did P. oppose Roosevelt so furiously? Was he, as Stock says, 'of Republican stock' or did he truly imagine that FDR had harmed the republic which, on any commonplace measure, he rescued from despair? Not all P.'s poundings were without force; the rock-drill left durable marks. No one could have looked at the course of modern kulchur and education and said that all was well. Yet, nervously treacherous to the priority of aesthetics, I prefer muddle to mania.

Behind old Ez, and not far behind, one can smell roasting flesh, and in him an appetite for it. The man who insists on definitions generally uses words wildly (he craves politico-metaphysical conclusions which the innocent do not yet perceive, and for which his apparent respect for language is already scheming). Those who harp on dirt and corruption do not so often dream of cleanliness or honesty as of punishment and the pillory. The true charge against Pound is not treason against the United States; it is treason against humanity, against the individual in the name of individuality. His treachery is at once majestic and petty, grandiose and spiteful. As for Stock, his fault is more banal: he has made a mansion from a fallen house of cards. Amassing material may build a career, but baulks at depicting the poet as intellectual *gauleiter*. Such biographies breathe life into the novel, which need not be a footnoted stockpot.

5.12.75. Christopher Morahan, the new Head of Plays, has not said one enthusiastic word to me about *The Glittering Prizes*, either as scripts or as finished articles. On Friday, during rehearsals for the last of them, I was conscious of a large man beside me: the boss. 'Freddie,' he said, 'you seem depressed.' 'No,' I said, 'I'm OK.' 'No, I can tell: you're feeling rather down.' 'Well,' I said, 'it's the end of six months of pure pleasure. Six months of having one's own set of living action men and women. It's sad to think that it's all over.' 'Of *course*,' he said. 'Of course it is. You really must write that stage play, you know. You really must.' 'You're right, Christopher,' I said, 'it's silly to go on having fantasies when the opportunity's there. It's like being in a brothel and not daring to have the beautiful girl when she's offered to you.' 'Yes,' he said, 'and, well, when the moment comes, you never know, *I* might be interested in directing it.'

He sugared his gall by murmuring of a scheme he had for writers to come in and direct their own films at the BBC – not in the immediate future, but in a year, eighteen months. 'But, of course,' he added, 'I shan't always be here.' One hopes not.

Philip Oakes, that soft-shelled turtle, has written a new novel. It was received by his regular publishers less than flatteringly. Philip is furious. 'It's not an easy book. It's got a lot of explicit sex in it. It's the best thing I've ever done.' I believe him, but then what has he ever done?

The old 60s hand. His mind is an unmade bed in which he has left his socks.

Peter Hall. He has been so abused during the last few weeks that one is almost persuaded that there is some good in the man. He was arraigned as an enemy of the people for having gone on an expensive recce to Norway. Soon they will bring back the death penalty for having your Dundee cake and nibbling it too. Peter has only one manifest failing: he has no charm and yet will continually wrinkle his nose. There must, however, be more self-indulgent ways of abusing one's office than by visiting Ibsen's homeland. If he had stayed at home to audition a couple of comely drama students, who would have said a word?

Peter always cuts me very politely. He fears he may have seen me somewhere. I have rarely enjoyed his productions, but don't doubt his competence. He resembles Denis Compton, of whom everyone spoke (rightly) with great admiration. On no occasion when I saw him bat did he make more than 13.

Losey was never done a better turn than when, after being a

humdrum Hollywood director, he was put on the blacklist and fled to Europe before he was obliged to testify in front of McCarthy's committee. He took on the allure of a martyr, unfairly accused of what was largely true: he *was* a Communist and he *did* want to subvert the constitution of the United States. For the New Left in London, however, he embodied the victim who had been denied free speech. That he advocated (and imagined himself empowered by) Marxism, which denied pluralism as a *principle*, was not regarded as either comic or grotesque. A man of dictatorial vanity, he had a romantic idea of the Artist (himself) as lone, incontrovertible, visionary. After a number of indifferent Pinewood films, he was liberated for better things by the collapse of the Rank organisation. He did nothing remarkable until he teamed up with Harold Pinter on *The Servant*, which merited its success and its fame.

We were living in Rome in 1964 when I received a letter from Joe asking me to do some dialogue on a script which needed improvement. Tears in my eyes, I took the invitation as an accolade. I was working with both Schlesinger and Stanley Donen at the time, but *Losey*, wow! I replied that I was not interested in being a rewrite man, but should welcome a chance to work with him on an original. When back in London, I went to see Joe in Wellington Square. He was enthroned, at length, on a *chaise longue*, blanched and beached. We exchanged civilities but I don't think we liked each other. I hardly recall anything we talked about, but I do remember him saying that he did not believe that there could be a 'genuine relationship' between a man and a woman in a bourgeois society. I assumed that he was joking, but he was not a man who made jokes. He showed little sense of humour (i.e. I did not amuse him) nor had I an impression of great intelligence. Like most directors, his talent was, in part, in the shrewd selection of those on whom (especially Pinter) his ability could feed. The director is an inverted ventriloquist; his dummies speak through him and he earns applause for their eloquence.

The French made him their totem: the unAmerican American. Vanity (and want of imagination) never allowed him to wonder whether the French had ulterior, political motives. A Marxist who could not imagine an insincere ovation, he was, in many ways, a provincial American (from the same state as the junior senator who, by putting him to flight, had contributed to his triumph). His Communism made him feel he had come to town.

When Jo Janni began to believe that I could direct a film myself,

it was necessary, as a preliminary, that I become a member of the
ACTT's directors' branch (I was already a member of the union,
which was a closed shop in those days, but only as a writer). To vali-
date my application, I needed to be sponsored by four directors.
John Schlesinger and Clive Donner were kind enough to put their
names on the form (signature implied no endorsement of my merit),
but Joe refused. He said that there were other people who deserved
a chance ahead of me. That may have been true, but my availability
to direct did not entail that others would be denied their chance.
Losey was being asked to make me *eligible*, under union rules, to
direct a film if selected; my selection by a producer was another
matter entirely. In keeping with his Marxist 'principles', he believed
not only in a centralised economy but also in a bureaucratically
(dictatorially) controlled art establishment, an academy in fact, in
which he would have *pleins pouvoirs*. His refusal to admit me to
membership of the union was of a piece with Soviet practice. It was
his refusal to scribble his name on a form, which would have
procured me no *advantage* whatever, that prompted my angry letter.
He did not answer it, but – as biographers have been happy to
declare – he went about declaring that I was a 'dangerous fraud'.

Whatever Losey's revised opinion of me, he asked me on a couple
of subsequent occasions to consider a project with him (I remember
in particular Roger Vailland's *La Truite*, which struck me as jejune
eroticism). In the event, although we remained distant acquain-
tances, I had little to do with him. Our sons, however, went to the
same school. As a result, Joe's son Joshua came to stay with us in
France. He had much more charm than his father, whose paternal
responsibilities were secondary to his mission to expose the false-
ness of personal relations in bourgeois society. Joe did, however, call
me to discuss the boy's career prospects: he was particularly
concerned lest Joshua fail to get a regular job, cut his hair, etc. I
ironised, sympathetically I hope, at Joe's suburban anxiety: surely,
it was not to be hoped that our children should find themselves
compatible with a decadent social system. He was neither amused
nor placated.

Tom Wiseman and Joe worked together on a version of Tom's
novel *The Romantic Englishwoman*. There are aspects of Joe in
Wiseman's latest novel, *Genius Jack*. On one occasion, in order to
attend the Cannes festival, Joe and Tom travelled together on the
Blue Train. Joe was upset by the lack of air in the sleeping compartment and wanted to open the window. Since the train was
air-conditioned, Tom pointed out that this was impossible. Joe

asked him to ask the conductor to come and unlock the window. Tom did as he was requested, but – as expected – he reported that the conductor said that it would disrupt the air-conditioning. Losey said, 'Did you tell him who I am? Go and tell him who I am.' Tom did; but the conductor was not a subscriber to *Les Cahiers du Cinéma*. He had never heard of genius Joe. The window stayed shut.

'When you think that I have betrayed you, you become angry; when I think you have betrayed me, I become resentful.' Who loves whom?

The poet described the city,
Falsely, said the journalist.
He made the warriors
Taller, braver, than they were.
The poet's lies came true:
The towers grew to top-
lessness, the warriors,
Faceless louts, put on
Nobility:
Hector, Achilles, Diomede.
Eyeless, the poet saw
The world make shift
To match his vision.

When her old man's about, Lesbia gives me hell.
The fat-head thinks it 'tebbly funny!'
The ass. If our thing were off, she'd be quiet,
Temperature normal. But: bitch, bitch, bitch.
Ergo, it's not. It's gone further than that:
She's in a passion. The hots. Hence: talk, talk, talk.

(Catullus 83)

18.12.75. Alone in Paris (after a meeting with Philippe Labro) I go to see *Nashville*. Excellent, immensely enjoyable; I come out *ravi*. I walk down the Champs Elysées in the December cold, with my hairy new trousers (brown check flares) chaffing my inner thighs to rawness. I take the Métro, change at Châtelet, and finally go to dine at Le Port St Germain. Why? Why not? I listen to a man who says *tu* to everybody in the attempt to persuade himself that he is with

friends. His mistress has refused to dine with him; a business associate '*m'attaque partout*'. He has eyes like Maschler: he expects
prompt attention in return for insolent intimacies. I eat *coquilles*
smothered in garlic and parsley – the Parisian idea of *provençal* – and
chicken on a spit, a gristly sight. I remain in a good humour. It is
two hours since I left the cinema. What was so good about the
movie? It was just like America. It was pretty funny, *un peu vrai
d'ailleurs*. It was all right. There were excellent scenes, weren't there?
It passed the time. What was wrong with it?

1976

12.1.76. Almost a month since I put pen to this or any paper. Holiday or deprivation? A lacuna during which we have given an almost great party (for the cast of *The Glittering Prizes* and a few displeasing hangers-on attendant on the producer, one of whom – Helen R. – stole make-up from our bathroom) and driven some 2000 miles through Spain. Stee has gone back to school in Grives today, tense with ritual apprehensions. Last night, faced with the blank pages of his *cahier*, he called out anxiously to know where we had stayed and what we had done on this day or that. I find myself, before my work table, in similar case.

For almost a month I have lived without Pharisaic recourse to a sealed study, without reflection, *en bon touriste et père de famille*. What does a tourist do? He drives too far, tries to see too much and spends more money than he intended. We expected a severe examination of our luggage as we crossed the frontier at Hendaye. Might we not be carrying munitions to our Basque friends? We were waved through with indifference. Not to arouse the slightest suspicion seems rather humiliating.

Has Spain changed? Spain has. The roads are largely excellent, the facilities are much more *facil*: the drainage works, there are *Cambios* everywhere, the shops bulge with goods, the butter is no longer rancid; we scarcely saw a *Guardia Civil* from Irun to San Sebastian. There is less of that bruised, defeated pride so obvious a generation ago. Spain is rich, in prospects, hopes, resources. Each town and city was horny with tower-cranes and skeletal buildings. Spaniards have learned Europe's game and wear the latest gear to play it. Even Loja, low-slung little *pueblo* between Granada and the coast, bulged with development; its ancient uniform roofs, of sun-baked tile, floored the valley, but they seemed to be confined in a dated ghetto by the new apartments and factories adjacent to them. The old Loja is an antique alongside the highway to *calamar* and chips.

How can one visit the Prado without a sagging sense of reporting for duty? With more Japanese than pictures, the circuit is a jostle;

aesthetics matter less than agility. All private appreciation is swamped in sanctimonious babble. Guides set the tone with their word-perfect recitations. Of the black paintings: '*Goya, dit-on, souffrait d'une depression mentale au moment ou il peignait ces tableaux.*' 'He was not,' says another, '*asked* to paint these pictures – they were not commissioned.' Got it, got it: we are in the presence of those who would never work except when they had to. Furthermore, since they – *we*, the people – are not suffering from mental depression, we have no reason to be ashamed of not having produced all this dark art, fruit of the anguish of an old nutter. How did he dare to inflict such uncalled-for images on a world with quite enough to worry about?

No one will ever overcome these swarming canvases – unpack them, with ideological explications or dig out their psychological motivation. The black paintings rebuke, if only incidentally, those who think that genius should be, can be, the issue of tradition and discipline (or cannot). It is easy to find the line that links Goya to Velasquez, but what hangs on that line? Art history, *nada mas*. No greatness threatens any other greatness. Art is not a competition, except in the most etymological sense: a common quest by men who need have nothing in common.

The *Guide Michelin*: '*Goya n'était pas précoce.*' Hope for us all.

13.1.76. Sharansky has been allowed out, a stumbling, almost comatose figure to prove that not all patients consent to their treatment and that not all doctors wait until they do. Remembering Sartre's *Nekrassov*, what smart tricks could Poulou play now? How would he transform one of the barely walking wounded in the battle of ideologies into a figure of fun or into the corrupt fabrication of the *bourgeois* press? The odiousness of Sartre's depraved sentimentality with regard to Progress achieves critical mass: how does such a man live with the truth of what he once declared – and still seems to believe – malicious fiction: the existence of an unbridled tyranny in the land where the future is supposed to work.

Science fiction would not have to be very witty to devise a plot in which some visitors to the Future – a land where all conversation is so forward-looking that it is conducted exclusively in the future tense – find their return path closed; they are obliged to live in their dream of Utopia. Sartre's position is inexorably this side of such a future state. No prayer, or act of will, can create for him the martyrdom he so craves here and would so quickly find there.

There remains a perversity so thorough in his cruel humanism that he cannot see that he wishes upon mankind a fate he calls the future; History is the Jehovah with whose appropriated thunder he threatens us. His paradise will be a torture chamber. He is the cultural commissar in Kafka's penal colony.

The announcement of Franco's death was followed, on French TV, by two cartoons. This incidental (unintended?) subversion of the obsequious recalls how Attic tragedies were followed by satyr plays, in which the heroic became ridiculous. Tragedy and comedy remind us that there are tears and tears.

We did not plan to see H. and C. in Spain. We had not heard from them since the spring; it seemed likely that they had gone to the US, or perhaps to London. The drive over the mountains to Malaga always used to be so arduous that I almost hoped that it would be unnecessary. I sent a telegram late one afternoon from the gloomy, well-staffed *Telégrafos* in Granada, asking H. to call the Guadalupe by 10 the next morning. With regretful relief, we had heard nothing at 10.15. We were all set to go when, at 10.20, he called. He said that all the previous day he had been 'unable to get you people out of my mind'. We were immediately excited and promised we were on our way. Odd, but true.

The *carretera* had been transformed. Where we once twisted on a narrow trail of polished tarmac, there was now an elegant highway – *el nuevo accesso* – which eased us into Malaga a mere hour and a half after quitting Granada. Once, when we were in the Standard Ensign, we drove the old road in thick, impatient traffic. A Spanish family, in a Seat, overtook a truck on a hairpin bend and the driver misjudged the angle as he cut back into the stream. Suddenly his car was airborne. It flew across the front of the truck and over the precipice on the right of the road. It was *gone*. I didn't want to stop, but I did. So did the lorry, whose driver came walking back with a length of chain in his hand. I hated to think what we were going to find at the bottom of the ravine. We looked over the edge (it was almost sheer) and there, halfway down, wedged with its boot in the angle between the cliff and one of the rare saplings on the slope, was the Seat. The driver had wrenched the wheel so violently that the car had actually spun round and had fallen *backwards* down the ravine. The lorry-driver and I scrambled down and found all the passengers tilted backwards, the women with their skirts in their faces. As they recovered from their shock, they began to abuse the driver who had been decent enough to come to their rescue.

We lunched dawdlingly in Malaga and drove along the coast highway towards Fuengirola. A terrible ugliness has been born where, not so long ago, there was the picturesque squalor of poverty and Franco's callousness. Fifteen years ago, the airport sported the tattered relics of the bombers which had won him the civil war. Gerald Brenan – Don Geraldo to the locals – had his *finca* where one of the runways now gouged the landscape.

Fuengirola still had its Casino bar, inset like a miniscule absentee team-mate botched into a group photograph in which everyone else looks more than lifesize. The *Calle Tostón*, where we lived fifteen years ago, still exists, but even Salvadora, our old cook (whom we saw the next day) can hardly find it behind the mammoth super-market where the Cayetanos have made their fortune.

Mijas is harder to obscure. The battlements of the village, rigid and denture-white, rest their long chin on the knees of the hills. The crests of the mountains behind the *pueblo* frown down over the purple and grey escarpment and glower at the hazy coastline. It was a fine afternoon which the villa-owners might have rented to gild their newly built lilies. A sign still pointed to Lew Hoad's *campo de tennis*. However, all the hotels now have their own tennis courts, and pros, and Lew is not having an easy time. I played with him (or was it *near* him?) years ago in a doubles game. His place was Andalusian with pretty ornamental pools. It must have been designed by an architect – was it Aubrey? – with scant knowledge of tennis. They had a lot of wet balls at the end of the day.

We went along the Benalmadena road to San Anton. Elegance became pot-holed. We saw the Gordons' house, lost it behind other buildings, went down a track to the right, reversed our decision, tried another track. We were fifty yards down it when a big puddle – how deep was it? Who knew? – blotted the rumpled track. I turned into a side track and then tried to back out. Sarah warned me of the ditch. When did I ever go into a ditch? The earth behind the rock surface was soft from the rain. I went into the ditch. If the ground had been dry, I wouldn't have; it wasn't; I did. The front axle was lagged with heavy mud; how to get out? A young Spaniard stood and stared, blank-faced, at my rage. There was nothing to be done except to do something. We began to fill the ditch with stones. The young Spaniard, at whom I had glared, helped willingly. So did his mother, who came out of a house behind the car.

H. had warned that the approach was difficult and I wasn't keen for him to observe my clumsiness. Paul understood my reluctance to be any more of a laughing stock, but Sarah set off down the lane towards the house (we had been on the right track after all). Paul and I and the rest of the now large cast continued to fill the ditch with timber and stones. Finally, thanks to Paul's herculean thrust, which helped me to get the car backwards onto the level again, I managed to edge clear, just as H. and his sons arrived.

H. has the the assimilated swagger of those who are at home in foreign places. We left the car and walked up to the house. The sunset had not waited for us before doing its gaudy number over beyond the Pillars of Hercules. It was dark as I stepped through the kitchen door and saw the dried herbs hanging against the limed wall. C.'s kitchens are always fragrant with gathered surprises. The G.s deck a house with charm, never quite as one expects, asymmetrically; the practical and the decorative feather their nests with functional levity. Who would not envy them their workshop/house decorated with such easy, seemingly casual aplomb?

14.1.76. Jesse and Ben were big and well and as normal as glad recipients of new Action Men could be expected to be. Soon Beetle was reading a manuscript. She passed the finished sheets to Paul. Both seemed to consider them with legal gravity. What significant new work was this? I slumped on the divan before the handmade fireplace. Had H., painter, designer, handyman, now produced a literary masterpiece? It was a children's story, handsomely typed, about J. and B. and their relationship with the *genius loci* of San Anton, decribed as an 'elemental'. It was touching, and it was laborious. It was not a masterpiece. Can I deny a certain sense of relief? It's hard to convince oneself that writing is not rather an easy trick. You can't help believing that most people could turn their hand to it; and nor can they.

H. and C. depend, in part, on the income from the Hamilton Terrace house, where the Jamaican High Commissioner is living behind drawn drapes, shutting out the light which H. arranged to admit. H.E. is due to quit in June. There are squatters in the next house. If 34 is known to be empty, there is every chance that there will be an invasion. Once squatters are in a place, they seem to have nine points of the law. The police will not act; a court order takes time to procure and enforce. We began to think about Seymour Walk; we'd be well advised to get rid of it while there is still someone living there. Can squatters *really* take over a property, change the locks and exclude the true owners? H. tells of a couple who worked for months renovating a derelict house they had bought. They finished the decoration and went away for a week's vacation before moving in. On their return, they found the place occupied. It still is.

Along with *bourgeois* apprehension – if property isn't sacred, what is? – there is the spark of a plot with which I toyed as far back as *Mr Frazer's Ducats*. H. says that the only effective way of evicting squatters is intimidation. They have acquired your place by force; it is by force that they must be expelled. One method is siege. You wait till one of them comes out and you pick him off. You follow him and threaten him and if he heads back to the house, you beat him up. Can I really see myself and Paul trying to thump some yobbo on the street? Knowing my luck, I should end up either with a broken nose or being arrested. Another solution is to employ some friends of your friends, on a commissioned basis, to take care of the intruders without you knowing anything about it. But once one has hired muscle, isn't one likely to have some nasty bruises to show for it? Who can intimidate others can also come round and intimidate you. How does one escape from that particular wheel without being run over? The 'porters' who patrol the flats where my parents live have metamorphosed into Security Men, whose own record is not always one of friendly persuasion. *Mr Frazer's Ducats* was conceived when the world seemed on the verge of nuclear war, but at least you did not have to lock your front door when you went out to be incinerated.

Every long vacation when I was at Cambridge, B. and I went to the Mediterranean. We were poor, but she was working and we could rent a room or a cottage for very little. Each summer I began a novel. I never finished one because our lease on paradise was limited. By the next year, I was embarrassed by my earlier manuscripts. For the summer of 1952 B. had managed to rent a cottage overlooking Menton. It had a narrow terrace where, every morning, I sat with my portable typewriter and worked on *Mr Frazer's Ducats*. In the afternoons, we moved the table and played 'cricket' with a tennis ball and a wooden batten. If you hit the ball too hard, it went down the hillside. We played defensively and scored runs by hitting the kitchen door. We were very happy, even when we had drunk water pumped from the well and suffered dysentery which required frequent hobbles down the narrow path to the outside loo. The terrace was shaded by a vine whose grapes were known locally as *framboises*; as they ripened in early September, they became succculent with a rich, red juice. They popped in your mouth and filled it with the flavour of raspberries. We called them 'sex grapes'.

Mr Frazer's Ducats was inspired by Rex Warner, a classical scholar and teacher whose novel, *The Aerodrome*, had been left in the cottage. A rare instance of an Anglo-Saxon writer influenced by Kafka, it has a facetious ferocity which is very English. At one point, the leading character's father is killed at some kind of a charity fair run by the Air Force (a sinister, neo-fascist outfit) and the news is brought by an officer who says, 'I'm afraid something rather rotten has happened. Someone's potted your old man.' This solemn frivolity seemed to indicate a way of writing about anti-Semitism in a way which would avoid self-pity, indeed self-reference of any kind. My leading character was called Sandheim, a Jew of no great charm who wished to protect himself against some business associates who were not, I fear, any less unscrupulous than he. It was part of my programme, so to say, not to claim 'equality' for Jews because they were sympathetic but rather because – bravo Orwell! – it was absurd for some people to be more equal than others. Hence I made Sandheim something of a caricature of the kind of Jew which anti-Semites disliked. The fun of the story lay in Sandheim's hiring muscle which, after no very long period of deference, became the very persecutors against whom they had been rented to protect him. His daughter was forced to serve their sexual needs (and to be naked at all times) and his house became a base for all the nefarious activities which my naïve imagination could conjure. One of the thugs was called Fonseca, who said only 'Yep'. He was based, with no justice whatever, on a pleasant South American with whom I played hockey in the St John's College Second XI.

I never finished *Mr Frazer's Ducats*, but I did get so far as to sketch out a final scene in which Sandheim, now totally compliant with the criminals who have victimised him, and rather revelling in their company, is playing bridge with three of his parasitic cronies, in his fortified flat, all of them wearing Hitler masks 'for security reasons'.

We are going to see heavier locks on England's doors and windows. *Neikos* becomes dominant; the 'community' falls into factions and fractions. Freedom and liberty cease to be synonyms (were they always, or *ever*?) The rise in taxes, the threats of VAT-men, the *rafles* of the Revenue, the demands of this authority and that, these things will lead to increased furtiveness, and – in the innocent at least – a sense of guilt like that of Joseph K.: our original sin will be the possession of anything at all. Expect contempt for property, and beauty, for any kind of value outside usefulness. The hopes of architects, such as Herb Oppenheimer, that beauty would procure civility – that the tenant would come to be worthy of his high rise – have proved empty. Property without ownership leads to grievance and contempt. What am I saying? What *am* I saying? That possessions create values? That a property-owning democracy is the only one in which virtues can prosper? The effect of vandals is to make one wish either to crush them or to join them.

Who is now going to do anything about anything? We cannot trust the ruling class; we can scarcely locate it. Bureaucracy acts in its own interests, not out of greed necessarily or corruption or malice, but because it is the only thing it *can* do; it becomes a thing-in-itself, able only to check its own machinery and discipline those paid to service it. It cannot be answerable to anything outside itself because it has already absorbed all the available power. It is a machine without product; it whirrs but it does not *work*.

His character is so thin one could not spread half a piece of toast with it.

Why do people find the success of fascism so difficult to understand? No tyranny which promises to divide the goods of the opposition among its zealots has a recruiting problem. The attraction of all class regimes (not least those proclaiming an end to classes) lies in the prospect of evicting the heretic, the unbeliever, and appropriating his stuff. When such a regime collapses, so does the strut of its officers and the credulity of its rank and file. Suddenly *no one* believes a word of what was previously received with respect by professors and *pères de familles*. There *are* no fascists; there *were* fascists.

Reverence without social context is sentiment. Piety, in the Roman sense, was not mere respect for ancestors; it was the conscious use of their usage. Rectitude in Roman society had *nothing* to do with states of mind. Ritual unites society by precluding self-consciousness.

15.1.76. Notes for an Icarus. Begin with the bronze muscles of the

Icarus Michael brought and installed here. Winged image, changed and refurbished as the maquette hatches from prototype to final form. Meditation of Daedalus on the means of escape from temporal domination. Flight as assault; the fighter plane (Dassault!) as returning D., the artist armed. Icarus, less vain than naïve, is an athlete with his trainer, unaware that gravity is a final call on man (he is much given to laughter, I.) and that aspirations to immortality must pay taxes to the flesh. Did I.'s laughter get on his father's nerves, inciting the master to tease the adolescent into overreaching himself? 'Careful!' implies 'Obey me', and inspires carelessness. Encouraged to caution, the boy mocks his father by flying into the eye of the sun; cynic and dog-fighter.

Minos' response to the news of the flight: 'Don't tell me.' Anger that he did not have an invitation to flee his own tyranny. Envy of other men's freedom is strong in tyrants; they dream of escaping their own dominion. They crave the freedom even of those whom they torture. The victims, as long as they live (and mythically after that), have the infuriating liberty of being other than the tyrant; he can be only what he is. D. an abstract figure feathered with specificity, yet mutable: Jeremiah smelling of onions. Minos to be an American (guy who built the big house, right? Big House is prison too. So?) Daedalus and Philoctetes (cousins?). We live as we fall; the Fall is now.

Many years later I wrote a piece for radio, in the days when it was still feasible to do long, serious work for the BBC. It was called *The Daedalus Dimension* and was a belated elegy for Michael Ayrton. Later, I reworked it for a volume of recensions of Greek myths published by the Folio Society, *Of Gods and Men*. If there were an adult Disney studio, what a subject the Cretan cycle would make for reanimation!

FINAL DEMANDS. The attacks of the Revenue on a man with a clear yet uneasy conscience; the official blackmailers, one of them appeased, another not; the grinning greed of the righteous publican. How to respond? Arrogance? They will skin you. Candour? They will gnaw your bones white. Flight? Even in decline, England makes other calls on one than that for gold.

F. came to supper, a young figure without youth, charming and appealing (in shirtsleeves under the false smile of a January evening, so that one said, protectively, 'Come in, come in'). He told us that he had been in Ipswich, considering the purchase of a Datsun. He approached another driver, who had just parked one, and asked for his opinion. The man replied in the voice of a friend of F.'s, and proved to be his brother. He told F. what the friend had not: that one of his nephews, a brilliant student, had just been diagnosed with multiple sclerosis.

F. had seen Jacqueline du Pré in a TV interview and was, he said, embarrassed by her (as he claims) 'bitter' unwillingness to concern herself with others suffering from the same disease. According to F., she was not solid with those who bore the same badge, preferring to be the solitary martyr rather than another case.

If this is true (*if*), why should genius be downgraded, on such unconditional terms, into mere membership of an afflicted class? The desire to herd together – ghettoise – those defined by age or 'handicap' or by affliction is pseudo-speciation, more convenient to the untainted than comforting to the minority. (Somewhere we can hear the judge who says 'Take them down.') J. du Pré has been robbed of her finest gift and responds – *how dare she?* – ungratefully; she rages against the coming night and refuses a forced wedding with her statistical peers; arrogance that might have been art must now be pain. And those who might, and should, have been in awe can make themselves her critics. Somewhere, horrible, horrible as these diseases are, and genuine as their pity may be, people tend to feel a kind of shameful gratitude that the mighty have been brought down.

We write down possible titles like storing teabags in a jar. One day we shall need only to add boiling water, *et voilà!*

Life, death and money; *Final Demands* takes shape as if by chance. One of the horrors of the incurable is that it proves that there are things money cannot buy; the charm of the mundane is that it proves that there are nice things that it *can*. Money is a way of being in society; it is the *permis de séjour* of the outsider. Modern taxation tends to strike more punitively at those who earn than at those with possessions, thus furnishing a legally proper form of social exclusion: we shall never have the acres which sovereigns allotted to whom they pleased, and who pleased them.

To dock the *arriviste* of easy means of *entrée* inhibits a surfeit of arrivals. Those who *gamble* in order to amass the entrance fee are more liberally admitted, perhaps because people always hope that luck will be infectious, perhaps because they believe, like ancient Hellenes, that the gods signal their favour by giving fair winds to the fortunate (odd that *fourtouna* is modern – meiotic? – Greek for a storm).

With today's explosion of public employment, the state recruits a higher percentage of interested voters than it did when it was only administrative and magisterial. The government becomes a constituency, composed of those who either cannot be, or are determined not to be, evicted from their places. In this Britain is less democratic than the US, where – since they are elected – officials, no less than judges, have insecure tenure. This leads to more corruption but less impunity. The conservatism of England is expressed most clearly in the Old Tyme dancing of the Labour Party, paying off old scores by incurring new debts.

The humiliation of those who maltreated the working class when Britain was rich is more important to Michael Foot and co. than the cohesion, or feasibility, of contemporary society, which is impoverished and confused by the oppositionism of its actual government. The policies of Wilson's cabinet are sentimental, not only in being bent on avoiding unpleasantness at home (strikes) but also in disregard of the world at large. Petulance in the face of mundane facts (American power, the influence of Europe, the wickedness of the Soviet regime) issues in the assertion of Britain's abiding *moral* leadership, as if any state ever led the world by its moral qualities or as if the abandonment of Cyprus to the Turks, contrary to undertakings given when Callaghan was Foreign Secretary, was an example of abiding rectitude.

The reactionary's charge recurs: socialism is finally, and maybe before that, the elimination of opposition. Contrary evidence becomes merely statistical; the truth is something to be embargoed, *pro bono publico* (the public interest being that of the government), by a journalistic union from which the maverick is either excluded or faces expulsion. The machinery of repression will be licensed and built by a faction without principle (except to *have* principles to parade, as the Soviets did their constitution to the credulous Webbs). We shall witness the eviction of Fabian intellectuals (too slow, too slow, yet unwilling to stop) from the leadership. The new tyrant will do anything to retain the Doge's cap. Perhaps some (Trades Union?) Napoleon will come along and make Harold chuck his hat into the sea. The Bucentaur of the Labour Party will be broken up to make camp fires for wreckers who prefer to burn the ship of state rather than see a capable captain on the bridge.

In the *albergue* at Aranda del Duero. A displeasing face watched us as we drove up. When Paul went, halfway through the meal, to pee, he met someone who asked whether he had come in the Mercedes. P. answered in English and the man continued in the same language. 'I think your silencer has blown,' he said. When P. reported this, I was furious; but I feared immediately that the man was right, though I had no impression, during the morning's drive from El Escorial, that anything was wrong. Perhaps he had observed another Mercedes, but I doubted it. Shit.

After lunch I went into the bar to order coffee. A man was standing there, in strict slacks, a light blue turtle-necked sweater, addressing the bargirl with peremptory bonhomie. 'Are you the owner of the Mercedes I saw earlier?' He told me later that he was sixty-five; though he looked younger he hardly seemed like the pissing companion of whom Paul had spoken. 'I think your silencer has blown.'

'Oh?' I said, at once disdainful and ingratiating (would he care to join me in a coffee?), 'I don't think so.'

'I've had fourteen Mercedes,' he said, 'and the silencer goes on every single one of them. I think it's gone on yours. It's not an expensive job.' He asked the girl for a cigar. 'My father,' he went on, 'was (I thought he said) the *ugliest* man in the world.'

'I beg your pardon?' I said.

'My late father – we lost him in 1948 – was the *luckiest* man in the world. Why? He owned three Hispano-Suizas. Three.'

'Have you still got them?'

'Still got them? I wish. I'd be a bloody millionaire.' He stood up straight and smiled; I smiled back, unsure which of us was the candidate and which the examiner.

'Are you driving a Mercedes at the moment?' I said.

'My present Mercedes...' He paused to select a cigar from the obsequious box offered him by a grey-liveried waiter. '... happens to be in England. I can't bring it out; they won't let me. And they won't let me bring it in.'

'Why?'

'Impossible,' he said. He had, it seemed, left England in some haste. 'The Revenue, they wanted 89 per cent of my business.'

'What business is that?'

'Shipping. We're in shipping. I've lived most of my life in England. Spanish father; English mother. I said, 'Right ho, you want 89 per cent of my business, I'm on my way. I'm a Spanish citizen, I'll go to Spain'; and so I did. I've got business interests here; I'm perfectly happy. I'm Spanish after all. I came back here to fight in the little rumpus we had. I came back and fought in that.'

'You mean?'

'The little rumpus we had. 1936. I was twenty-two years old. I came back to fight in that.'

'And what's going to happen in Spain now?' I said.

'Happen?' He looked at me with dangerous eyes, his whole face contracted with the task of drawing smoke through the brown tube which plugged the puckered mouth.

'Are there going to be changes? *Las cosas van a cambiarse, no es verdad?*'

'Changes? What changes?' He looked as he must have at those who try to sell him something, their sisters for example. The plump, powdered cheeks, so cleanly shaven and something rubicund behind the pampered skin reminded me of the Baron de Charlus; I realised (not too quick of me) that he was homosexual. 'We'll have *changes*,' he said, 'when we're ready to have changes.'

'Parliamentary elections,' I said. 'Democratic elections, what about those?'

'When we're ready, in two years' time perhaps. But I'll tell you one thing, my friend; one thing I'll tell you, *por nada*, we'll have them when *we're* ready, not when Giscard d'Estaing or Harold Wilson tells us we should. Harold Wilson has a civil war on his hands, in Northern Ireland, and he's not coming poking his nose in here and telling us what to do because you know what they can do with their advice?' His speech skidded into a mirthless laugh. 'They can go and wipe their arses with it.' This was in English so as not to offend the modesty of the bargirl. 'Ha ha ha. Two things I hate; and that's politics and journalists. I'll tell you one thing, this little man we just lost, he wasn't simply a good thing for Spain, he was a bloody *miracle*, old boy. A bloody *miracle*.'

'Who was that?' F.R., the straight man, said.

'The little man we just lost. A bloody miracle. It's thanks to him that Spain – have you seen what's been happening here in the last five, six years? – it's all thanks to him that Spain is one of the most prosperous places in Europe. So don't talk about politics to me. I have my opinions and my English friends have theirs. We're jolly good pals, jolly good; we have a drink and we have a chat and they tell me what they think and I jolly well tell them, OK, you think one thing and I think another and that's how we'll leave it, we'll agree to differ. And that's how we stay pals. Because nobody – and certainly not Master Wilson – is going to tell Spain how to run its affairs. I'll tell you what it all comes down to: law and order. The whole thing's about law and order. That's why Spain is as strong as she is today, because we've got law and order, and that's all thanks to the little man who's just left us. We don't need anybody's help; we don't need anybody's advice, thank you very much.'

He had just come back from three days of 'tremendous fun' with some friends on Formentor. He was the most contentedly livid fanatic you could hope to meet. He was right about the silencer. I changed it as soon as we got back to England.

Henry de Montherlant remarks in his *Carnets* on the ignoble element in van Gogh's earnest boast 'No day without a line.' I found recently, in an old notebook (written long before I read the *Carnets*) a remark to the same effect. How odd to have an affinity with a writer so uncongenial as H. de M. A rare case of imaginative sympathy? Or an obvious thought?

With H. de M. you are aware all the time of the undeclared aspect of his character. What is not said trims his prose. There is something unearthly in that sang-froid: the transformation of heat into chill. He was not, and meant not to be, a *type sympa*. A writer who forever advertises his respect for silence gives his produce the rich allure of a fruiterer who stocks only what is out of season, a jeweller of the vegetable world. M.'s scorn for the quotidian becomes his daily habit. The sequestration of pleasure, its fleshiness, from the heart of the written matter makes for an unchaste celibacy; he was a doctor of death, the lover of the exact, the exacted, the moistless; his vanity was in a style which informed him in both base and noble ways; his prose aped the walk of the matador, which rehearses pride. When the *torero* runs, scampers to the *barrera*, one does not hoot necessarily (*I* don't), but one sighs; one senses his shame and feels it for him. ('Ach,' Dick Lederer used to say of a bad bid at bridge, 'it's like a discord.')

When H. de M. struts after doing too little or bows after doing less, one is ashamed. What can it be like to exist only to dominate or to be disappointed? No, he is not, does not care to be, *sympa*; he is good or he is bad. He is bad, and one sighs; he is good, and one is chilled and applauds as people do a winter parade, to beat out the cold, but without removing their gloves.

The bandannaed slimness of the matador held in the belly of M.'s prose; pride was his cincture. Pleasure for him was the discharge of a debt: cocked flesh found its target and was satisfied. To give pleasure is not always generous; *always* to give it is the annulment of humanity. A cold man always comes on time; hot blood makes mistakes. M.'s hero is inhuman; faultlessness his flaw. A world of Montherlants would make sentiment a heroic heresy. His appetite for suicide was a feature of his dandyism; he defied the world to find it unstylish, the last trick of the stoic magician who says, 'If you know how to do it, you do it.' He admired Seneca and made of society, gross and materialist, a hydra-headed Nero meriting only a last dry gesture of disdain.

Ronnie Geary told us of a renovation which involved the provision of a 'dressing room'. It turned out to be a separate bedroom, which was eventually sited on the ground floor of the house. It was, in fact, for a husband who drank too much to be acceptable in his wife's bed and often too much to make it up the stairs. The architect, like the doctor Ronnie might have been, sees life in the raw; he flirts with a will, though he often meets a won't.

H. and C. have lived up on their plateau outside Mijas for two and a half years now. I asked her if she was as happy as she looked. 'I've been stuck up here so long,' she said, 'I want to see some people; I want to see a movie.' When was Paradise enough? She makes necklaces, threading copper-coloured beads and *penne* of home-baked clay onto nylon. People are, she says, 'very excited' and someone has promised to sell them in a boutique (Beetle bought one). C. has courage and slim, ingenious fingers. She has constructed an arch, a high hoop of pottery forms, on the edge of the plateau overlooking the despoiled majesty of the coast. The arch reminded me of the metal hoop through which one is now obliged to pass, for security reasons, at airports. Stepping under it, passing from nowhere to nowhere, you half expect the gotcha ping of the metal detector.

When H. first built the house on San Anton, mostly with his own hands, he brought water and electricity from the village. He had to tunnel the pipes past several Spanish homes, whose owners he told that when they wanted to 'plug in', they'd be welcome. One by one they have taken up their options. Power and water have been connected to washing machines and TVs which the tourists first imported. They dazzled the natives like the beads of technological missionaries. H. and C. have neither washing up machine nor TV. They have made bad bets and are the victims of bad debts. H. told me that the logo which he designed for Cinecenta (he was in the team that made the first one, in Panton St) earned him only a thousand quid, while the little tune which accompanies its regular

appearance on the screen earns a royalty for its composer every time
it is played. H.'s brains are often picked, his services irregularly
rewarded.

Poverty is harder to bear on the *Costa del Sol* today than it was
when we were poor there; our poverty – we lived on ten pounds
a week – allowed us to live like petty princes. Salvadora laughs when
she thinks of what we used to pay her: 300 pesetas a month.
Salvadora looks younger than she did then. I gave her some apologetic money, now that she doesn't need it.

Muchachas are paid by the hour these days. C. cannot afford help.
She had a severe ear infection and barely escaped being permanently
paralysed. It began with an earache, wrongly treated by the same
doctor whose insanitary hands I fled, back in 1960, when I had a
lump in my throat. We drove into Gibraltar and I saw an old Guy's
man instead.

The local doctor alleviated C.'s pain briefly, but it returned in
agonising form; soon the whole of one side of her face had 'fallen'.
She could not close her eye. A specialist in Malaga said, as special-
ists say all over the world, 'You've only just got here in time – I
hope.' They had, but it cost them 1,500 pesetas a visit, plus the antibiotics. '*Dinero, dinero,*' Salvadora used to say.

I have never been a smoker, though I did occasionally smoke at
Cambridge, in order to seem as grown up as those who had
acquired the habit doing National Service ('Smoke if you want
to,' was almost an order). My first experiment in smoking was in
the loo adjacent to the tennis courts at Manor Fields, the block
of flats where my parents moved in 1940, after being bombed out
elsewhere. I played tennis, and afterwards played at smoking, with
Dorothy Tutin, who had an excellent forehand. I also smoked
chocolate biscuits at one stage, at Charterhouse. We discovered
that you could bite the ends off chocolate fingers, light them and
draw the smoke through the biscuit. It was not addictive.

When we went to live in southern Spain, in 1959, we had very
little money, but it cost very little to buy Havanas. It was an affec-
tation hard to resist. Some months later, I developed the persistent
lump in my throat which took me, in trepidation, to Gibraltar. I
was directed to a specialist opposite G.H. He was a Scotsman who
inspected my throat with antique solemnity and then said, 'You
think you've got cancer, don't you?'

I said, 'It ah did... occur to me.'

'Well, you haven't. I know what's wrong with you and I can cure it.'

'I'm very glad to hear it.'

'You should be. The only question is, when shall we do the operation?'

'How long will it take?'

'How long are you here?'

'We just drove in for the day,' I said.

'Can you spare twenty minutes?'

'Twenty minutes? Of course.'

'Then we can do it right away.'

'Um, should I... tell my wife?'

'Tell her when it's done. There's only one problem.'

'Yes?'

'In order to do this operation, I need three hands. As you may have observed, I only have the two. One of them will have to be yours, are you prepared to do that?'

'Do... *what*?'

'Have you ever had your tonsils out?'

As he was speaking, he had opened a creaking cupboard whose shelves contained his stock in trade. He removed a large brown box in which, as he put it on the table, I saw a big blue battery, of the kind which used to fuel not-very-portable radios.

'Yes,' I said, 'when I was a little boy. In America.'

Attached to the battery was a device which had the form of a large, curved pair of tapering tweezers: metal praying mantis.

'That explains it,' he said. 'American medicine. What you have is a post-lingual tonsil, as the result of incompetent surgery. It's a lump of scar-tissue which has been left behind by, if I may say so, a botched operation.'

'What exactly do you, ah, want me to... do?'

'As I shall need both hands,' he said, 'to conduct the operation, what I want you to do is perfectly simple. It requires no medical training. Just a firm hand. I want you to hold your tongue.'

He was now attaching the leads to the giant tweezers to the battery and tightening the screws. Soon the ends of the device were glowing red hot.

'While you do what exactly?'

'I'm going to burn it out,' he said. 'Scar tissue contains no nerves, hence you won't feel a thing.'

'Um, but... aren't there, ah, surrounding areas which ah... do contain them? Nerves.'

'I shan't touch any part of your person except the target area,' he said. 'Do you doubt me? Would you prefer to have a swab of cocaine?'

'I don't doubt you,' I said, 'and, yes, I would.'

'Oh ye of little faith,' he said, and was soon swabbing my throat with impregnated gauze, the touch of which had a strangely caustic coldness. 'And now, and not before time, are you ready to hold your tongue?'

He gave me a folded gauze and instructed me to stick my tongue out as far as I could and hold it there, sandwiched in the gauze. He took the tweezers and guided their red-hot convergence past my teeth and tongue and down my throat. There was a mild sizzling sound and he retracted the instrument.

'You can let go now,' he said. 'The operation is over. You'll have no further trouble.'

Tentatively, I said, 'Thank you.' My voice still seemed to be there. 'How much do I ah owe you?'

'Normally,' he said, 'that would be three guineas, but in view of the fact that you helped with the operation, we'll say three pounds. What are you going to do now?'

'Go across the street,' I said, 'and find my wife in Lipton's. And then we'll probably have a cup of coffee.'

'Just what you shouldn't do,' he said. 'You ask me – quite unnecessarily, as you will have observed – to anaesthetise your throat and then you're going to go and pour hot liquids down it. You'll probably damage the lining of your stomach and create the ideal conditions for a carcinoma.'

'I'll have a fruit juice,' I said.

I gave him three pound notes and shook his hand. I have never smoked since.

In Fuengirola in 1961, *I* was broke. One day, sitting in the memorial garden by the old Somio café, H. boasted modestly of the job he had been offered in New York City: 'Six thousand a year. Six thousand *quid*.' In those days that was almost 18,000 bucks; real money. I could not afford to live in England and it seemed that I should soon be unable to pay the rent in Spain. H. not only had access to huge salaries; he was also a confident artist: he had accumulated a loft pendent with dozens of large canvases, each likely to fetch at least a thousand dollars. Dealers in New York had been very excited by the earliest examples of a style perfected during nearly two years working in Fuengirola. He seemed certain of success when he returned to the big city. Juliana had said in her fluently eccentric English, 'One day he will be hung in a muse-you-um.'

But some time a little later *Time* magazine came out with an issue on Art. The featured article made one firm declaration: 'Hard edge is dead.' I remember mocking this curt obituary: as if journalists could announce what painters were meant to do, or not do! Did artists vary their line as couturiers the length of their skirts? The answer is, they did, and do; I was too naïve to know that, in America in particular, fashion *was* art, art fashion. H. knew; so did the group of Bohemians who hung out at the Casino. H.'s paintings were *all* hard-edge. He never did find a dealer for the rows and rows of canvases hanging from his studio rafters like a Perigordine *charcutier*'s stock of hams.

We took H. and C. to what they said was 'the hippest restaurant in Mijas'. I said I was happy to go anywhere they proposed, as long I could use my Amex card. 'They've got all kinds of stickers on the window,' H. said. 'I'm sure they'll take it.' On the way into the snazzy little place, I asked if they took Amex, and they said yes. We ate, and drank, and then they didn't take the card; they took Amex traveller's cheques and that was it. I did not have enough cash on me, so H. wrote a cheque, for which he was cordially thanked by Feliz, who happened to be his neighbour. The meal gave me acute indigestion (moral: when there is only one portion left of something – pheasant in this case – at the beginning of an evening, it was cooked for lunch and will blow nobody any good). Feliz said goodbye perfunctorily to me, no doubt imagining, if he imagined anything, that I had stiffed H. with the bill. The next morning I went to the bank and changed enough money to repay H. *Dinero, dinero.*

17.1.76. We have been married twenty-one years. I have never seriously imagined that our marriage might, would or could come to an end. We have children whom we love and who, I believe, love us. We still desire and enjoy each other's company. I count my lucky stars as if they were small change.

The Glittering Prizes is about to be shown. My mother telephoned with her usual congratulations and an excited account (how gathered I don't know) of what the *Sunday Times* would say in its preview tomorrow. Jeffrey Bernard appears to have been generous.

The *Radio Times* has already kept its promise and we are featured on the cover. Mark Shivas has puffed us in *Sight and Sound* (shite and sound, as Schlesinger calls it, except when it speaks well of him). I seem to have dozed off and found myself a bit famous. I am pleased especially for my father, to whom – at least since he worked for Shell as press officer – cuttings are the proof of local distinction. When he congratulated me on my petty rise on the *bourse* of fame, I said, 'If I were you, I should sell my shares now.'

20.1.76. I went to Paris on the Capitole in the morning, wondering why one does such things, and I returned the following evening, still wondering, but not much (*vanitas vanitatum*). I went to the BBC's Paris studio to be interviewed, down the line, on *Start The Week*. I was there less as a dramatist than as an unpaid huckster for the BBC's own programme. When Richard Baker asked me, with candid cunning, what it felt like to be famous, I had no problem in dodging a trap which was not my size. I have no delusions of celebrity, though I did experience them, briefly, when I won the Oscar. I was more *recognised* when I fronted *Film Seventy* or whatever it was called. People looked at me with insinuating intimacy in the underground. As it is, Terry Wogan is infinitely more famous; so is the man who does the weather forecast.

I had driven to catch the train at Brive with a certain elation. I drove home with a feeling of eager excitement (at the prospect of seeing B.) that would not have disgraced a *ressortissant* from the Trojan War. I am reduced rather than liberated by solitude, which I imagine will prove so luscious. I have no gift for picking people up, whether women or in conversation.

I am not stimulated by my own company. I fail to amuse myself; I have heard it all before. I wander about and ask silly questions, as if – for common instance – searching for a particular book were evidence of useful purpose. In Paris it was Robert Aron's *Histoire de l'Epuration* (would I have searched so diligently if I hadn't thought him some relation of Raymond Aron?). I discovered it finally in a discount *librairie* near the Gare St Lazare: four volumes. I also discovered, quite as if I were not hoping to find it, a street – the Rue St Denis – lined with whores, lounging in daylight outside the hotels where they took their clients. One girl leaned against a wall and was remarkable for the length of her outstretched silky legs. Was I tempted? I was; but *only* tempted. Flaubert gave me a literary warrant for voyeurism, though G.F. had already contracted syphilis when he resigned himself to a spectator's role.

J.L. was staying with us. It would, I suppose, have been charmless of him not to propose himself for B.'s bed during my absence. She had foreseen such an offer and had granted Stee nocturnal rights in her bed, thus making up her mind before a decision was required. How hard, even for a novelist, to accept that his wife's fantasies at least might be as disreputable as his own!

J.L. is dungeoned in cheerful unhappiness and kept in by the firmest of marital locks. This requires him to deny that he is imprisoned at all. Why did he marry S.? To what did she give him access except to the cold buffet of her body? She seems a nervous, snobbish, Hayward's Heathy woman. The register of her charm would be a slim volume indeed. Her classiness – vested in a *slightly* shrill tone – is all borrowed. The usual prejudices roost in her like bats dangling in a deserted belfry. The blind, folded mice of anti-Semitism and other sociable sentiments hang upside-down from the rafters of her largely empty head.

M. Drabble's smug biography of Arnold Bennett, which I read on the train, remarks on A.B.'s elaborate travel arrangements: he supervised the laying of his own red carpet.

J.L. was an editor in New York and worked, for a while, as a script consultant in LA where he shared an apartment in Santa Monica with at least two chicks. Why did he not escape permanently from the tight little island and its predatory middle-class women? What made him come back to publishing in the UK and to life in Mogador with *her*? I suppose that *finalmente*, or rather sooner than that, he is an Englishman.

Ronnie Geary was in the Navy. It gave him the confidence which Neasden had not. He spent a longish period on the lower deck and recalls how the 'Killick' – a kind of dorm boss – used to receive 'sippers' from everybody's rum ration; 'gulpers' if he wanted to show disapproval of what his underlings had been doing. This warning was rapidly 'hoisted inboard', as they say in the wardroom if they want to know if you got the point. A 'long ship' was one where you waited a long time between drinks. National Service gave a whole generation a quick opportunity for social advancement. Even I look back smugly on my 'career' as an Under-Officer in the Charterhouse JTC.

In the decaying property in the Perigord which A. comes to renovate (to measure, first) is a death-bed, relic of an illness requiring phials and bedpans and the dated paraphernalia of intensive care. He also finds a cache of weapons and – under the floor – a bag of sovereigns (HMG loaded their agents with gold because it was the only currency which French patriots would accept). He wonders whether C. knows of the guns (still serviceable) and the money (still tempting). Alone, A. has the feeling that he is being watched. He is liberated and shackled by the freedoms which seem to dangle before him and with which he does not quite dare to make free.

22.1.76. I came back from driving Stee to the little school in Grives and found B. on the telephone. Eight a.m. London time; my mother was reading the reviews of *An Early Life*. They are unanimous raves. Success? No one will be very impressed on the Coast. I am still sick at the newsreels from Lebanon, but – God forgive me! – it makes me happy to be the toast, and possibly the marmalade, of London. Fame, however brief, makes a nice salt on the long porridge of rejection. *Carpe diem*; a day without carping.

23.1.76. But, as Joe Levine said of *Darling*, 'Baby's gotta walk'. One play is not a series. Call no man happy till the final fade. For *real* success, you have to feel rich enough to go out and adopt André Previn. The notices are not *all* as good as the best of them. The man from the Express says that *The Glittering Prizes* is 'a milestone in the history of television' (you can hear the copy-taker 'Is that milestone or millstone, old man?'). In the world of journalism, there is a milestone every ten yards. Yet I did manage to make a personal statement in a public medium and that is what matters. The deluge of praise from strangers is enough to wash off the memory of a 'friend' like Karl Miller who, in 1960 (of *course* one remembers), dismissed *The Limits of Love* in a TV programme which we could only *hear* in East Bergholt, so dim was the signal. Joan Bakewell (who called me on Sunday) told me of a recent meeting at which Karl said, 'I should never have had anything to do with literary criticism; I should've been a novelist.' Everyone wants the downhill runs, don't they?

Joan (Rowlands) and I played tennis together once or twice at Newnham. We sat side by side at a strange dance in David Gore-Lloyd's rooms in 1953. David Ridley had put coloured bulbs in the light sockets and cushions on the floor. It was a prototypical disco. I assumed that Joan was spoken for, and made a virtue of my own fidelity to B. Joan grows younger by the year; when she reaches twenty-one, she will be eligible for the old age pension.

You can understand why Harold Pinter never talks about his work: his plays do the talking, not that they say very much. He has reduced himself to a minimum; his work is a trick of personal disappearance. The Jew David Baron – here we go, folks! – seeks to create *another* name for himself: famous, respected, with no tangible history, a phenomenon announced in lights; nothing but a name. *Ou-tis*, but a Name!

Jonathan Miller said that *My Secret Life* was the autobiography of someone who thought of nothing but sex. I disagreed; it was indeed a book mostly (but not entirely) about sex, but the same man could have been a dedicated lexicographer, a theologian or – to judge from modern instances – a cabinet minister. The telephone book lists all subscribers, but does it prove that they are always on the telephone? Wittgenstein's notebooks suggest that he thought only of philosophy (even on Christmas Day 1916, in the trenches, he was doing his enigmatic stuff); who would guess from them that he was also a fan of Betty Hutton? ('Can you do a flick?' he would ask). Jonathan's cleverness lies less in what he knows than in what he knows *about*.

24.1.76. At nine in the morning, I was sitting in the Connaught, waiting for Peter Fiddick of the *Guardian* to come and interview me, when in swung the tall doctor himself, Miller J., in a khaki overcoat and scarf and looking remarkably khaki himself. His face elongated itself into a smile. 'What are you doing here?'

'What are you?'

'I've come to see Susan Sontag. Are you *staying* here?' He put the question with a stretched neck, arched eyebrows: an exclamation and a question mark made flesh.

Oh for the right to have replied, 'No, I'm buying the place.'

Susan Sontag came down. I met her seven or eight years ago at an André Deutsch party, just before *Two for the Road* came out in England. She told me that she wanted to make a film and I said, 'Why don't you then?', as if everyone did, and could. She was a dark and deliberately dangerous lady then. Quite soon, she became a leader of protests against the Vietnam war. She learned to be expert with banks of microphones; she turned into a veteran of the podium, a yes–I'm–darkly–attractive–but–aren't–there–more–important–things–to–think–about? kind of an *engagée* intellectual.

She *was* staying at the Connaught. She had aged into a Jewish Mary McCarthy, with less than even teeth and a grey-white flash in the famous-but-never-mind-about-that hair. I shook hands in a courtly way and remembered, like any crawler, to mention her book *Against Interpretation*. I said that I often thought about it, and sometimes I thought 'She's absolutely right' and at others 'She's completely mad'. Aside from 'often', it was true, though I do not know why I bothered to say it.

Was she – is she? – some kind of power in NY or has the market gone back on bright bright Jewish *intellectuelles*? She has just shown her film on Israel and the Arabs at some (Jewish?) gathering and bore the rueful scars of those who try to show both sides of a question to people who will accept only one answer. We talked, awkwardly amiable in the carpeted heat, while I wondered whether the *Guardian* would keep its tryst.

How little I know J.M.; though we do our best to be friends! When we were at Cambridge, I visited him at home in St John's Wood and we tried to confect a sketch for the Footlights. It depended on a joke about the temperature on the Air Ministry roof (then the Greenwich, as it were, of London weather). Our fantasy was that it had a climate unlike the rest of England and became so freakishly tropical that monkeys began to swing around its mini rainforest while bananas ripened. Invention could not match the *donnée* and we did not pursue our collaboration.

When Fiddick arrived, he and I went into the dining room. It no longer has the plush blush of unostentatious showiness which was sustained by the elegance and polish buffed onto it and by the smooth progress of the waiters. Our order arrived incomplete and the foreign waiters did not read English signals.

Fiddick is an Oxford man with the shining face of a bow-tied embryo which has not quite decided whether to be a boy or a girl. He was attentive and passive and had the sort of alert nullity that you might see in a slip-fielder to whom the ball rarely flies. I talked in an unguardedly wary way, mixing information with anecdote and wondering what the real purpose of our breakfast was. I knew what it was: I still hoped to be lauded in a paper which did not even review my new novel. So? The *Sunday Times*, to which I have contributed for more than ten years, was sour about *The Glittering Prizes* (who is Peter Lennon, and why?). Clive James dented my complacency, but did not puncture it. The flow of praise glistens with an attendant scum of malice, but so what? Less thrilled than relieved, that was the impression that I tried to give Fiddick; even though it was true, he may have believed me.

Douglas Orgill was an unexpectedly nervous *Express* staff man; also

Oxford-educated, in his fifties and manifestly a friend of distillers everywhere. He was astute and almost sentimental. He drove down in the snow to Langham and arrived at seven; he left at midnight. He had an air of practised loneliness, as if mixed financial fortunes had obliged him to accept a life for which he had no appetite. He was staying at the George in Colchester. Short and bowed, he wore a rumpled pinstripe suit. Hair and complexion were white where thirst had not rouged him; eyelashes as pinky-white as a Labrador's. The telephone rang frequently until, during dinner, Beetle took it off the hook.

We dined off Beaverbrook anecdotes, like schoolboys, or old boys of the same school who attended it at different times but are reconciled by laughing at the foibles of a common master: who could be more common than the Beaver? I worked, surreptitiously, on the *Sunday Express* between leaving Charterhouse and going up to Cambridge. My father knew the news editor, so I was smuggled into the newsroom without the NUJ asking any questions. I worked as a runner for the industrial correspondent, Alan Brockbank, one of the last working-class journalists. He had a small vocabulary and wrote his stories in longhand, with very few lines on a page. Brocky's merit lay in his energy and his willingness to dig for dirt, rather than have it handed to him by informants or delivered, sanitised, by PR men. We went to dingy pubs and met senior members of the Labour party and the TUC eager to gossip about their comrades. Indulgent and educative, Brocky cut my polysyllables, shortened my paragraphs and eliminated my semi-colons.

When I began to go out solo on stories he would tell me loudly to take a taxi and then whisper that I should go by bus and send in an expenses chit for the taxi. In that way, despite not being salaried, I made five or six pounds a week. On one occasion I was sent to the British Industries Fair at Olympia. My mission was to find ways of suggesting that it was a waste of time and money. The Beaver did not want to hear of the selling achievements of which the press people were eager to assure me. I hung around the bar and got hold of a rumour that the Germans, although officially not invited (it was 1950), had sent 'buyers' who were, in fact, selling German manufactures at undercutting prices. A story!

I wrote a damning piece, with (in principle) no sentence longer than three words and no paragraph longer than three lines and, after Brocky had subbed it, passed it to Stanley Head, the news editor. The previous autumn I had won the Major Scholarship which supposedly testified both to my intelligence and to my integrity.

How easily I hurried to obey the Beaverbrook party line and to deliver to my masters what his Lordship wanted to hear and see!

Scholarship? Integrity? I wanted to see my words in print. And I did. The early editions carried quite a long piece 'by *Sunday Express* reporters' (we advertised the wealth of the Beaverbrook press by seeming to be legion) in which I quoted anonymous sources (which I had indeed interviewed) who denounced German treachery. When the proofs came through, the assistant news editor – Bernard Drew, who was well cast and always wore sleeve garters to keep his cuffs out of the wet ink – and Bernard Harris, the chief features editor, and Brocky himself, took me out for a beer at the little pub opposite the old *Express* building. Their congratulations were much more sincere than those of my fellow Carthusians when I earned them a half-holiday with my Cambridge scholarship. There was an old drunken Scots feature writer, famous in his day, leaning against the bar while my elderly friends drank to my journalistic future. Another drinker accused the old Scot of being subservient to the Beaver. He turned on him with savage r's and said, 'Dirrrty old *News of the Wurrrold!*'

I grabbed a freshly minted copy of the next day's London edition home with me in the tube. When I turned to the page where I had been featured as '*Sunday Express* reporters', I found my piece had already been spiked.

Orgill was on 'the back bench' at the *Express* for some time as well as having been chief sub. Once, as night executive, he was manning the telephones when the red light indicating 'the old man' began to flash. There had been a budget that day and a tax had been put on ice cream. When answering the Beaver's phone you always had to put a tape-recorder on as well. Orgill lifted the phone and pressed the button. 'Yes, sir?' 'Who's that?' 'Night executive, sir.' 'Well, Mr Night Executive, I want a recipe for homemade ice cream on the front page tomorrow morning.'

The subs on the *Daily Express* were a famous clan of NCOs. The Beaver's faith in them was revealed not least by their lack of respect for famous contributors. On one occasion, Randolph Churchill, whose rudeness to secretaries was notorious, came in and reduced one of the girls to tears by the violence of his tirade. One of the subs turned from the long table and said, 'Know your trouble, Churchill? Your name begins with C,h, in *Who's Who* and S,h, in what's what.' One of the great anonymous put-downs of all time.

28.1.76. A friend of Orgill's was invited to Cherkley, the Beaver's country home, for lunch. The summons was welcome; to be asked was to be promised, before the end of the meal, a rise of at least five hundred to a thousand a year, especially if you had had the wit to make the Old Man laugh. Orgill's friend acquitted himself well; the Old Man split his sides. He beamed with bonhomous intentions. Lunch came to an end. The conversation fizzled on the last reminiscential chuckles. It was time for the visitor to leave. D.O.'s friend stood up, 'Well, sir, it's been…' Money was yet to be mentioned. The Old Man usually said that he had given orders to the cashier, etcetera. The Beaver said nothing. Then, as Phil's pal turned to go, Beaverbrook said, 'Mr X, do you have a car?' Phil's friend did have a car, but he was a quick thinker. 'No, sir,' he said. The Old Man grinned. 'Quite right,' he said, 'sensible fellow. Nasty dangerous machines. Good afternoon to you.'

Another of O.'s stories about the Old Man. Charles Wintour joined the *Daily Express* as a senior executive. In those days, under a certain high ceiling, you could, on joining, ask for any car you chose. 'What car do you want, Mr Wintour?' came the Old Man's expected question. 'A Zephyr, sir, please,' was the premeditatedly spontaneous answer. In due course, C.W. was informed, at the office, that his new car was in the yard. He went down and found an Armstrong-Siddeley Sapphire; a better car than the editor's. Sometimes it pays to speak indistinctly.

As chief sub., D.O. had on his desk a list of the Old Man's interests. Items concerning tomatoes, pigs, strawberries, Empire free trade, New Brunswick and roller skates (to name the most obvious) were to be favoured. The blacklist? I didn't question D.O. (fool!), but no doubt it existed, even if not in written form; the paper was to be filled with what pleased the Beaver, so what need was there to specify what did not?

D.O.'s happiest years were in the Army. He was in the 14th Lothian and Border Horse, which had an idiosyncratic walking-out uniform, complete with spurs; it sounded like a positive Sabre Squadron (Simon Raven's fictional outfit), of which D.O. took a dim view. He likes women; his wife is as dear to him as the prospect of an occasional dish on the side. He is often alone. Not long ago he was in a Scottish hotel and was aware that a couple was taking an interest in him. After a day or two, they left the dining room at the same time as he did and the woman said, 'We've been wondering about you and I've come to the conclusion that you're a man who's nursing a secret sorrow.' He laughed at the absurdity of so grand a role: 'Probably I didn't have an idea in my head.' But he *does* have a secret sorrow and his name is Boyd.

Boyd was his driver in a Sherman tank. They had been all the way up Italy together. Tank squadrons consist of five 'troops' of three tanks each. The troops take it in turns to lead. When a subaltern first joined his troop, his troop-sergeant led, but when he was played in, the second lieutenant took over. The lead tank was generally knocked out (so did the troop commander *always* lead?). Douglas had had Boyd as his driver ever since he joined the regiment, which was part of the Eighth Army. Boyd was a quiet, capable man who spoke Russian; a lance-corporal, he had been a student at London University. On 23 April 1945, the regiment was in action in northern Italy, attacking German columns retreating across the Po. Douglas's troop sergeant had been killed the previous week. I think he said that it was the troop sergeant's turn to lead the troop, and O.'s troop's turn to lead the attack, but O. decided that the new man couldn't be expected to take command; he decided to lead himself. They advanced in early mist across a bridge over a tributary of the Po. It was 'an ideal shoot'. The German columns were strung out along the adjacent road, trucks and half-tracks: 'a dream target'. Douglas was firing away when, out of the corner of his eye, on the stretch of road ahead of them, he saw 'a very brave man' get out of a ditch with a bazooka. ('He was drunk actually.') O. began to traverse his gun back, left, to fire on the man. 'There was an over-rider on the turret, but in the nature of things, it took time to swing the gun round.' Until he could do so, there was no defence. The bazooka man fired first. 'I could see the thing coming. About 900 feet per second, but I could see it coming.' The rocket went straight through the slit of Boyd's compartment. The explosion set fire to the stuff at the bottom of the turret. O. felt an urgent thrust on his heels. The gunner wanted to get out. He pushed O. through the turret hatch and they piled into the ditch. The tank blew up. 'Did Boyd get out all right?' O. asked as he and the gunner took cover. 'Yes, sir. He's in the ditch on the other side.' 'You're sure he got out?' 'I saw him, sir.'

O. stayed in the ditch. He was wounded: shrapnel in the face. As he was climbing out of the turret, he had seen freckles of blood falling on the yellow panels (aircraft identification, for the benefit of). There was enough blood for it to roll off the surface of the tank. He lay in the ditch, shocked and frightened, but even then, if present memory served, he knew that he ought to go and see if Boyd needed help. Boyd was, as it turned out, in no need of help; he had not got out. The bazooka shell must, *must*, have taken him full in the chest. O. had noticed – he *thinks* – that Boyd's face looked 'strange' on the morning of his death.

Meanwhile, the bridge had been blown up between the two first tanks. O. and his surviving men were taken prisoner. They joined the German retreat north. O. had surrendered to a German officer called Schreiber, who turned out to be a Trinity man, though Oxford had not made him immune to the *Führer-prinzip*. (O. was at Keble.)

The Lothians' tank crews had all been issued with asbestos suits which resembled flying gear. Since the RAF was constantly strafing the column ('killing people'), casual German soldiers adopted a menacing attitude to O. and his crew. '*Flieger?*' they would accuse them. '*Nein, nein, panzer-truppen,*' Schreiber would say. As the retreat continued, O. tried to persuade the red-haired Schreiber that the war was over and that the obvious thing was for him to surrender to O. so that he and his men would come under British protection. The hills were full of partisans. Schreiber was reluctant (thinking of his honour) and also convinced that some deal would be made allowing Germany to join the allies and fight against the Russians. At last, however, he realised that the game was up. He surrendered to O. and his men.

Soon the partisans came down and began to shoot the Germans in the column up ahead. They shot them all. When they came for Schreiber and his men, O. said, 'Oh no, you don't.' The partisans insisted they had to shoot all the Germans. One of O.'s men had lost a hand in the explosion in the tank ('We put a tourniquet on it and it didn't seem to bother him a bit'), but he drew his revolver with his remaining hand and said, 'They're ours; shoot them and I shoot you.' The partisans buggered off.

Schreiber sent O. Christmas cards for several years after the war, 'a big chap he was, with red hair'. D.O. had to write to Boyd's parents. 'Of course one always said the same things. Killed instantly, doing an absolutely vital job, that sort of thing. But I've always wondered, was it true? I should've gone to see; I should've checked. He might've needed help.'

The Rifle Brigade came along later and they told O. that Boyd was in the tank and that the bazooka shell had gone clean through him. But… 'Shall I tell you something? Not a week passes but I think about it. Every three or four days.'

The Rifle Brigade killed the chap with the bazooka. How did they know he was drunk? Did they smell his breath?

O. guessed that my method in writing fiction was to investigate *character*. Hardly your idea of Expressman on the spot, he was hesitant, grateful, apologetic to B. for keeping her out of her own drawing room. He had read *Lindmann* and *Who were you with last night?* and all my cuttings (ah the morgue!). He said that he wished he was Jewish, or wished it sometimes. A friend of his who 'liberated' Belsen said that he felt in the presence of evil itself, and yet at the same time he had a strong conviction, as if from the same source, that God, or good, existed. I had to say that the universe was not *necessarily* constructed on a binary principle. Would the inmates of the camps accept that their sufferings served to indicate the existence of Higher Things?

30.1.76. O. said that he didn't know much about art when he was in Italy ('Don't know much now'), but as the allies advanced, hidden treasures were brought out. He was very struck by the Caravaggios he saw. He had an introduction to the de Gasperi family, of whose importance he was not aware (the head of it would become Italy's first post-war Prime Minister). He told the daughter how impressed he had been by the paintings. 'Oh,' she said, 'do you like him? We've got a couple upstairs.' There was no electricity, so she showed them to him by torchlight.

After the press on *The Glittering Prizes*, I shall not, I am sure, be so well spoken of again by the *presse écrite* until my eightieth birthday celebrations ('Forgotten but not gone…'). I have escaped whipping, though I have been lightly scourged; the *arrivisme* of Clive James was ever served by abusing fellow-travellers. I also received a fat jeering anonymous letter. 'How dare you?' its prolonged message, though it claimed to have been written 'for your entertainment'. *Au pannier?* Montherlant's reaction to anything he disliked, especially charity appeals with *fautes d'orthographe*. I am not made of such arrogant stuff; I read, and am wounded. (X quotes Neruda: 'We are Many.' I'll bet you are.)

Another correspondent, Julius Hogben, has an elegant script. His envelope promised refinement, but it contained only spite and grievance, bad fish in a fancy wrapper. Hatred, especially of the BBC brass (Jonathan Miller and Humphrey Burton in particular) rose rankly from the page. Why did I spend a full hour replying, vexed, to such vexatiousness? I had better things to do and flattering sincerities to acknowledge in a clutch of unanswered letters. *Et pourtant*, Master Hogben – pointing the finger – two upward fingers – disturbed my vanity and ruptured complacency. Well, it was good for the triumphant to be reminded, by the slave at his shoulder, that he too was mortal. At the same time, however, the slave was reminded of his slavery. So it is with the sullen, unapplauding mechanical who hands you frank opinions like a dose of refreshing hemlock. 'Life is all very well for the effortlessly superior,' he wrote. 'For the rest of us, it is not.' One of *them*! (He could be a windscreen smasher in the fifth of *The Glittering Prizes*.) The angry uneven pages – written on the back of some dead screenplay – are loaded with unappeasable grudges. One day, I fear, the mob will come for me (and they will not only be Old Carthusians). I fear cowardice as Juan fears impotence. What justice is there in Julius' charges? I am reminded that the work is far from perfect, but then 'the perfect map', what would that show us? The English are the most 'realistic' people ever to have a language sumptuous with metaphor; realistic in the banal sense that they want their paintings to be 'like' and their drama and film to be documentary (bugger *Nightmail*). They are indeed empirical; they will see something only if they can suck it. Hogben – has he ever suffered from being Jewlius? – threatens me with the brotherhood of the *damnés*: his fellow-technicians (he is an assistant film-editor). They want revenge; they want to be heard. And all excellence frowns on their desire. What are they to do but frown back? The class war is alive and sick, and living in the East Tower.

Orwell saw the metaphorical richness of the BBC clearly enough; nothing has purged it since. Success seems to those who do not enjoy it to be epiphenomenal on privilege. The derision available to Mr H. is unlimited. In part, one hates, fears and despises him for exactly the reasons he declares: he is not of our persuasion, nor susceptible to it. The collapse of bourgeois society would leave him where he is, provided he can dodge the odd tiles as his comrades toss them from the roof. The *sans culotte* makes us all check our flies.

Jack Lambert asked me if I'd heard the news. 'News?' 'I'm leaving this job in April.' Of course I had heard. He offered me a book to review and asked me to call him at home on Sunday. *Nel fratempo*, he volunteered that Peter Lennon had not much liked *The Glittering Prizes*. However, at Harry Evans' suggestion, they had conducted a round-up of ex-Cantabs, who had largely endorsed my work (the beginning of reviewing by numbers?). I called Belsize Park next morning and Catharine answered, 'Freddie!', *so* friendly and lively. She might have had the strength, I could not but think, to thank me for the flowers we sent when she was in hospital. Jack told me at the time that she *had* written, but when she reached the post office to buy the necessary stamp for France (where we were at the time), it had closed. And never reopened?

Jack came to the phone. They hoped we'd come to this 'small thrash' they were having. Their daughters were doing the catering. J. told me that he had first been approached by Harry E. in November, with the suggestion that he relinquish his post on New Year's Day: six weeks' notice after twenty-eight years. He countered with the announcement that he had already decided to give up when he was sixty, in April '77 (I always had the impression – and so perhaps had he – that J. was much younger than that).

H.E. was embarrassed and uneasy; he had clearly made promises elsewhere like all those who wish both to maintain their power and to be popular with everyone. He was determined to overthrow J. without upsetting him. J.'s suggestion of a date for his own departure satisfied neither H.E.'s critics (who thought him indecisive) nor his own sense of power. Jack had asked his executioner for a birthday present. H.E. offered him one, or at least the wrappings: Jack would become an associate editor, on full (or fuller) pay and the paper would bulge with his contributions: a middle, a review, a column on the back page. He reckoned he would be writing a quarter of the paper before he was finished. Yet finished he is; his friendliness had the warmth of those who sense that they are being hounded into the cold.

Beetle is stern and even contemptuous: 'He is no friend of yours,' she said with the stored scorn typical of her integrity. Jack, in power, never did me a good turn; he allowed Julian Symons to savage three novels of mine, one after the other, while glorying in affectations of officious impartiality. I should be disposed to acquit him of amiable malice if I were not aware that the books of cherished names – Snow and van der Post – fared favourably at his hands. To the unreviewed, however, my treatment seems evidence less of indifference than of favouritism. But Beetle *knows* that the man kept me down and primed apprehensions he could have allayed. She does *not* want to go to the Lamberts' thrash. Why do I? Should I, like

Daniel Meyer in *April, June and November* after Victor Rich gets fired, declare my *quondam* patron a fart because he can no longer thunder?

'One rather likes the old thing,' said Michael Ayrton of Jack; and so one does. On the other hand, Jack said of Michael, when he asked me to review *Fabrications*, 'No one much likes him.' It invited a sour notice, so I didn't write one. My review of a kindred spirit led to our friendship. The *Observer*, which M.A.'s father had edited, headed its notice of *Fabrications*, 'A Bit of a Borges'. That's the way, smart bastards. Jack did at least publish an obituary dose of Steinerian verbose compression when M. died.

Jack affected to be more amused than crushed by the arrival of a death sentence so soon before his natural term came to an end, but John Peter promises that he is deeply hurt, not least because (he imagines) no clear successor is in view. Is it all unnecessary? The senior reviewers are senior indeed; grave and reverend dust due for a *coup de balai*. Harold Hobson had only to be asked to an ominous lunch to volunteer that he had had 'a good innings' (what else?). Dilys is made of sterner stuff. *Her* lunch ended with Harry promising her that the column was hers until the day she died. So cordial were his assurances that it seems that if she could phone in her copy from the Other Side, he might well agree to her continuing posthumously. B. Glanville says, and I somewhat agree, that the arts pages are a geriatric ward. A lot of these oldsters still turn in excellent pieces (Raymond Mortimer not least), but Harry has a middle-aged desire to prove himself on the side of youth. He wants pieces like Martin Amis's last week, bovver-boyish chic. He fancies young Turks conducting massacres on the arts pages; so first, he must have the old Turks' heads.

Jack's lack of urgent feeling or severe taste made the literary pages prudently eclectic, but King Log was always both easier to despise than King Stork and more agreeable to live under. What do I care? Do I fear that I shall no more be asked to field at third slip/long stop by the new skipper? Success (on TV!) is a drug of *courte durée*: how many jealousies are arming themselves with righteous ruthlessness at the way I have been 'overestimated' during the last week?

Jack was in the Garrick when he saw Harry Evans with James Margach, the political correspondent, in the pay-out queue in the dining room. Someone went up to 'Jimmy' with crowing bonhomie and said in a loud voice, 'Good God, Jimmy, you're retiring!' Jack, from nearby, called out, 'Yes, like me.' 'You're not retiring for God's sake,' Harry said, flinging his arms around Jack's neck, 'you're not retiring at *all*.' Jack's bitterness attempts to cover its tracks like an old bitch using its hind legs in a dry field; it raises a lot of dust and hides nothing. The paper is full of rumours of a new supremo: one leading runner is Bruce Page. '*Arts*' pages? Never his patch; so he's probably a shoo-in.

2.2.76. Paul is a voter. Eighteen years ago today, a Sunday, I was having lunch with the Nimmos. Fathers did not attend births in 1958. Beetle herself called at a quarter to two. Standing at the phone (were John and Dudy, as she then called herself, decorating their flat in Upper Addison Gardens?), I was amazed to hear B.'s voice. Being the fruit of a Caesarean, I thought of childbirth as a kind of operation, not as a natural process. 'We've done it,' she said, with conspicuous generosity (after all it was a long time since I had made my contribution), 'a boy.' 'Wonderful,' I said. I hope I sounded proud; I was, but I was also conscious that a girl would have been a daughter; a boy was going to be a Jew. I had marked my son with a taint which would last him forever. (Beetle has *none* of these feelings; her pride is unclouded by my well-schooled dreads.) It would be nice – because ironic – to believe that Paul has never felt saddled with Jewishness, that it has never been a source of fear or embarrassment to him, but I suspect that is not so. The 'discovery' by fellow Bedalians that he is a Jew has been made easier by my work, and its recent rather loud reception. Was his early anguish at Dunhurst caused by dread that his 'secret' would be revealed? I hope he has reconciled himself to a condition more interesting (let's hope) than damning. He now seems strong and confident, intelligent enough to face life without my assumptions of rejection and habit of suspicion. He has wit, energy, and adolescent zest. His then headmaster Juckes said, eight years ago, when he was unhappy at Dunhurst, that Paul would succeed in life. He has been supportive (*ut dicunt*, and *saepe*) with regard to *The Glittering Prizes*; glad, it seems, that the success was mine, not his. Perhaps knowing that I need it more than he does, he is *amused* by the tide of acclaim. Less selfish than I, he deserves his vote.

Notices, notices; why does one notice them? How can one not? I was so well, or at least so thoroughly, reviewed for the first episode that I could expect either nothing or nothing but cries of disappointment for the second. Silence was my best hope. Doll (my sister-in-law secretary) called at eight on Sunday morning. Clive

James, who has criticised the first episode on account of fundamentally important errors, such as the fact that Letraset had not existed in 1950 and yet it was used for the names at the foot of Adam Morris's staircase, had returned to the charge. But with (almost) reversed lance! He had had to confess that many of his readers had been outraged by his scorn for the first episode. If he was not converted to admiration, it was not for lack of missionaries. As for the second episode, he was enthusiastic, particularly – and rightly – about Angela Down's 'superlative' performance. There is still no shortage of malice (who is Eric Korn and why does he write in the *Statesman*?) but also some disarray among my enemies. (Nabokov: an enemy is someone who does not like your work.) This morning comes an invitation from the *Statesman* to renew my subscription. *Au pannier!*

Munk's *The Passenger*. Brilliant and distressing still, but there is a certain sense of *relief* as one watches the horrors. The uniforms of the camp inmates whom one actually sees are remarkably clean; they might be beach pyjamas from the 1920s. The conditions are less than terrifying. To some extent, the chic is necessary to set off the ironies. The unspeakable and unseeable take place elsewhere. The little Jewish girl stroking the Alsatian (German Shepherd indeed) of the SS man who is supervising her death had a poignancy that was also sentimental: the image was both telling and too deliberate. It is a great strength in Munk that he faced us with so much of the unendurable. His narrative has, by the chance of his death, the unrubbed originality of the incomplete. It remains a weakness that he recruited a death camp into something 'personal': he sentimentalised it, as Dickens did his blacking factory; and hence he somehow humanised the inhuman. You still have to admire the unsqueamish daring of the man: he plunges his hand in the shit, like the RAF corporal whom T.E. Lawrence celebrated in *The Mint* when the bog was blocked.

The progression of Munk's plot made as many demands as that of a romantic comedy. The twists and dramatic hesitations are the result of messages and timely accidents of 'fate'; you are conscious of a man *visiting* Hell on a tourist visa rather than enduring it, imaginatively but without privilege. Failure of such a noble order makes one suspect a *systematic* flaw in the aesthetic claims of the cinema to be art. If *The Passenger* isn't art, what can be? The fullness of the frame and the clarity of the image, the regular obligations of lighting and sound, mean that too much has to be made plain to too many people. In the cinema, documentary reference thins and 'averages' the specific; the demand for drama pumps up understatement into rhetoric. The novel may be moribund, but it transcends such mechanical problems.

All the same, Munk's film leaves strong marks in the memory. The silent image of the man in the camp yard with the high-sided, horse-drawn cart remains indelible. At first you have no means of guessing what those unnaturally high wooden sides contain and then the driver, with an air of casual tidiness, takes a long, long forked stick and reaches up with it to where a single dead-white arm hangs over the very top of one of the wooden sides. With no more emotion than a park attendant tidying litter, the driver uses the forked stick to push the arm over the top of the side and into invisibility. We can see and yet not *see* that the whole volume of the cart is filled with corpses. The driver urges his weary horse out of the compound. That is all we ever see of the horror, and it is enough forever.

As I mention in *Eyes Wide Open*, when I was writing *Eyes Wide Shut*, Stanley said to me once, 'The Holocaust, what do you think? Can we make a movie about it?' I said, 'There have been one or two.' He said, 'Have there? I didn't know that. What?' I mentioned *Nuit et Brouillard* and *Schindler's List* ('That was about success, wasn't it?' Stanley said) and then Munk's film. He had never heard of it.

A las cinco de la tarde,	When did they come
As he had conjured,	For the other
They came for Federico.	Garcia, *campesino*;
They came for the poet.	Who died at dawn
A las cinco de la tarde	At the hands of the *guardias*?
At the house of a friend	Did don Federico tell him
They hunted for Lorca	The things he knew
Lover of men they hated.	Or did he Federico?
He was afraid, and trembled;	Did he feel fear, or what,
Proved to a point their point:	When they knifed him
Who would care to die	With their headlights
So early in the day?	And shot him at dawn?

Habia luz en Granada,	It was dawn in Granada,
A las cinco de la tarde	*A las seis de la madrugada;*
Treachery requires	No accuracy
No acquiescent smile.	In the anonymous.
He was a coward, queer	He was brave as a lion,
And a coward, Granad-	Said a *Guardia* later.
ino; complex lover	He threw, as artists should,
With a single flame.	A devious shadow.
Jaca negra, luna grande	No moon; no eyeing *burro*;
Arab, Christian, Jew;	*Sin nombre, sin historia.*
We cannot let you be	*A las seis de la madrugada;*
A constellation.	He died without a shadow.
Trinidad? Unidad	He died Federico's death
The uniform is black	As the poet his life.
Arab, Christian, Jew;	One immortal in line;
Camino no hay.	One mortal in deed.

Love is perishable; hatred – provided you take proper care of it – can last forever.

Shackleton Bailey's *Cicero*. How hard to abandon reverence for the scholarly style! The care an academic takes to avoid error gives his text all the signs of maturity, except *depth*. Its chronology smacks of the filing cabinet. S.B. is hardly more than a supervising editor. Oh for a traveller who is more than a topographer! He has visited all the obvious sites (though he has not trudged through Sicily as Peter Green did when he scaled Epipolae in *Armada from Athens*). S.B. is reticent when it comes to telling us, for instance, how Cicero conserved, or acquired, his fortune. Who were his friends (and paymasters) and what did their friendship imply, and buy? The truth is that S.B.'s book gains its authority from his other work (the edition of Cicero's letters in particular) but never justifies itself. Finally he abandons admiration for M.T.C. just when he is most touchingly admirable. Reticence dwindles into treachery; he seems glad to be done with the old windbag. He sides finally with Kingsley Amis (whose ex-wife Hilary, S.B. married) in a fibbing, lame effort to end on a modern note. I see more genuineness in Cicero's sense of loss (of Tullia and of the Republic) than in his championing of

Republican institutions when he imagined himself their guarantor. In the keenness of his regret he is the father of modern literature, whatever the windiness of his periods and the emptiness of his hopes. At the moment when he realises that there is no future, that all is lost, his character is redeemed; he becomes worthy of the tragi-comedy of his life.

The analogy with Proust (instantly scorned by Steiner, when I floated it to him) is only a little forced. Cicero is a prime instance of the snobbery which knows itself to be deceived, which wishes – as Proust and Waugh did – that what it wants to venerate were worthy of veneration (think of Cavafy's *Thermopylae* and of how many Ephialtes can be found to sell any pass you care to mention). The *boni* are the ancestors of the Guermantes; Cicero's snobbery is a kind of wishfulness typical of men from Arpinum or Illiers. Cicero's soldiering is grander than Marcel's and yet both are patently soldiers *malgré eux*: civilians posing for history, furnishing passages for their books rather than gaining spurs. Cicero's finally decisive courage – after so, *so* many changes of face – seems to annotate history from a portable condemned cell (he was in his litter when Antony's hit-men caught up with him) and parallels Marcel correcting proofs as he lay gasping for life in his cork-lined room. Informed by the doctor of his impending death, Racine is said to have flung the papers on which he was working into the fire. Cicero, trembling, tongue-tied for want of applause, found in superb lamen-tation an opportunity for the Philippics which built a verbal monument to an ideal Rome that he could neither rescue nor preserve. His Rome had existed only in his appetite. He was a man of letters who, had he stuck to that role (was Léon Blum another such?) and merely observed the events in which he chose to take a losing part, might have been a Roman Thucydides, with an ampler sense of nuance. His misfortune was that, for a brief season, it was plausible to take rhetoric for a means to power, and a treasury suffi-cient to sustain it.

Those long – let me *not* finish, he seems to say – sentences of Cicero are cousin to the Proustian periods; both launch great streamers of language, dressed overall with gallant phrases, that wave and wag like signals from departing passengers who never agreed to go. The great orator produces one final flourish, and one more after that, in the hope that the past will keep him in view (and young?) as long as he continues to show it deference. Many-decked sentences are the vessel of nostalgia; home is sweetest to those who have never quite been able to get back to it.

Restaurants: mouth brothels.

Neck amphora. Two rows of animals. Tyrrhenian group by the Pointed Nose Painter (570–60 BC).

I have sentimentalised Cambridge in the 1950s and so have become its eulogist. In truth, I speak only for myself, and not quite candidly then. Who would guess that I had ever been uncomfortable there? I recall being in a very odd play (*Musical Chairs*?) which was set in the Romanian oil-fields between the wars. I played an American business man. When the play was evidently a flop, I intruded a crowd-pleasing, *sauve qui peut* imitation of Jimmy Stewart into my performance. Afterwards, backstage, I bumped into someone who congratulated me on having been 'such a perfect Jew'. Should I have struck him? I thanked him and hated him.

I also recall a party being given in a mansion near Wittlesfield by a prancing prawn called Kim Tickell. He was a hanger-on in theatrical circles and, so far as I know, I had been properly invited (possibly on a group ticket), but I heard him say, with carrying shrillness, though not to me personally, 'I will not have my house turned into a synagogue.' I neither objected nor left. I had no transport, a mistake I seldom make today.

Many Jews were quickly at the heart of things in Cambridge. Peter Marchant officiated over Cambridge writing (all he had to do was start a magazine with his own, or his father's, money). Jim Ferman drove without difficulty (he had been in the US Air Force and already had that soft-topped MG) into the heart of the acting world. Bob Gottlieb, later a powerful editor in New York and, later still, the brief successor to Ben Shawn at the *New Yorker*, lorded it methodically as a director at the ADC. I never got to know him, though I lampooned him in my *Varsity* column. He never forgave me and contributed to my exclusion from publication in the US. Our only personal contact was after I had made a disobliging remark about him in a private letter to an American agent who affected to think highly of me. I cannot remember what I said, but it was witty (or cheap) enough to be sold to a newspaper by my opportunist correspondent. I wrote to Gottlieb to apologise and received a civil enough response.

My jejune attempts to introduce the question of anti-Semitism (strictly for the sake of example) into my philosophical essays for Renford Bambrough were glossed over with what seemed to be embarrassment (perhaps my own). Years later, Renford recalled how I had cited Macaulay's pro-Semitic speech to the House of Commons in a discussion of C.L. Stevenson's *Persuasive Definitions* (how often I used his argument about *ignoratio elenchi* by higher – or lower – redefinition!). In general, however, philosophy was not an *engagé* pursuit. Its chaste rigour was not undignified, but it chimed with the caution of English intellectuals at a time when the Final Solution was not ten years in the past and almost never mentioned.

The return of the Conservatives (Churchill was again Prime Minister during my last three years at Cambridge) justified a tendency to stop the ears to any disagreeable truths discovered since his finest hours. The horror was forgotten, if it was ever remembered, in the joy of red meat and jettisoned ration books. What a relief it was to connive with wilful reaction! Nervous adults may have taken my long hair and green corduroys for evidence of a dangerously buccaneering spirit, but I had small inclination to shake the pillars of the temple if there was any chance of a seat among the elders. I still called dons 'sir', when Mark Boxer was shrieking out 'Dady!' and 'Noel!' to grandees proud to be acknowledged by the outrageous epicene who was dating Sarah Rothschild.

Mark was only the most reckless of a generation of climbers. Nothing was more repugnant than suburbia, from which so many of us had come. Almost *anything* would be better than a *retour aux sources*. If we were impatient with our elders, it was because they were the snakes between us and the ladders which led to Fleet Street, the BBC, the Treasury and Sunday reviewing. My generation had no common purpose. Although they may share an ambition, a thousand Rastignacs do not constitute a band of revolutionary brothers; there is no orchestra of one-man bands.

Oh, I did remain, as many did, determinedly on the left. I even read the *Daily Worker* in the JCR, though I never dreamed of contributing to Walter Holmes's 'Fighting Fund'. I did not quite believe that the Americans had used germ warfare in Korea, but I did not quite disbelieve it either. The middle ground can be marshy too. I was fearful of German rearmament, but never a wholehearted ban-the-bomber. My loathing of those who had murdered the Jews was hardly greater than my muffled contempt for those who had done so little to prevent them.

The elimination of metaphysics was a passionate cause. The reproduction of Ayer's trenchancy or Wittgenstein's tentative urgencies was a soft militancy, but it was certainly sincere (as if sincerity were a method in philosophy!). The destruction of English illusions was an intellectually respectable style of revenge. I had the idea that to refute religious belief (and, under Popper's influence, ideological dogma) could kick away the premisses on which genocide had been licensed.

Renford Bambrough, my philosophy supervisor, was only a few years older than I, though – by virtue of his office and tenured intelligence – he seemed antique. I wrote essays for him quite as if he had not taught me the careful daring which I fed, and read, back to him in ill-typed weekly doses. I was never sure whether he liked me or whether he endured me; perhaps both. He was himself a man with a secret; it was no shame to have come from Scarborough Grammar School (many male pupils were sent to Oxbridge, though equally clever females were denied the chance) or to have been a Bevin boy (so, by conscription, following previous generations into the pits), but was it anything to be proud of? If Renford did not pretend to be more than a good scholar and an ambitious academic, his accent was carefully modulated and he certainly did not draw attention to his northern provenance. It was a time when regional tones did career prospects no good: Joan Bakewell has told, charmingly, of how she went into the loo at Newnham with a Brummy accent and, by an effort of will, emerged with the right voice for the BBC, where she has since sparkled volubly.

If they were, in principle, opposed to the class system, those who craved advancement were wise (and hence eager) to learn the ways of their betters, on whom preferment depended. The ambitious are the most dedicated preservers of whatever might disqualify others from competition with them. Not necessarily prejudiced, except in their own favour, they maintain the barriers which they plan to hurdle, in the hope that less high-flying runners will trip over them. The ambitious may call for careers to be open to all the talents, but their wish is that nothing be allowed to stand, institutionally, between them and their aspirations. Those who have been selected have no abiding objection to others failing: is not ostracism too a democratic process?

The 1950s before Suez had no clear character. I remember being shocked at the reception of a line I had written in a Footlights Review in 1953. Impersonating Michael Foot, at that time a regular TV panellist on a programme called *Free Speech*, I came out with, 'We in the Labour Party will do everything in our power to get everything in our power.' The first night audience howled and stamped its feet. I still defined myself as a socialist and yet... what is more intoxicating than to receive an unexpected ovation? The charm of anti-Semitism lies, not least, in the ease with which orators could get applause by pandering to it; Karl Lueger, the Viennese mayor who literally popularised anti-Semitism, was not *personally* disagreeable to Jewish friends, but the dividends of malice were too great not to be banked.

A certain bad faith was fostered by uncertainty of heart and mind. Marriage was the mature Leavisite solution to sex, but did we all embrace it with *quite* the same zeal with which so many of us were to go into it? Socialism was our naïve notion of justice, but – fortunately – it seemed unlikely to come into demanding practice. The cold war was still cooling, but the barrack-room world of the wartime generation was not ours. By 1950, when I went up, few undergraduates had actually been in battle. As a result of National Service, however, the squaddy's vocabulary was still a *lingua franca*: 'You've got two chances, a dog's chance and fuck all chance' was a commonplace. If active service was rare, one of the dimmer members of the Footlights had won an MC in Korea. He had been in a tank which had *almost* shed a track under Chinese fire. He had managed to tilt it off the road in such a way that the track re-engaged and he and his crew were able to get away.

National Service was the public school of those who might never otherwise have escaped from the provinces. How else would X have screwed the queen of Mogadishu or Y the wife of his company sergeant major? Would Z have had a shot at some Mau Mau in Kenya – and never known whether he killed a man or not – unless he had been conscripted to maturity, if that is what it was? Would a maths scholar have been disposed to say 'up your gongah!' as often as Tony B., if he had not gone from Cheltenham to Cambridge via Camberley? 'Just because you've got a penis and two testicles, that doesn't mean you're a man,' the drill sergeants used to yell. Getting some service in guaranteed manhood.

One realises that one belongs to a generation only when the first member of it dies. How close a friend was David Gore-Lloyd, on whom I based the dying Catholic boy in *An Early Life*? College friendships were often a case of *juxta hoc, ergo propter hoc*. The element of *noia* is often tactfully omitted in memoirs and, especially, in elegies; one remembers long afternoons, but discounts their length. David was remarkably free of the usual ambitions; he never had his eye on the main chance, perhaps because his family was rich (they had once had a steam yacht), perhaps because he was *so* happy to be an undergraduate. He was not very clever (today he might well not gain entrance) but he was expected to be a good oarsman.

The Lady Margaret Boat Club had thirteen eights on the river when I went up, and six blues in the record-breaking University boat (coxed by Tony Armstrong-Jones). David had been in his school eight, but his appeal to the selectors ended when his 'wrists packed up'. Tadge Leadley, President of the CUBC laughed when I suggested that D. had been unlucky – 'Rowing is about your wrists *not* packing up' – but I remained sympathetic. D. was converted to philosophy by Tony Becher and me; curiosity became fervour: I still have a typescript somewhere of a paper he wrote on Intention.

His own innocent intention was to mix with 'the smartness'; if he rarely said anything witty, he liked to laugh. He enjoyed the silly games of Oneupmanship which, under the influence of Stephen Potter's slim volumes, were painfully frequent. The idea of U and non-U speech and speech patterns was another of our toys; D. liked to think, with some justice, that his family was very U: they used napkins and never serviettes, though I do not know that they claimed to put their Christmas cards on the *chimney-piece* rather than on the mantlepiece.

D. bit his nails with the steady application of someone who would have liked to make his living from it (I am a more surreptitious nibbler of what my mother always called 'hang-nails'). D. laughed and sucked in his breath almost at the same time, so that you could hear the tide of his humour seething between his teeth. A joke was greeted with a sound like yes-yes-yes-yes, as if he were agreeing with your wit rather than being amused by it.

He was a seconder of others' remarks. If never a toady, he did defer; he was not a sycophant, but he did hang on. Did he ever have a woman? He scarcely had a beard; he was often pink in the face, but he never exactly *blushed*. We were a *pudique* generation, little given to sport; I never saw him undressed. He as good as failed the first part of his Tripos, when still reading maths. Because the college knew that he was fatally ill, he was not sent down. Despite his poor showing, he never seemed a dunce. Moral sciences, with its arcane freemasonry and its ill-defined subject matter, suited his enthusiasm. The happiness which he found among the philosophers in particular was the unenduring stuff of youth, but young was all he was.

D. had been weighed down by the moral handicap of Roman Catholicism. To be licensed, by therapeutic positivism, to throw aside those heavy crutches was as great a joy to him as the sense of not being *just* a Jew was to me. He was a gooseberry – I recall evenings *à trois*, when one (two) longed for him to be gone; after Cambridge was over for us, he stayed up. He was full of speculative curiosity of the kind to which Magnus Herschfeld and Dr

Kinsey had most of the answers (no one imagined that any of them had been falsified or *parti pris*). By the time that he was more practically involved, at least emotionally, with Puny's sister, Pussy, he was already a victim of the surgery which postponed but could not prevent his death. He had been 'innocent', in the Catholic sense, for a long time, perhaps for a physiological reason linked with the onset of his disease.

What is most memorable in him is still his innocence: joy in simple social pleasures, lack of guile. He loved to play poker and billiards (not snooker so much), though he had no great aptitude. He loved arty society, but not art; actors, but not acting; he came often to Footlights smokers, but he never wrote a joke or a lyric. In a generation Gadarene with ambition, he (like Tony Becher) never rushed towards fame and fortune.

I am not sure that Tony Becher ever really *liked* D., but he certainly did his duty by him, not least when it came to visiting the Westminster Hospital (I never drive past it without thinking of David). There were others who, when the cancer began to kill him, simply turned away. His dying was prolonged, and terrible. I can still see the fat grey bottle of painkiller which he carried with him during the months of remission. Jonathan Miller, with a medic's knowing shudder, called the mixture a 'terminal cocktail'. D. remained bravely willing to be amused; but we never had a serious discussion, except on abstract subjects (not the *Phaedo*). I never saw him in the very last days, but I did visit him more often than, God help me, I liked. Once, when I came out of Westminster Hospital, I found a copy of Brian Glanville's first novel, *Henry Sows the Whirlwind*, on a secondhand stall, and was envious that a school-fellow had already made it between hard covers. When D. died, I was in Lucca with Beetle, and happy. The testicular cancer of which he died is now among the easiest to treat and, often, to cure.

I might have run foolish risks,
Shafted witches and princesses,
Spent ten years beside Scamander;
Gulled the archer, buried Aias,
Played a double game and won.
Then have sailed for Ithaka,
And memorised the siren's call.
I stayed at home, loved Penelope
And died in bed, of boredom.

3.2.76. *The Glittering Prizes* is an unmitigated hit. Have they ampu-
tated my grievances? I count my stigmata as others their blessings,
or their spoons. How Jesus must have dreaded that 'the Jews' would
call for his release and not for that of Barrabas!

Hardy's youth ended, he said, when he was fifty. His biographers
seem to find this somewhat comic. Yet I have no sensation of having
yet entered my middle years. Whose fantasies, today, are of growing
up? What non-ideological writer does not cling to the stuff of his
youth as the basis of his fictional personality? Hardy's renunciation
of fiction is said to have been a sulky reponse to the critical reception of *Jude the Obscure*. Yet perhaps fiction had done as much as it
could for him, and he for it: he had been boosted, without risk of
return, from the namelessness (despite Admiral Hardy) in which he
had been born: Jude stayed obscure, his author not. He was enabled
to renounce fiction for poetry, in which the anguish of his loveless
life could fuel a less Latinate persona.

    The divide between his heroic/romantic principal characters and
his rhubarbing rustics was too wide to straddle. Being without
metropolitan affectations, and the classy tones that cloaked them,
left him marooned on the provincial side of the fence. As he was
never going to be the gentleman a novelist was supposed to be, he
had to resign himself to being a poetic genius. He returned to live
in Wessex, but ceased to depict it, prosaically, in his work. He
installed himself in his native haunts, but so feared being haunted
by the natives that he surrounded himself with reclusive walls and
a screen of gloomy trees. His house was a base for expeditions only
into the past. Lacking the nerve to be a revolutionary, or the class
to be a reactionary, he became a fatalist. Mean to his servants, lack
of belief in human progress kept him true to his Muse, if not to his
social responsibilities. Knowing the miseries of the Dorset labouring
class, he depicted them only pictorially. The influence of painting,
and of architecture, inhibited his fictional style: he could never make
a coherent connection between the passions and ambitions of his
central, tragic characters and the clogging folklore of peasant life.
Having recoiled from the sophistication to which the successful
novelist had access, he retired into a divided world (by dividing
himself from the world) in which his Muse could be preserved. That
he came frequently to London, and dined in literary circles, suggests
that, like Ramsay Macdonald, he was not impervious to aristocratic
ladies. Yet he said little; at dinner parties, he was the mangey lion
who had achieved eminence, but who never traded on it.

Poetry – of which *le tout Londres* rarely makes much (Byron was a verse gossip and travel-writer more than a bard) – continued to flow from a pen uninhibited by concern with metropolitan opinion. Instinct warned Hardy that, with the intelligentsia, intelligence is never the passport it seems. He played possum, the passive part which, in nature itself, always fascinated him. What he loved or desired was always beyond him, a social/sexual 'beyond': he could not love what was not above him, nor desire what was not beneath him.

The generalisation of desire, a passion undeclared to a single, desired object, leads to daydreaming. A facility for fantasy is common to the masturbating male and to the novelist. The singularity of Hardy's social position created a kind of aggressive shame. Necrophilia armed his genius. Poetry – the medium of his super-ego – came to express the woeful passions of an *id* which lacked the nerve to descend to the loins. When he invented Sergeant Troy (cock incarnate, as Lawrence was bound to see him), he had finally to kill him, to demonstrate the 'impossibility' of unpunished desire, of unrepentant masculinity.

The renunciation of prose was a happy castration: exasperated with the humbug of late Victorian publishing, he cut himself off. He had endured Leslie Stephen's condescensions as long as he could. Success makes writers impatient with restrictions which are tolerable only when they are the conditions of initiation. Hardy's anger seems as much social as aesthetic: he turns his back on a society which deplores sex with/in those whose blood is not of their group. Mr Gifford seems to have served him notice here, calling his daughter's suitor 'a churl'.

Emma must have seemed a catch, when he first wooed her. Gittings composes his biographical narrative skilfully enough to enchant the reader with the first impression of a busty babe at the vicarage (how sweetly symbolic, in the Hardy manner, the location of their first encounter!). Hardy could not believe his luck. Yet almost as soon as he was married he felt cheated and dismayed. The catch had caught him. He railed more against marriage than against his wife, not that she could be expected to mark the distinction.

What is singular in marriage is that it is a *particular* relationship. It cannot endure as fantasy, though any enduring marriage is, to some degree, imaginative. Hardy had to come down to earth. And then the earthiest of English novelists could not reconcile himself to the animal he perceived so clearly in others, and in nature. His parsimony was another wall he built around himself: Emma's querulous childishness suggests that she was, as they say, not getting enough.

That he made allowances for children even in his 1922 will is no more evidence of his having sex with Florence than does the homosexual's allusion to his girlfriends imply that he is kicking his habit. Hardy was not uxorious. He dreamed of fair women, but was not fair *to* them; he treasured above all what might have been. There was creative perversity in his rejection of Alain's advice, to love what *is*. He harped on what had not happened. He was a fervently negative writer; all of his rockets were aimed at the dark side of the moon.

How narrowly – and *how* narrowly? – D.H.L. escaped Hardy's fate! Childless also (unusual in those who marry young), he found his sexual liberation in a mother, a foreigner (hence exotic) and an aristocrat, who lent him social promotion from the lower-middle class. His device for emancipation was more effective than Hardy's, but to profit from it he had to exile himself from the countryside whence his vitality derived. In flight, his fiction was enfeebled with ranting and hyperbole. He sought vicarious Paradises in sunny places and challenged censorship at a distance, where he was immune from social and legal consequences. He exposed himself indecently to Britannia, but at a sufficient remove to be safe from the Bow Street magistrate.

A man will live more happily with a woman who has a sound digestion than with one who has fine opinions.

When the prisoner was tied and quiet, he kicked him hard in the balls, like a Mexican training a horse. 'They understand only one thing – pain, no pain.'

The cat goes on tiptoe at the door, to thin itself.

13.2.76. Lunch with Peter O'Toole at the Intercontinental. He is going to do *Rogue Male*, since Alan Bates has, it seems, passed; he says that his father is dying. It may be true, but he is famous for vacillation. O'Toole was late. Mark Shivas and I sat in the red plush restaurant, the Soufflé, with the air of patient penance which a late star imposes on those who need him. He arrived before the deadline I had proposed after which we would eat, and fuck him. He burst in without haste, an actor's sketch of apologetic bustle. Taller and scrawnier than I imagined (all actors contrive to be *slightly* different from what is expected), he wore a big, houndstooth overcoat, as one might a dressing gown flung on before quitting a burning house. Steel-rimmed glasses dressed him as a Mr Chips who is going to need his notes; and his disshevelment gave the impression that he had forgotten them.

He started off, hurriedly, with 'One story, OK?' It was all about how he had taken the ashes of his father back to Ireland a week before. First he had had to send a spoonful to be sprinkled on the pitch at Roker Park. His father had played for Sunderland before the Great War. He spilled some of the old boy on the floor (his Jewish accountant somehow came into this, baffled) and left another spoonful behind to be buried with his mother, before setting off for Dublin. He claimed that all the bells rang as he walked through the metal-detector. They rummaged in his father's ashes for deadly weapons.

When I said that I didn't want any wine, he said, 'Are you on the wagon?', as one might ask an old soldier whether he too had been in a certain battle, probably a losing one. He had turned out the lights of stardom; head down, he solicited no admiring glances from the room. He wanted to be liked, and to be businesslike. He praised *The Glittering Prizes*, and I accepted his compliments with a nod: no need to go on. He did have a couple of points about the script of *Rogue Male*. Well? Cue for the notebooks. 'Always carry a notebook.' Bloody small points they turned out to be: I can't remember what they were – oh, about the recurrence of Rebecca and something to do with the fishing.

He had admired Household's book for years, 'had a script done on it once'. I had written the script in just over a week, and rather felt that I had lingered over it. He told us how busy he was, and how this major film he was about to do might cramp his timetable. He looked so anxiously for anxiety in our eyes that one felt obliged to oblige. 'X quality,' he said, gripping my arm, 'that's the other thing I wanted to say.'

'I'm hoping that's what you're going to provide,' I said.

I realised I had left my sheepskin coat in the lounge, where I had earlier had a meeting with Karl Sabbagh, the young, very pleasant ex-Palestinian Arab producer of the BBC programme to commemorate Michael. I ran back – remembering that the pockets were arrogant with cash – and found it still draped over the arm of the chair where I had left it. We had been searched on the way in (the Inn on the Park, across the street, had recently had a bomb), but the heavy lining of my coat could easily have concealed explosives. No one had remarked it.

O'Toole was in no hurry to go. I was forced to make the first move. He would have talked all afternoon he was so busy. He liked Mexico, where he had made a couple of films. It was all a question of the *mordido*. 'The whole place is completely corrupt. Doesn't bother me. All you had to do is find out who you have to take care of. I got hold of the local police chief, discovered what his favourite charities were...' He looked us in the eye, first me, then Mark. 'Sealed envelopes. Anonymous contributions – as long as they all knew where they came from. No trouble at all. Ten weeks, all finished, everything wrapped up on time.' He was the guv'nor on that film (*Man Friday*, almost certainly – to judge from a clip – a clinker), but on the other Mexican piece, some Americans were in charge. No *mordido*: they went seven weeks over, trouble all the way. 'See the point?' He took Ben Travers to some first night, eighty-nine years old. Asked him what the message of his new play was. Looked at me. Like this. "Fucking isn't a sin," he said. Sat down. Eighty-nine years old. "Fucking is not a sin." I liked that.'

George Steiner, the well-beloved, has declined to appear in the programme in memory of Michael, on the grounds that two minutes is not space enough to expatiate on Michael's genius. He may be right, but it is time to vote Michael into the pantheon to which England was so unwilling to vote him.

16.2.76. We went to the Lamberts' party, their first invitation to us since we stayed with them almost four years ago. They have a pretty, flat-faced house off Haverstock Hill. Other couples scurried, from small cars, out of the dark London cold. Among them was Maurice Cranston and his handsome, bold-eyed wife, a lady quite unintim-idated by years in the academic moil. I cannot recollect where I first met Maurice nor why, over the years, we have always greeted each other with polite enthusiasm. How old was he when he came to the Moral Sciences Club and delivered a blameless paper on John Locke, after which he was savaged like a goose in a fox raid? Did I find a good word to say for him, and can it possibly have mattered?

Age and a settled reputation have bent his back like a coalman's load. His face creased, his jaw slightly out, you could not take him for a young man, yet – for all the professorial glasses and watchful-ness (he has learned the wisdom of the delayed response) – there is a humane decency in him, a tender virility which his wife Iliana's looks suggest is not imaginary. One always had the impression with Maurice that he was very keen on sex, and rather good at it.

Catharine was alight with excitement at our arrival. '*The Glittering*

Prizes' burst from her lips like a *vivat*. 'You *are* a clever boy,' she said, eyes as brilliant as those of a *contessa* whose new gigolo has really (and at last) done the trick for her. Bernard Levin, as huge-eyed as a tropical fish that has lost its stripes, hair crimped like a black hat of carbonised meringue, recognised me, for once: 'What does it feel like to be the most famous man in London?'

'My dear Bernard,' said I, 'I was just going to ask you.'

Beetle later reminded him of our campaign (for which she supplied key documents) against the CU Appointments Board. 'We did rather well there,' he said, apparently oblivious of the failure of his trumpet to shake down the walls of that particular Jericho. Journalists can keep up their fire-rate only as long as the editor's yawn is postponed. B.L.'s vanity is considerable: when I asked him about his capacity to be brilliant three times a week, he told me – like a Don Juan who has been advised to cut down – that he could easily manage five times a week if need be. The worst was once a week (as Perry Worsthorne had told him) because then it was necessary to make a statement for eternity, which always takes longer.

Catharine could not bear to see two of her stars twinkling at each other and introduced us, separately, to duller company. There was no one much duller than the Secretary-General of the Arts Council, who had been a lecturer in economics at Keele. Flew flew into my mind; and he had indeed been a friend of theirs. 'One disagreed with almost everything he said, but one couldn't help liking him.' Easier, I observed weakly, than agreeing with what he said, but not liking him at all. This seemed to pull the plug out of the already shallow conversation and we found ourselves drained of words.

I had been looking forward to an exchange of heavy artillery with Julian Symons, but the bore had been struck off. Dilys Powell, doughty as a dowager with a good solicitor, saluted me, remembering my disagreeable views on Greek politics (in *Like Men Betrayed*, which I had sent her). She now conceded, with sudden girlishness that revealed how she still managed to write with such verve, that my ideas were probably correct. Convinced that I am a fanatical leftist, she seemed unpersuaded by my dull claim to be concerned with truth rather than with ideology.

The Lambert girls had done the food and the party came alive from the trouble they had taken. There must have been something to celebrate, but our host – in a silk judo robe slack about his hollow chest and unclosed over his sagging stomach – looked sunk in chalky gloom. The poor man has taken his fall badly. As Michael once said, 'One's fond of the old thing.' Not everyone, however: John Peter hates him with the specific hatred of those whose devotion has enabled their master to take advantage of them. When in power, Jack was a bad winner. I am, J.P. promises, the only person of whom he has never spoken ill during the long courts-martial at the triune desk in the arts department, where the Lord Chief and his assayers sit in diurnal deliberation.

George Steiner is royally ribbed. Jack even went as far, one day, as to write to G.S. to comment sarcastically on the title of a lecture G. was to give at the ICA. 'It verges on self-parody,' said J.W.L. (Quite as if G. himself did not verge on it.) George was unamused; Jack's comments were 'uncalled for': the title of the lecture had been chosen by the ICA. and relayed without permission. Jack would do well to remember that people such as G. agreed to write for him not because they respected his intellect *but because they loved him*. 'Jack was delighted,' John Peter said.

'*Delighted?*'

'He regarded it as a victory.'

Jack runs the department on Tonbridge lines. George's ignorance of house rules and *mores* turns him into that standard figure of derision, the swot: clever enough to do you an essay better than you could do for yourself, but cornered by his inexorable qualities, a butt for everybody's ifs.

John P. looks as John Keats would have, had he been a Hungarian Jew. His hatred does not preclude pity for Jack. The ambitious need to distinguish the snakes from the ladders; but they must also be alert to the springs of human conduct. Unlike moralists and defeatists, they have to act rather than judge. J.P.'s ambition is to be drama critic of the *ST*, a position now up for grabs. His advocacy of John Whitley for literary editor is a move in the game of grandmother's footsteps in which the coming men stalk the editor and come ever closer to hoped-for offices; half blind man's bluff, half musical chairs.

Jack's old number two was of the company. He had liked the first play, and said so in *The Times*. We greeted him warmly, as one might an old acquaintance who had made good. He was larger and wider, like a shop that had done well enough to expand into the one next door. When he has time to get his teeth aligned, he will look like Fortnum and Mason.

Beetle liked him and feels that we treated him badly by asking him to Seymour Walk and then not asking him again. I prefer to be aggrieved: he never reviewed my novels in *The Times* when he was Lit. Ed. and never invited me to review for him. It now occurs to me to wonder whether Jack exacted a promise not to poach any of his critics.

Marina Vaizey insisted that I introduce myself to John. 'He's much too shy to come and talk to you.' I went up boldly to thank him for his kind words in the *ST*, which had torpedoed Lennon. He jumped up, a lean-faced man with the asymmetry of someone who had undergone major surgery. 'You're a genius,' he cried, 'an absolute genius.'

Maurice, who had been on the sofa next to J.V., smiled nicely to himself as if to say that geniuses come and go but professors are always in season.

The Vaizeys drove us in their Renault in pelting rain back to the Intercontinental, where we were staying overnight. John drove in determinedly manly style while Marina, in back with Beetle, shouted instructions, SHOUTED as if to a deaf mute chauffeur of dubious IQ. Vaizey drove like a novice, so delighted to have the car moving that he ignores all directions and gives the machine its head, like a child pretending to command a wilful donkey. We laughed and laughed at nothing very funny, as people do at the beginning of a friendship when they have nothing more in common than the wish that it will come about.

Marina and I had both yielded to John Peter's incitement that we should write to encourage Harry Evans to appoint John Whitley literary editor. J.V. thought our intrusions unwise; so do I, but in honour, I had no choice. I am aware, with prudent anxiety, that I am getting very good billing these days. May the new man not treat me as James I did Sir Walter, who was 'left over from the previous reign'. A shrewder operator would have agreed to endorse John Whitley but been wily enough not to post the letter, from which he could quote freely if his candidate prevailed, but which would not be on the file to soil his reputation with another.

R.A. Butler was on the selection committee for the Cape thriller competition. He argued at length for a story which was not chosen as the winner and finally agreed to another having the prize. T.M. drove him back to his hotel. He apologised for the long time spent in deliberation. 'Oh, one's used to that,' said R.A.B., 'but at least there's the satisfaction of knowing that one's got one's man in.' Had R.A.B. repressed his defeat or had the whole thing been a cunning blind and his money on the eventual winner all along?

The Vaizeys were asked to Sir George Weidenfeld's on the second Wednesday of *T.G.P.* Marina refused to go. John, less immune a moth, could not resist the famous flame. He made Marina's excuses, saying that she had not been well. The Weidenfeld party was no great shakes. Towards 10 p.m., John told his host that he was not feeling all that well himself. 'I think I'll be getting off home.' Weidenfeld said, 'Oh don't be so silly. If it's *The Glittering Prizes* you want to see, it's on in the bedroom'.

18.2.76. *The Book Programme* with Robert Robinson. With us, as they say, was James Gibson, a Hardy scholar who has spent the last five years on an edition of H.'s poems. A lecturer at Kent, in his fifties, he had never been on TV before. In the hospitality room he talked fluently, denouncing the authors of *Providence and Mr Hardy*, whom he clearly regarded as meriting transportation. Ephemeral celebrity and *quondam* screenwriter of *Far From the Madding Crowd*, on which tweedy, pipe-smoking Dr Gibson did not fail to pay me a scholar's compliment, or two (but no more), I suggested to our very made-up chairman that he allow Gibson to do most of the talking. The latter seized his chance: we were, in a word, lectured. I managed to intrude a good word for tittle-tattle, but remained heroically self-effacing.

Philip Speight, the director, came down and asked, would we do it again, and this time would Bob direct the first question to me? G. still had his say, but not before I had somewhat raised the temperature in the tomb. He thought he had done well, but wished we could have had half an hour. 'One couldn't really say anything, could one?' he said, as we waited for the taxi which would take him to Victoria so that he could get home in time to see and hear what he had had to say.

I regretted not having time to develop my insights into homosexuality in Hardy's fiction. 'Just as well you didn't,' the scholar said, 'because I would have shot you down in flames.'

'Oh really?' I said. 'I shouldn't bank on that if I were you.' I adduced the Boldwood–Troy relationship (citing D.H.L.'s untypical error in failing to notice that – contrary to his own denial of the fact – Boldwood did indeed have a Christian name, William, and that it was to Troy that he revealed it). There was also the passionate conflict between Henchard and Farfrae which gives *The Mayor of Casterbridge* a tragic thrust. Here indeed was the love that dared not speak its name. Well? Mr Gibson was silenced, for a moment, and then, with an aggrieved, honourable, blink, declared that I might have something.

Mark Shivas, Rob Knights and I previewed the sixth of *The Glittering Prizes* in Christopher Morahan's office. It was the first time I had seen him since the press and the public took the series to their fickle hearts. He received us as coldly as a bank manager who had already decided to foreclose. He watched without a smile, stirring vexedly whenever one of us – especially when I – laughed. After the lights went up, he looked grim. He did not think that the public would sympathise with the main characters. The only person with whom *he* identified was the au pair girl. I listened with cowed contempt to solemn anxieties about whether or not we had 'lost our audience'. I muttered that if you are going to lose your audience, the end of the last play is not a bad place to do it. *His* problem, I was reminded, was to get people to turn on *next* week, when my plays were finished. If I had alienated the audience so that they were too disgusted to come back for more BBC2, well, that mattered to him, if it didn't matter to me.

He then commented pusillanimously on details of the play (about which nothing could now be done) until I asked if he was looking for a quarrel, because I was very happy to have one. 'We're not quarrelling,' he said, 'we're having a discussion.' I sat tight, but didn't like myself for my prudence. I said only that I would remember his sympathy with the au pair girl and next time we had a dinner party, he could come round and do the washing up. I added that I didn't give a shit if no one ever watched BBC2 again, as long as they watched to the end of the series.

'You certainly got him,' my colleagues assured me, as we left. I was ashamed that I had not told him what was what and then walked out. British office-holders, even when scarcely gentlemen, still seem to have a hold over me which must date from Charterhouse. As soon as Morahan loses office (his departure is said to be imminent), he will discover who his real friends are. Does he *try* to be dislikeable or does it come naturally? Will his new marriage, to the lovely Anna Carteret, and the child that is due in July, alter his lofty, crabby, miserable character?

19.2.76. Joan Bakewell telephoned to apologise for what she appeared to have written in *The Sunday Times*; they butchered her copy and printed only the tag. 'I too have written for newspapers,' I said, and then told her that I *had* been faintly piqued by her condescensions. She then asked us to dinner, which Beetle converted into an invitation for her and Jack to dine with us, and the Sullivans, at the Wick. Joan disclosed, as they say, that Karl Miller had been asked to give his opinion of the verisimilitude of the first play, but declined: 'How can I be expected to remember what Cambridge was like in 1850?'

On Noel Annan's instigation, Karl has been appointed Professor of English at King's College, London. He has never run, or even taught in, a university department. The best claim he has to his position is that he can be trusted never to make a joke about it.

At dinner, Joan was amazed when I said that if she had spoken ill of my work, I should never have spoken to her again. She assumes that a friend will understand if you blackguard him for guineas.

Sullivan's new wife, Judy, had said on the phone, when I invited them over, 'After seeing the plays, I don't know whether I want to meet you.'

'Are you disgusted or intimidated?'

'Intimidated, I guess.'

She did not seem very intimidated, unless timidity made her garrulous. She knew very well that Bill Bourne and J.P.S. had been born back-to-back. The first thing she asked me was did I know what 'a knee-trembler' was; she had been informed by John that his R.S.M.'s wife had instructed him. Sullivan is over here researching in Cambridge libraries.

When I first saw Judy come out of the darkness, I had to look twice. At first glance, I thought she might be black (like Bill's wife, Joann, in the fifth play) but she was white and from Texas, in a flouncy red dress that displayed young legs, and thighs. She teaches school to five year olds. She exchanged no more than a couple of sentences with Joan all evening. Afterwards, she declared her fellow-guest 'a phoney'.

John is plump, in a tight-buttoned floral shirt, professorial glasses, black beard, flop of dark hair with a flash of grey in it. Why are they married? *Are* they married? They are together; amiable but not loving, along for the common ride. John huddles down into himself. A short man keeping it short, he does not really need a private life. The university provides for his social, if not his sexual, needs. The first Judy was dark and rather prettier, and I guess more vulnerable, hence likelier to wound a man who took her for granted. She left him for another woman. This Judy is tougher and thus more easily retained. Neither Judy appears to have wanted children. John has the air of boyish elderliness common to childless fathers: a secularised Jesuit, *malgré lui*.

Joan's new, young husband, Jack, runs a fringe theatre and wears his hair as long as a *légionnaire*'s sunshade; his beard would do for Dr Knock. He was at Keele, where he read maths and theology 'for the style not the content'. His wariness rehearses hostility but never quite gives the performance. They have a cottage in Cornwall, where they go to repair tissue frazzled by metropolitan life. They were shocked recently to hear that it had been listed in an anarchist publication as suitable for occupation by squatters. A man called Heathcote Williams is said to be responsible for making that kind of trouble for the famous who own, or talk, too much. Loyal neighbours had called, however: 'Don't worry, Joan, anyone tries to break in, they'll have us to deal with.'

The gossip columnist. Shallowness is the secret of her charm: she will never embarrass you by running deep. She runs a neat journalistic kitchen, with just enough of everything bottled and to hand, but little fresh. She wears her years lightly. Her miraculous consistency of appearance suggests a petty compact with the devil. She left her provincial accent in the loo and nothing has been heard of it since. She presses herself against, and hopes to be becomingly reflected in, the glass which fences her from the London smartness of which everyone assumes her to be a part. Incapable of intimacy, she is everybody's best acquaintance.

25.2.76. Note for the Daedalus Dimension. Pasiphae was daughter of Helios; leading to Icarus' infatuation with the sun? The magic knife of Daidalos, belonging to Peleus, could not be used against its master. Androgeos killed by the bull of Marathon, hence young blood-money exacted by Minos. Minos (Callimachus notes) ordered the flutes to cease playing when he heard the news on Paros, during sacrifice to the *Charites*. Labyrinth originally a spiral; tie-up with Nautilus legend; repetition, *in parvo*, of the same trick. Minos' defeat of Megara; Nisos' purple lock, shorn by Skylla, his daughter, who fell for Minos (when he took her water-skiing). Nisos becomes a sea-eagle; Skylla a *ciris*; ever after the two birds pursued each other. Talos had a single vulnerable spot, a knuckle or (?) a vein running from nape to knuckle, closed with a brazen nail (when it was removed, he leaked to death). Talos in ancient Cretan meant the sun: cf. Zeus Talleios. Zeus Cretan sun-god; the bull the same (?) god in night form.

30.3.76. Harold Pinter, in black suit and purple woollen tie, black boots with silver buckles, minatory spectacles, came to rehearse *Rogue Male*. The fear which might have been present, had he been less successful, has been converted into intimidation. If he were not such a dandy, what a mess he might have been! Not altogether easy in his superiority, he began by asking if, where I had his (minor) character, a Jewish solicitor, say, 'Robert, what *is* the matter?', he might say 'Robert, what's the matter?' After prolonged thought, I agreed; and then, when we came to do the scene, he said it the way I had written it.

O'Toole is conscious of his age; the famous face hangs gaunt on his long skull. His career has brought him everything except kudos. He has the wealth and fame and careful step of someone who no longer falls down: his drinking days over, he prefers to eat. Lean but not fit, billiards is his likeliest form of exercise. I had no large hopes of his performance in *Rogue Male*, but after a few days' rehearsal was convinced of his qualities. He gave Pinter one excellent hint, which he attributed to Robert Atkins, at whose name Harold winced. Peter retorted, giving scorn for scorn, that Atkins had been the first actor–scholar. The hint was that when you don't know which of two adjacent words to emphasise, pronounce them as if they were a single word, and emphasise that.

The phrase in question was 'Don't blame yourself'. With bleak gracelessness, H.P. made blameyourself one word, and the problem was solved. He makes ingratitude a kind of elegance. Refusing connection with the common world; his incorrigible autonomy is a form of avaricious solipsism. His style demands a world in conformity with his incorrigible specifications.

1.4.76. Thanks to Joan Axelrod's new realtor role, we are in Tony Richardson's house, on King's Road, a block up from Sunset strip. He bought it only two years ago for something like £30,000 pounds. It is on a steep hillside, subject to earth-slips, and had been neglected for years. They dredged the detritus below the house and unearthed a tennis court and an Olympic-sized swimming pool, which had a car in it, a Lasalle apparently (Julian English would have recognised it).

The sitting room has what Joan calls 'a cathedral ceiling' and is lined, high up, wih Hockneys, effusively inscribed to Tony. They can't be stolen without a ladder. Richardson's English Sunday papers continued to arrive during our tenancy. What better morning than April Fool's to take delivery of an MGM typewriter, the machine on which many a good man has been racked?

'Ah, Monsieur Proust, je suis desolée: plus de madeleines!'

What is plagiarism, but free love among the Muses?

Byron and Shelley. How about if the ghosts which haunt them that
summer on Lake Geneva do not appear merely in flashbacks and
flashes forward, but roam the terraces and rooms of the villa Diodati?
The bedroom will be full of ice when Mary Shelley opens the door.
Its domesticated crepitation is far more unnerving than the usual
location shots of mountains and crevasses. 'And it saves money,' one
of my producers said. He greeted my ideas like a man who recog-
nises the fish he has caught only when it is being weighed. Will
MGM ever make this movie? Burt and Bob swear they are very
keen, though they are keener, surely, on Scorsese than on a movie
about two limey poets in nankeen breeches.

MGM. The executive floor is as quiet as if somebody's hopes had
just died there. Each Lord of the Lion has two secretaries. We went
in first to see Ray Wagner. Tall, greying and slim enough to go
easily through closed doors, he paraded his creative credentials: he
produced *Petulia* and he knew John Schlesinger. Then Daniel
Melnick arrived, much the same age (early middle-) with a smallish
head, draped with more skin than it needs. The forehead falls into
creases like a bouncer's suit. His eyes have the air of frankness which
comes with being used to dodging the question. I had sworn to
myself that I would not unleash my ideas (since we had no signed
deal yet), but the tedium of the occasion, unrelieved by the commis-
sary hamburger which lay like an underdone sandal on my plate,
unbuttoned my garrulity. I assured them, all smiling menace, that if
my ideas didn't appeal, they should say so, and I would go home.
    Melnick said, hey, sorry, but he had the idea, from earlier discus-
sions, predating my involvement, that the movie would be a trinity
of ghost stories, told by the leading players. I said, fine, but that
wasn't something I could or wanted to do. Marty, exhausted by
some unexplained crisis, dark eyes like bruises in that bearded,
boyish face, little guy with broad shoulders and it had to be a buckled
belt, sat beside me in silence. He can afford to be quiet: *Taxi Driver*
is a big hit, even though it didn't hit me all that big. Marty wears
success with furtive complacency. Does he know that his movie is,
in some respects, shameful? Violence supplants sentiment: Alice
really *doesn't* live here. Yet in some ways *Taxi Driver* is downright
soppy. Cybill portrays a dream girl such as Jerry Lewis might covet.

De Niro's fine performance is of a character whose civilian sincerity is ridiculous; war is the only world where he is completely at home. He drives his cab like a yellow chariot. He goes into battle with his head shaved in the style of the Special Forces in Vietnam, the ghetto boy transformed into the vessel of paranoid wrath, but directed against an enemy not undeserving of it. What makes an artistic claim is the ambiguity of the character, its potential decency. Yet the future life of Cybill and the taxi driver was hardly likely to have been one of realised harmony. How long before she was practising tap-dancing in the bathroom?

Marty is surrounded with a cohort of ancillary workers. De Niro cruises the office, ostentatiously saving the lights of his stardom. The actor who plays the gun salesman in the movie also hangs out in the office, colourless face ridged with unproductive effort. He wants to 'get into production', a kid in his twenties, prepared to make all the tea it takes. Marty goes to an analyst four times a week. He has a child, or children, from an earlier marriage, and remarried last year. Julia was a journalist sent to interview him after his success. He asked the last question and now she is pregnant, with no small opinion of herself and a maternity smock to make room for it. Sensing that Marty could be turned off the project if she were excluded from the huddles, tactful shame led me to address many of my remarks to her. *Beh, le donne!*

   Julia has the blue eyes of a juvenile who has already seen most of it. She parades like the boss's wife who knows who is boss. She not only knows her way around, she knows her way right through. Marty is trying to budget a very expensive movie not in his league, a musical with a title *New York, New York* I wrote down years ago, with Liza and De Niro, the Italian jobs. Irwin Winkler, my once-bearded tennis partner, is the producer, as he is of the next Bogdanovich. Peter wanted to produce it himself, but Irwin owned the script. Irwin is producing. Irwin is grey and downcast, but he gets there just the same. At Disneyland, he would be a wise little mole: nibble, nibble, scratch, scratch, that's how he gets around, and brand new heaps of money mark his passage.

10.4.76. The labyrinth is language; the poet makes wings from words, and gets away with it. Coil of the maze like the print of a key; the lock as a vertical maze. Babel was to be the labyrinth of labyrinths, a universal dictionary that would have put everything under human control. Babel and honesty should spell everything out. Was sexuality, and its binary implications, what brought the tower low?

16.4.76. We have been in Tony Richardson's house for three weeks; doing what? I have persuaded everyone, apart from myself, that the Byron'n'Shelley project is the most exciting thing imaginable. This is less the capital than the Capua of the Entertainment Industry. All the clichés are true: one runs in quicksand, swims in treacle, warps like wood. The single-storey minds are primed by a single motive: money. Only lettuce is kosher. What is the difference between one drive to Metro (down Pico to Motor, and thus to Culver City) and the next? Marty's mock-modest office is lurid with old posters – *The Man Between*, script by Harry Kurnitz, faces his desk – and has the stale air of a restaurant that isn't serving right now, even though *New York, New York* is in the oven. Julia's determination to be important, and reckoned with, puts a clove of garlic in the recipe.

Bobby de Niro, pigeon-toed, head down, goes in and out. Is he as anxious as he looks, or is he – like the movie – 'in preparation'? The 'pages' are constantly revised and refurbished. The script came in at 153 and has been savagely pruned to 147. The big blonde desk is covered with alternative versions. The writer (never seen, but constantly leaving fresh sheets for disapproval) has clearly reached term. It seems to be Julia who vets the new pages. When she decides a scene is brilliant, Marty goes along with her. In her loose maternity clothes, she will produce in September, whatever Irwin manages. A journalist, she is about to do her first piece for *The New York Times*. Wow, right? I foresee nothing but trouble from her intrusions.

I was going to lunch with Judy Scott-Fox at La Scala when I met Bob Shapiro on little Santa Monica, bound for the same place. He was due to lunch with Jo Janni. My reaction was, might it be better if Judy and I went elsewhere? No, the reservations were in different parts of the house. When I went to Judy's table, J.J. was sitting there with her. He was slumped down, in an open-necked shirt which sorted ill with his jacket. He had the plumpness that comes of too many hotel breakfasts and inconclusive expense account lunches. It all smacked of an ambush.

'Hullo, Joseph.'

'Don't worry, I'm not having lunch wiz you.'

'I'm not in the least worried, and not in the least sorry. I've had about as much boredom in this town as I can stand.'

My charmlessness startled even me as I poured scorn on the slouched figure, quite as if I had prepared the ambush.

'Well, what can I do for you?' he said. 'If zere's anysing – '

'Luckily, there's nothing. And I can't think of anything better. The great thing about nothing is, it takes so much less time than anything. And I don't have any more time to waste.'

'Zen we leave you.'

'Please.'

I had no idea that I harboured such venomous feelings and I would never have believed that I would give such cruel expression to them. Am I a bit of a bully? Had Jo called me when I first came to town, and made me no matter how specious a speech, I might have been more flattered than impatient, but the knowledge of his silent presence (he did speak to Beetle, without knowing who she was, when he called the house hoping to speak to Anthony Page) reminded me of past slights. I was also, I daresay, a little bit guilty over the portrait of him in *The Glittering Prizes*. My chance to get even with him and John had eliminated an inhibition, and I cut cruelly loose. Had I been told that things were going well for him, that I had insulted someone who might have done me a favour, I should not have felt so bad. But Judy told me that things were, in fact, going badly for him: *Jane*, that piece of bogus modernity, had been set to go, but had gone into the trash can. When Columbia didn't want Ted Kotcheff, Faye Dunaway, the ubiquitous, had not been willing to commit.

I have been tempted, of course, to suppress the above note, which is why I have included it. What on earth was it all about? I cannot recall what specific tinder was ignited by my chance encounter with Jo, of which I now have no memory whatever. In a novel such a violent clash would require plotting and explanation, neither of which I can provide. A man who always likes what he sees in the mirror is not taking an honest look.

We had another meeting with Ray Wagner. Danny Melnick was absent, but Ray declared the closeness of their rapport, which was like declaring an affinity with last week's towels. Wagner is as young as a diet can make you. He likes to think of himself as a creative person, something of an artist even. In other words, he has a failure to apologise for. *Petulia* was his idea of a picture 'like *Two for the Road*, ahead of its time' (another word for failure). He saw us as two of a kind; I did not. Sherry whatever, the MGM script supervisor, was also at the meeting. She is a great-looking, long-legged girl in loose fawn pants, connected sexually with one or the other of the bigshots. She takes the exaggerated pains with her appearance typical of the girl who wants be judged exclusively on her brains. Her wide mouth emits thoughfully spaced clichés. With plenty of shampooed dark hair, she thinks like an ad. I talked like a man trying to win parole: it's all meant to get me out of this place, with the money, and back to Europe.

The new Buck Henry script is called *Ape*. It is, in the wildest sense, a rip-off of *King Kong* on the remake of which Dino (di Laurentiis) is said already to have spent more than twenty million dollars. And they have yet to shoot any footage of K.K. himself: the giant ape remains to be weaned from the bosom of the special effects department. In an access of urgent naïveté, Buck Henry sent his script to Dino to be sure that he agreed that Henry's ape was no relation of K.K. The Laurentiis people admired the script so much that they will go to any lengths to prevent its being made. It is essential, in Staney Donen's eyes, that it be made before November, since it concerns a presidential election during which the incumbent is drowned in ape shit.

Lucky Lady has been a disaster. The Huyks, Willard and Gloria, for long Stanley's close companions, were among the first to denounce him to the press. Can they honestly have believed that the film might have been Art if the ending had not been changed? A script so confected to cater to every cheap hope aims only at financial success. S.D.'s sole failing was that he did not procure it. Burt Reynolds and Liza see themselves as the victims of vulgarity, when both are the incarnation of what people will pay money to see. Stanley is convinced that the movie was unfairly treated. He associates his disappointment with the reception of *Barry Lyndon*, which he holds to have been insulted because it gained no significant Oscar. He has, he thinks, been humiliated as Kubrick has. He should be so lucky.

Stanley Donen campaigned openly for *Barry Lyndon* and even had campaign buttons made to promote it. 'The other Stanley', he said, had made a masterpiece. And so he had; even though critics continue to call *Barry Lyndon* a bore, you have only to see a frame or two to recognise a masterpiece.

No one could accuse *Lucky Lady* of being unfairly consigned to oblivion, but I still recall a line about its being 'so quiet in here, you could hear a fish fart'. Stanley rang Gloria Katz, Willard Huyk's wife, when he read what they were said to have said to the *Los Angeles Times*. He asked her, 'Did you really say those things?' 'Yes, Stanley, I'm afraid I did.' 'Oh Gloria,' Stanley said.

Hickey has cancer. He came out here almost three years ago and decided not to return. He was tired of England and, I suppose, his family. He soon learned the way of California. During the energy crisis, he directed us to the most genial pumps and was a prompt grader of the supermarkets. He had not liked Adelle and found Yvette a delightful change. Now he has cancer of the prostate. He was operated on by the most expensive knife on the coast. The surgeon made things worse by tearing the rectum, exposing his patient to a severe risk of infection and even more discomfort (the soft term for agony). Had H. been in London, he would have been treated with drugs and, I suppose, radiation. I saw Hickey sitting in the sun in the driveway of 300, Stone Canyon, wearing invalid blue trousers and shirt, thin but smiling, hair brushed back, brilliantined, from the pale brown face. The blue eyes, the slightly hawked nose, the thin amiable lips and sharp jaw reminded me of somebody else: it was an old David Gore-Lloyd sitting there, unsuspecting of his fate but, in the style of his body, resigned to it. When I left the house, I had to manoeuvre the car between the parked cars. Hickey, still and stiff in the healing, desiccating sun, indicated with his hands how best to do it, the beached chauffeur waiting for the next twist of the knife.

I went with Charles W. to play squash, in the UCLA courts. He used to be fat, but went on a crash slimming course and is now half the man he was. He plays regular and, I found, effective squash. I took only one game, though two went to eight all. He prides himself on his wilful fitness and has a new young wife as proof of his puissance. A squash player of a few, well-executed strokes, he stands in the right places, and sometimes in the way. When I struck a firm ball into him from the back of the court, he allowed me a let, though I always thought obstruction lost you the point. We played and talked like old friends, which we are in a way, though we have little more than a cuttings library knowledge of each other. When he walked naked to his shower, through the puddles of other athletes' feet, I noticed on his plump buttock the prunous imprint of what looked like a salacious bite. Lucky professor, to have so passionate a bride! Then I realised that it was I who had administed the tell-tale bruise: the tale it told was of a well-struck ball, for which I was given a let, instead of the point.

As we walked out, I saw the empty squash court as a maze without walls, through which one lurches and stumbles in pursuit of the killing stroke.

Peter Green told me a story of the days when Michael Ayrton moved bibulously in the company of Dylan and one would never have guessed what a sage he would become. Michael was travelling with Minton in a wartime train. The journey was long and made longer by delays. The two artists had their colours with them (and their bottles) and ended by climbing onto the luggage racks where, recumbent, they set about transforming the compartment into the Sistine Chapel. The journey went on and on. Having covered the ceiling with colourful obscenities, both artists fell asleep in the luggage racks. They did not wake till it was daylight.

'Where the fuck are we?' Michael said.

Two old ladies, who had taken seats below them, in what they took to be an empty compartment, jumped up and pulled the communication cord.

We gave only one dinner party at King's Road: Louis Malle and Alexandra; Pauline Kael and Bob Towne; Peter, who claimed once to have been a '*cineaste*' and Carin, to add some Attic salt. It was not a success, though it did go on and on, until Peter said to his wife '*prepei na phygomeh*' (modern Greek for 'we ought to go'). I have used the same formula with B. and I was faintly insulted by the assumption that I wouldn't understand the code. Pauline Kael, one of Hell's most garrulous grannies, was the centre of attention, if not of attraction.

Girlish and cute, she wore tortoiseshell spectacles and a floral top and a black skirt. Bob Towne was her beau for the night, but a beau that refused to be tied: he left, alone, towards midnight, after the usual cryptic phone call. I had thought to throw her into the melting pot of the evening, but she merely congealed there. Her contributions served only to stifle everyone but me. I am a more forthright host than guest. When she asked what American films I had liked recently, I could think only of *Nashville*. but said that I preferred *Lacombe Lucien*, at which Louis covered his face in a wince of modesty, or dread. Was he thinking of his dead actor who would never have had that fast car had he not served in Louis's *milice*? Or was he reluctant to concede the contribution of Patrick Modiano (in whose praise he had spoken loudly, at least in private)?

I had been unguarded about the artistic affectations of film-makers, and their crass, greedy ambitions. Louis reckoned that I was being 'cynical'; making films was an essentially naïve activity. I first met Louis immediately after seeing *Lacombe Lucien*. He seemed bright and brilliant, an imaginative intellectual, and French *en plus*. Weren't we lucky to have such a (distant) neighbour in the Perigord?

Now he sits all day in a little office at Paramount, trying to cook up a story about a wetback who comes to work in California. Freddie Fields has already advertised the brilliance of what refuses to come to life. Louis is confused by the success of *Lacombe Lucien* and the catastrophe of *Black Moon*, a low-budget, 'personal' film, which he described to Billy Wilder as 'a dream within a dream'. Billy looked at him and said, 'You just lost two million dollars.' And so he had.

Louis, says S.D., who has 'known him for years' is a bit of a bore. Alexandra's determined vivacity covers for his upwardly displaced constipation. Her sister is a professor of Italian in Montreal (?) and she has the family flair for languages. She became an actress because she was so beautiful, but says she cannot act. I suspect that L. is beginning to believe her. She trips gaily about; and on the day they got here, she tripped out to admire the sunset and broke her foot. Yet she flits around, all freckled laughter, and seems undaunted by Louis' mean mien: he gave her several looks of black malevolence. Myth, to be done with her, would turn her into a butterfly, forever ephemeral.

R. Towne told me that we had met before, at John Schlesinger's house, when he had been a gushing admirer of my work on *Darling*. He has a beard, pendent on a long, joyless face, the same lugubrious knowingness you see in W. Goldman, the picture-framer. Towne was consulted recently by John on *Marathon Man*. They finished the picture and then found they had no ending. He flew to NY with the missing part, the Towne mechanic. Later he went into a reti-cent huddle with Louis; maybe he had brought some spare endings with him.

Miss Kael thought herself so cute that the evening was sacrificed to her high opinion of herself. She drank heartily and would, I think, have stayed the night, had I not left the door open when the others departed. She was finally frozen out. She kissed us all goodbye, including Paul, lifting one girlish leg up behind her, like Andy Hardy's daughter. The advantage to be gained from entertaining critics is that one need never take them seriously again. Paul said, 'If she ever reviews anything of yours unpleasantly, we shall simply roll on the floor laughing.' I wonder.

22.4.76. I met Pauline K. by chance, waiting for a taxi on the back alley steps of the Beverly Wilshire, wearing her round specs and what I suspect was a West Coast air of girlishness; she is probably much more mature in NYC. She told me how beautiful and smart my wife was and advised me to 'take a more practical hand' in the making of my movies. ('What movies?' I should like to know.) She then boarded her car for Colorado, where she joins the lecture circuit and the gravy train. I went on into the hotel, where – finding that he was out – I left a note of apology for Jo Janni: I wished him the kind of success which would make sure that old friends greeted him with admiration and affection.

Yesterday I heard that *Jane* is supposed to be going forward with Ted Kotcheff directing, but it still depends on Faye saying yes; and she cannot, surely, say yes to everything offered to her, because everything is.

Alan Pakula's *All The President's Men*. The Axelrods proclaimed it a triumph, having seen it at a special screening. We went, as commoners, to see it in Westwood, and were very bored. The opening – blow-up of typewriter keys hammering into a sheet of paper – was sufficiently startling to make you believe that cinematic rhetoric of an interesting kind might be about to denounce the whole Washington circus, but dull good taste soon prevailed. Habitual tension was imported to endanger characters so revelling in their starred impunity that it was the audience that was in danger, of believing that Redford and Hoffman were its serious guardians and that their pushy arrogance was man's best defence against corruption. Were actors ever so unconvincing in a newspaper office, Balsam and Robards no less than the dynamic duo? Everything was clean except the chat which was overlaid with Goldman's mannered man-talk. Melodrama and irreverence are cousins: both embrace the forbidden and make overstatement a commonplace. Narcissism, aping virtue, replaces heroism. Pakula's 'seriousness' is that of the account executive: everything is composed like an advertisement for itself. He is inventive, where he is (and where is he?), only when it will not endanger sales. The balance that he passes off as style is inoffensiveness in a Baroque register.

The tension generated in the film is the product not of any dread of the agencies of evil men, but the fear of boring the audience. Having lost faith in Nixon, the committee to re-elect Alan Pakula relies on well-lit decorum. The only corruption that riddles their efforts is derived from vanity, caution and self-admiration. What is as clean as shitty elegance? Nattiness stands for nastiness: the portraits of Redford and Hoffman are so piss-elegant that they are a pair of non-toxic plumbers. When Pakula dishes shit, it is all chocolate ice cream.

The treatment of Watergate in terms of a well-made thriller is a way of avoiding serious questions, moral and political. What fuelled the journalists? To what degree was their ruthlessness an aspect of the same hard-nosed philosophy that backed the plumbers? What sour comedians might Billy Wilder, in his prime, have made of the good guys, with a little help from Hecht and MacArthur? Not a single detail in the whole cumbrous picture, so elephantine in its dexterity, so bleached of mischief, even hints at the real nature of Washington or of big journalism. It pretends to be *true*, but its truth is commercially sanitised, clean of purpose or judgement. So determined were the producers not to offend any cash-carrying customer that one of the reporters (the pretty *goy* of course) has to be declared a Republican, so proving that there is no intention of denigrating a political party run by men without honour or scruple dedicated to the perversion of the Constitution. The mention of Chappaquiddick could be said to come from the commercial sense of fair play on an audience-researched scale. Washington was less anatomised than glorified: the plethora of long-shots, of long-haul pullaways gave us a tourist's view of the city. The set-ups suited the taste of a postcard salesman. The top-shot of the interior of the Library of Congress was entirely pointless, but inspired the empty awe typical of fascist art.

The only noticeable black in the movie had to be a good Joe and hand over the Library of Congress cards, though no blame could be attached to him, since they revealed nothing. All you could say of him was that he recognised Redford and Hoffman, and knew how to tip his hat to the real talent around here.

The lack of any authoritative intelligence, of any stringent purpose or polemic fire, lay in assuming that *the* political scandal of

the time had to be depicted, in order to be interesting, in the style
of a TV serial: the panicky exit from the underground car park after
the meeting with Deepthroat (a name itself allusive to a porno
picture of which the audience could be flattered with naughty
knowledge); the fake menace of the finale in the empty apartment,
where the masking music was turned up to save the two news-hawks
from being overheard, this after they had been blabbing all over
town and announcing themselves like celebrities seeking a table at
Ma Maison at short notice.

All The President's Men is itself another cover-up, an elaborate
fake, denunciation as a pail of whitewash. It never comes within
spitting distance of the real origin and nature of corruption because
the film-makers are of the same persuasion as Nixon and his gang:
a parade of serious intent is sufficient to gull the punters into thinking
that they are in good hands. Delusions of worthiness fill the picture
with fake authenticity. The avoidance of naïveté has become an end
in itself for Bill Goldman. Frivolity masquerades as realism; the
unsmiling passes for seriousness, uneasiness for fear. The movie is
rancid with duplicity that, in a strange way, justifies the *auteur*
theory: the Janus-facedness of Pakula, symbolised in his literal
ambidexterity, is expressed in an attack on falsehood which is itself
false, in indignation which keeps its nose clean, and in the construction of a pillory so aseptic that every tomato thrown at its occupants
has to be washed first. All premeditation of this sanitised order is
conspiratorial, an agreement to concoct, conflate and, simply, to
con.

Joan Axelrod. She left a rich, dull husband (whose war service in
Germany ended with his acquiring the US distributorship of
Volkswagen, for the price of a signature) in order to hitch her inde-
pendent wagon to the starry future of the brilliant, witty author of
The Seven Year Itch. Money endures longer than talent: the ex-
husband has just bought the LA Design Center, off Santa Monica,
to (so says Joan's son, Jonathan) 'put her eye out'. As for the play-
wright, Stanley and Yvette went to his latest effort, *Souvenir*, and
felt they had to go round and see Deborah Kerr. 'You don't have
to say anything,' she said. 'Just sit down and have a drink.'

24.4.76. Alexandra and Louis are falling apart. He has been seduced
by a well-kept divorcée with a teenage body and a teenaged
daughter. Women of a certain (but not *too* certain) age are very
attractive to him; Jeanne Moreau the showiest. Alexandra was

suicidal on Thursday, but much better today, having meanwhile seen two casting ladies. One more child battered by selfish fates has been uttered into the world, Justine. Shades of the Marquis de Sade. (What else?) What will become of her? She will live and she will die. Who is different? Everyone hopes he is, or she is, and it all comes to the same.

Alexandra believed it, she told us, when Louis said they were not like other people. The girl who had been auditioned by Darryl Zanuck ('I couldn't believe it when he pushed open the bedroom door') was any little Fanny when True Love whispered its lies. Her tears were as childish as mine, or anyone else's, when L. could spare her only five minutes of a day crowded with squash and other pressing engagements. How terrified the erotic operators are when it comes to real emotions! Yet what man would not be Don Juan if he dared? To hurt others and feel nothing oneself, of such is the kingdom of carnal knowledge.

Alexandra will get another job and another man and she will avoid us, the witnesses of what she will then see as her lapse. How frail and small she was with age, a lovely woman among younger ones!

The Axelrods had fancy company when we went to collect and take them to dinner. Lord and Lady A. He, Geoffrey, a rather long-nosed, pin-striped smoothie, was smug with the title with which he had just been fitted, after a long law-suit which proved, if you accept the judgement, that his virgin mother was impregnated by the contents of a sponge that she had been unwise enough to share a bath with. Her ladyship is French and worked at 666, Fifth Avenue when she did PR for Worth. She was expensively dressed in autumn foliage, hair elegantly done, arched feet neatly shod and kept in by gold straps and chains. With eyes that knew all the exchange rates, she is descended (by a winding stair) from the Mellons, who were first respected millionaire swindlers, then philanthropists. She reacted without warmth to the fact that we had a house in France in the Perigord.

'I am very fond of *pommes Sarladaises*. Is it near Sarlat?'

'About twenty kilometres.'

'What's the name of the place?'

'You won't know it. It's very small. St Laurent-la-Vallée.'

'Of course I know it. Very well. There's a little bridge over the river.'

'No, actually; there's no bridge and no river.'

'When are you there? You're there only in the summer.'

'We spend time there all the year round,'I said. 'And there's no bridge and no river.'

'In the winter months...' she was all set to tell us that we didn't live in St Laurent-la-Vallée rather than confess that she was talking about another St Laurent (of which there are hundreds). Her husband, the lordly Geoffrey was indulgent to the point of complaisance. She had been in New York, waiting at 21 and lonely oases like that, for the famous legal decision. Would she have greeted hubby so sexily, had the case been thrown out along with the bath-water? They were perfectly charming, making much of their invitation to the Juley Stynes' *after* dinner the previous evening. The boss of MCA and his alcoholic Doris have a housekeeper who won't allow more than a dozen at table when she does her stuff. Lord and Lady A. were nouveau-richly delighted to have had a car and chauffeur put at their disposal, and embarrassed to have so few destinations to command. George advised them not to show the driver the smallest consideration and, though his callousness was amusingly expressed, he meant it. He admires Evelyn Waugh with masochistic veneration. He believes in the power of money and irritates Joan by saying that if he had been born rich, he would never have written a word. The irritation comes from her awareness that he no longer writes anything anyway, and is poor. Joan is now more of a scribe than he: she wrote a script which she sent to Alan Pakula (once the object of the Axelrods' hatred). Alan did not read it himself but Hannah, the scholar, told Joan she thought it was wonderful. Joan was torn between indignation (that a mere wife should pass judgement) and delight. Of course she and George consider *All the President's Men* a triumph.

I was determined not to invite his Lord- and Ladyship to join us for supper, though such an invitation – giving the Axelrods a chance to be generous with our pockets – was much hoped for. I should have sat there till dawn rather than pick up the tab for those particular parasites. We dropped them at the Beverly Hills Hotel and went on to Chuck's in Westwood. The Axelrods had never been there (and were, we realised later, chagrined at being taken to so unsmart an eatery). George abandoned his diet and sank martinis and white wine like a kid potting bottles with an airgun. Less amusing in liquid form, he was sour with the waiters. Bitterness marks J., and nostalgia for the days when G. was a producer and they were given four free cars a year. She drove a white Continental convertible. G. still insists on travelling first class, although it is no longer the Studio, but his empty purse, that pays.

Dinner with Charles and Helen in their rented apartment on Veteran. The building – yellow stucco, palm trees – could have been where a celluloid foreign legion defended themselves against the Tuareg supplied by Central Casting. Charles has the face of Dick Tracy in middle age and a new wife to go with it. The other couple, the retiring professor of classics at UCLA and his starched lady, were correct enough to make you feel that we were all in a period piece. They loved France and French cooking and had been to all the three-star restaurants, though their girth kept it a secret. Amiable, but not interested, garrulous but not forthcoming, the professor made the unremarkable suggestion that Daedalus' wings may have been sails, though the details of the myth (the wax, the feathers, Icarus' meltdown) hardly match the idea that D. simply invented the mizzen. Rescripting *The Cretans* was, he thought, a trilogy too far for Ken and me; why not work on *The Trojan Women*? When he rehearsed its merits, with keen accuracy, I suspected that he was manoeuvring the conversation onto well-turned ground.

They all talked briefly, but with sudden animation, about their colleague Quentin P. His English ex-wife, Cass, has refused to accept alimony on a sliding scale, to match the cost of living, and insists on being paid in sterling, not dollars. She impoverishes herself with every demand. 'She's got a mental age of six,' the gleeful Helen said, as if that closed the case rather than opened the wound. The distraught, unTrojan woman cannot bear to have her growing-up children leave her and threatens suicide if they do. Cass's parents were reported to be monsters who beat her up when a baby. To have been a battered baby turned out to be one more of those misfortunes that count against you when the going is bad.

When Beetle told of Alexandra's falling out with Louis, with whom Charles had dined at King's Road, he said, 'I know that kind of woman – ' (as that kind of man often does) ' – she can't get it together. I have no sympathy at all. I'm entirely on his side.' He treated B.'s decent sentiment with the same quick suspicion you direct against an insurance salesman who asks for your date of birth: what's this got to do with me, what're you getting at? How convenient it is when a woman *deserves* to be ill-used, when abandoning her becomes *the right thing to do*; you can then suit yourself and play the moral arbiter as well.

The academic expat. He is happy to be in America, but he hates waffles and pancakes, jam, maple syrup and butter. He would sooner eat a waffle as it is than pour anything over it. I was surprised by his vehemence on so petty a subject, but if he cares little about anything else, he sure detests batter.

Charles and 'Johnny' Sullivan are severally pickled in Catholic brine, which they affect to have shaken off. Men of sexual experience, so far as numbers go, neither is at ease with women. They have no time, maybe, for the courtesies of courtship; they need women as eager to get away as they are. John is the opposite of George Axelrod, who welcomes any opportunity to stop work. (He warned me that he never answers letters: 'I don't write on spec...') 'I'm a procrastitute,' he said.

Larry Turman had seen *An Early Life* and invited me to go and see him in Strada Corta Road, Bel Air. His house was close to the street, behind an apron of rosy brick forecourt. An old Ford station-wagon, full of junk, was parked there. The Georgian door of the rather small and charming house was opened by the coloured help. She showed me into 'the library', a large walk-in closet furnished with no more books than a bibliophile's bathroom. The prints on the narrow walls included one of King's College chapel.

When T. arrived, we went into the garden. A slim man with the creased neck and skinny arms of someone frightened into losing weight, he had a huge success with *The Graduate*. 'Was he hot!' Stanley Donen had said, and grabbed burned fingers away from the imagined touch of him. 'Hot as a pistol.' Then he made the mistake of directing a picture himself (*The Marriage*, was it, *Of a Stockbroker*) and cooled right down.

There was a brick-floored terrace at the back of the house, with outdoor sofas and loungers. The maid brought coffee in a silver pitcher, no spoons. Later, he took me to see the guest house. His wife was converting it into a projection room and office, oh and a guest house too. There were workmen and expensive furniture all over the place. It was charming; the ideal cell for a writer to do time in.

He apologised for the projection room, but it was so convenient. Those who enjoy this convenience can never project a movie without hiring the services of a 'projjy'. Where would they all be without their contract gardeners and pool-boys? Richardson's gardeners, as surly a pair of wetbacks as ever waded through false papers, made a habit of flooding the tennis court with inches of expensive water minutes before we wanted to play.

The Turmans have a large garden below the terrace, a tangled wilderness of hired shrubbery designed to supply a three-dimensional backcloth for the garden furniture. (Herb Ross's garden, being on the Beverly Hills 'flats', has lawns and rose bushes and automatically watered weeds.) A glaze of defeat overpainted Turman's successful style. Still rich and somewhat famous from Mike Nichols' movie, he has many development deals, but what else, aside from a new projection room and a new Mrs Turman? She was a middle-aged lady, with no orthodontic improvements, who joined us, with polite brevity, on the terrace. Why did I feel unexpected warmth for a man who had, *en deuxièmes noces*, chosen a grown woman, not a babe? There was a hint of sincerity in him, a lack of killing confidence: he would not be a bully, and might even be bullied. Yet the word from S.D. is that he was very difficult to work with. Jealousy or truth, or both? One goes to see such men as successful businessmen go to see their bank managers, when they don't need a loan.

The death of God is like the death of the father. Men wait all their lives to be free to do what they always wanted and then they discover that what they always wanted was to please their father.

When I hear appeals to come to the aid of ordinary people, I send my contribution, but who wants to go to the meeting?

Why does the literature of male Jeremiahs have a tragic ring, while that of females shrills like an unwanted telephone? Voltaire: one needs *testicles* in order to write tragedy.

How many reconciliations come about not so much on account of some access of magnanimity but rather because one old enemy sees another off guard, trudging along a dusty road or shopping for a demanding wife, and realises, not suddenly but with a slow burn, that he feels more *for* the other than against him? Enmity – like its cousin, desire – fades with a sense of mundane community.

The reason that many marriages work (and that Bertrand Russell was not a nice man) is that nice people, out of love, come to care. Caring may presage the end of desire, which depends, in part, on strangeness, but that does not entail that it *must*.

Could one argue that the more abstract a man's habit of thought the less likely he is to make a lasting lover? Oh, there may well be a Whitehead for every Russell (who, one can well believe, wanted not so much Mrs Whitehead as what the Whiteheads *shared*) and it

may be that the Carnaps were legendary for their conjugal blissful-
ness. Yet the higher the level of generalising, the more *bloodless* the
calculator: the biologist *must* be more tender, more attentive to
specifics, than the physicist. The mathematical mind such as
Russell's, turning to geopolitics and morals, thirsts for conclusions
which 'must be the answer'. How neat to find selfishness the *logical*
consequence of principle!

Iris Murdoch's weakness as a writer relates to her weakness for
people: her determination to see good in them leads her to assume
their capacity for love. A sublime John O'Hara, she fits every peg
to every notch, out of concupiscence with all the natural possibili-
ties of her *dramatis personae*. I.M., like O'Hara, has forgotten that
there is also a time *not* to embrace: when the presumption of
lovability, fuckability, is an assault on others' autonomy, a greed no
more irresistible than snacking between meals. I.M. lends contingency 'necessary' consequences; she makes existence itself mythical,
her version of Platonism.

In *The Sovereignty of the Good*, she proposes a hierarchy of values,
and perhaps of human feeling, in which daily life merely illustrates
some lofty and eternal scheme. Her novels are the soft porn of sentiment. There is no feeling for the agony of choice, which is the
essence of morality. We find affectations of seriousness, of the
anguish of lived life, but only as decor. Her idea of Love as paramount among human beings is so commanding, so peremptory and
pre-empting, that it becomes master of all the gods, the Good.

Who has ever finished *A Word Child* (Sartre's *Les Mots* on
steroids)? There are some surprises, but they derive from the agility
of the author, not from anything implicit in her creation. I.M.
attaches no personality to the work; if she is a narcissist, she addresses
herself in the third person. *Elle ne se tutoie pas.* The apparent elimination of herself does not leave her characters free; it means only
that she is ubiquitous: every novel brims with renewed romantic
self-esteem. She has elevated mental masturbation to the grandeur
of metaphysics. What disconcerts *chez* I.M. is the self-infatuated
verisimilitude of her fantasies. Believing that she deals with the
grammar of affection and desire in an observed world, she looks
down on the god/Good which she affects to venerate. She is *so* big-
hearted that she cannot criticise even herself. Oh for some
autobiographical 'lapse', a hint of lived life, a spot of washing-up,
some dirty knickers, a charmless child, *something* disorderly apart
from *eros*! Could nanny not stop *playing with us* and tell us or *show*

us something about herself, apart from how clever she is?

The self-portrait is an honourable habit in painting and can be in writing. Yet in fiction the self-portrait is taken to be, at best, only unintentionally self-revealing, and generally self-admiring or self-advancing. Velazquez' self-portrait is of a proudly handsome man, but does he simply admire himself in it? Yes? What about Rembrandt then? The self-portrait, no less than landscape, is a feature of the secularisation of Western art. Landscape climbs through the window of devotional painting. Seen first as mere background to figures pertaining to mythological or Christian significance, the pastoral is advanced, as if through a zoom lens, until the view fills the frame and displaces the mythic.

Does Spinoza's equation of God with Nature coincide with landscape becoming an autonomous form? Flemish art certainly seems to have become secularised (and market-driven) before that of Italy or Spain. *Simul ergo propter*? Nice to think so. Does Spinoza's (renounced) Judaism dispose him to express an aesthetic crisis in a philosophical way? He ground lenses, which enabled people to see without prescribing what they should; another pretty coincidence.

The portrait bust was common enough in imperial Rome. Did the deification of emperors not lead also to iconoclasm? Vandals wanted to break the power, the totems, of the empire they sought to dismantle. At the same time, the Byzantine iconoclasts, in an excess of veneration, feared to deflect reverence from Divine Truth to mundane imagery. The self-portrait then is a culminating stage in the desecration of art: rejection of the Platonic ideal of Beauty leads to self-examination which, in Rembrandt, makes a virtue of warts. Mimesis is truer than the ideal.

When artists make models of their wives or mistresses, they are not always painting the women they most admire in a moral sense, only the women whom they most look at. Proximity does not always make for flattery. So what are the objections to self-portraiture? Has it got something to do with Christian denial of the selfish prefix? Self-abuse, playing with oneself, that kind of solitaire is not a proper game. *Portnoy's Complaint* – the *ne plus ultra* of confessional fiction – acquired quick notoriety by having the first hero who masturbated in so many words. It became a hot book no doubt because most of its readers greeted it like an old friend who also had spots. It excited the laughter of relief among self-servers everywhere. Roth's self-portrait verges on self-destruction, if what the writer seeks is public esteem. He severs himself from those whose applause

he has won by whacking off in public. How could he *do* that? A
Jewish writer, acclaimed in New York (if *Goodbye, Columbus* was
tough to take, it did win the National Book Award), needs to make
violent gestures to free himself from cloying admirers, the posses-
siveness of those whose ideas are repugnant to him. Roth's
self/ishness – where ishness combines what he knows he is with
what he knows he dislikes being – reveals the quasi-self-portraitist
at a moment when he seems both to immortalise (success passes for
immortality) and to immolate himself. He can never hope to be
asked to a *barmitzvah* again. Jacqueline Susann, the pop-porn queen,
announced she admired the book but wouldn't like to shake the
author's hand. The hand, after *Portnoy*, takes on a specific use of
which women had to affect ignorance.

With Lee Friedlander, his shadow alone becomes a limb of the
self-portrayer. It has always been a rule that a photographer's shadow
does not fall into frame any more than a professional housepainter
leaves his hairs on your sill. Only the amateur signs himself so clum-
sily. Narcissus dispensing with his pool, Lee makes a *subject* of his
shadow. His sense of the comedy of the situation, and of the photographer's uneasy claim to be a serious artist, leads to toying with (and
breaching) what was an absolute convention. Having gone so far,
he goes further, and shoots himself. By taking himself as subject, the
'artist' chooses a model whom he need neither favour nor pity,
whom he can shoot and shoot without seeming callous or vindictive. Lee's *Self-Portraits* are remarkable for the detachment of his
self-regard. His agreement with himself that he be shot with the
same weapon he uses to shoot others recalls the old pulp fiction term
for a gun: 'an equaliser'. Without anyone else in the frame, he aligns
himself with all other subject-objects. Self-involvement and vanity
cease to be tautologous.

15.5.76. Anna Cartaret, who was in *The Glittering Prizes*, went up
to collect my Writer of the Year award at the Royal Television
Society Ball. Christopher Morahan's avuncular hostility to the series
will have been nicely capped by his being obliged to watch his wife
collect my prize. In addition, Huw Weldon, who blocked me at the
BBC for years, was also obliged to applaud, since he was being given
the Society's Gold Medal. Such unworthy considerations are more
directly enjoyable than any measure of mature praise.

The only embarrassing confession, in sophisticated circles, is one of
uxorious delight.

At the moment when she realised herself abandoned, she lost faith in herself as an actress. Every rejected sexual opportunity (for instance, with Warren) became the proof of fidelity to a man who did not deserve it, and hence regretted. Her eyes grew smaller, and clouded with yellow. Her lover fell from being an *auteur* to the status of a cheap waiter who impregnates a chambermaid and then skips town. I remember little Maria on the telephone at Seymour Walk, saying over and over again to some other Sicilian maid, '*Ma che vigliacco! Che vigliacco!*'

5.6.76. Jack Lambert's farewell party in Little Venice. I wanted to call the Wick first, to wish Paul and Sarah well for their exams. The first booth was full of a foreign lady with a row of numbers and 2p pieces. I crossed Warwick Road, where there is still a green shelter where cabbies cluster, and found Felix Aprahamian, one of those short, dignified, little men, at once ridiculous and impressive, who look as if they have been made by a short-sighted Gepetto: he makes only one or two a year, but they all bear his mark. Felix was feeding the coin-box like a man pressing fish on a crocodile in the hope of having it let go of his leg. He wore black, up to – not all that far, of course – the broadbrimmed hat, duly dimpled at the crown, which he says he bought at the St Sulpice hatter who provides the same article for the cardinal archbishops of Paris. Felix shows me such respect that it seems always that he knows something to my advantage of which I have yet to hear. He was *aux prises* with his accountant, his anxiety having been excited by two tax demands within a week, the second being an aggrandisement of the first by eight whole pounds. He was seeking urgent help ('I pay him a hundred pounds a year,' he said) like a man whose symptoms were suddenly so much more acute that he could not decide whether it was worth calling his specialist or whether, to avoid new expense, he should proceed directly to the cemetery.

Felix wears his dignity like galoshes in fine weather. Why he defers to me is simple: I am twice his size. When he appeared in *Darling* as a pretentious critic, he needed no make-up, but he did need the work. Like everyone in London, he speaks passionately only about money; after the Swinging Sixties, the Sponging Seventies. Felix has a grizzled beard and glasses with hinged lenses, like the windscreen on a reconnaissance car. Like George Steiner (who is of the same dimensions), F. is unmistakably foreign. He is marooned in a great bitter lake without issue, in which he manages to catch a few fish. Does he really make love in *Lederhosen*, as he is reported confessing, or was it *claiming*?

We walked together, the little Armenian and I, to the waterside where the newly ennobled Lady Vaizey, hugely delighted at her unexpected elevation, was sitting against the canal craft which was to take us there and back. The company was small, consisting of Jack's personal entourage. Derek Jewell sequestered me for a long time until I was rescued by John Peter. John is a paragon of considerate ambition: whatever he means, it is never trouble. No one native to English culture has studied it half as diligently. He lives a life in translation, but unlike Felix he has no unquestioned domain; he needs to be as agile as a squirrel who has all his nuts with him.

There cannot have been more than twenty-five persons at the party. The food was modest: veal and ham pie, permanently waved sandwiches. The white wine or the red? Derek Jewell paraded his Oxford origins and his classless accent. One thought what an excellent hire-car driver he might have made, had he been able to complete his education: he had the grey Che Guevara moustache, sideboards and an air of *rusé* obsequiousness. A jolly nice chap, he is a director of *Times* newspapers and, apart from making ten thousand a year from selling review copies of LPs (the figure was computed by Godfrey Smith, who estimated that one needed to make £60,000 before tax to have the equivalent amount), D.J. also devises and supervises the lucrative special offers which badge the paper's corners. Proud of his commercial skill, he is eager to be culturally acceptable.

Jack was given three Victorian watercolours, chosen by Marina and by Deborah, Jack's Courtaulds-educated daughter. Desmond Shawe-Taylor made the presentation with vivacious grace. He is an old boy as asymmetrical as the balance of payments. In a blue striped shirt and white collar, he looked as if he was halfway through changing for some arcane summer game in which he was going to bat number eight, but would not field. Jack replied with splendid *élan*. His speech might have been prepared long in advance, yet – given that the event was a surprise – it must have been largely spontaneous. Raymond Mortimer, creased as an old driving map, vulture turned vegetarian (it was said that, when he had his claws out, Cyril Connolly was afraid of him), went amiably about, seersucker-suited, complaining of the tourists in Venice, voice seemingly funnelled through the finest leather.

Jack said that his twenty-nine years had been remarkably free of friction, though Raymond had once taken exception to a headline, concerning a Shakespeare study, which ran 'Hey diddle, diddle, the play's in the middle!' It had taken a fortnight to repair that particular mischief.

I had hoped that Peter Lennon or Julian Symons would be there, since the pitch suited my bowling. I glared at a young man with glasses and black curly hair and blue eyes (he might be Irish like Lennon), but he was the new ballet critic. The previous *tenant du titre* had gone to Australia with the Royal Ballet and, according to John Peter, was struck by the male homosexual menopause while, appropriately enough, Down Under. He sent back scatological pieces and refused, via Reuter's tape, to eliminate the short words. Faced with an ultimatum either/or else, he chose the latter.

The in-and-out fighting in the arts department has not yet achieved quietus. Philip Oakes was not at the feast, though I saw him in Gray's Inn Road last Thursday. He too has reached a critical climacteric. He left his wife a couple of years ago, but it was a photo-finish: she was halfway out of the door herself. He decided to lead the full, honest, liberated life and has been in a state of despair ever since. He spends much of his time, and his budget, on the telephone to his ladies, asking them, in a purely speculative and disinterested way, why they are fucking other people. He wears form-fitting blue turtlenecks, but hasn't a great deal of form to fit. Having lost weight in all the wrong places, he resembles a length of sausage bought from a *charcutier* in which you are at liberty to insert your own knots, if you ever get round to it. He assured me that it was all true about Jeremy Thorpe. He has heard so many amazing stories that he is beginning to make notes of them. Considering how long he has been in Fleet Street, he can hardly be accused of being quick on the down-take.

One of his stories: when John Stonehouse was first made a minister, he asked a lady political correspondent to dinner at the Mirabelle. During the meal, he put his hand on her knee (one does not, it seems, look for unusual initiatives from members of the government) and said he thought he was now entitled to a mistress, so what about it? Since he had a *pied-à-terre* with red sheets ('Useful if you've got the curse,' the political lady was reported to have said), the smart couple coupled smartly between them. The flat was furnished from the G-Plan catalogue and sported a payphone. When Stonehouse went off to the ministry the next morning, he left the lady in bed. She called 'all her friends', so Philip said, and gave them three guesses where she was. When they had had their three, she said, 'No, I'm in John Stonehouse's bed, calling you from his payphone.' Hard to say which of the two sounds the more repulsive.

Hugh Trevor-Roper, in dark grey suit and with a silk scarf as a sling, drifted towards the dry buffet. Taller than I remembered, I asked if he had once worn spectacles repaired with adhesive tape. He denied it, in the Regius Professorial voice that needs no volume to drown others. He has a strange nose, straight with a sort of bracket at the end, as if to prevent his spectacles from sliding into the soup. With small eyes, and the pinkness of a pig who has gone up in the world, he is married to the daughter of an earl. I asked him if he hadn't been an examiner at Charterhouse in 1948 or 9. I had a distinct memory of his advising me not to attempt verse into verse translation in my scholarship, rightly, no doubt. I had the idea that he was a practising OC, but he said he had disliked Charterhouse. He had been a Daviesite, under a clergyman called Allen, the most reactionary man in the school (that must have taken some doing), but he was torn between disgust and gratitude: he had been very well taught, especially by 'the Uncle', A.L. Irvine.

He resented the indifference with which the school had greeted his ascension to the Regius Professorship. When the Uncle died, H.T.-R. sent word that he was coming to the memorial service. He was not pleased when there was no red carpet. No one addressed a single word to the professor all the time he was there. He was, he said, surprised when I told him of the prevalence of Carthusian anti-Semitism. He is a supporter of Zionism, but I wonder if it's not because he wishes to be disembarrassed of the Jews.

Trevor-Roper's still small voice expects others to fall silent before it. Not all Carthusians are bad, he said. For instance the ambassador to Spain. T.-R. and his Lady wife were on their way to London airport and dropped by the Spanish embassy, to see their friend the Spanish ambassador and found his British *homologue* there on a courtesy call. The OC H.E. asked how they proposed to get about in Spain. 'We shall use the buses.' 'Oh you don't want to do that.' The ambassadorial Rolls Royce and driver were sitting idle in Madrid. 'And there and then he wrote out a chitty for us to have use of both during our stay. As a consequence, we saw the whole of Spain from the back of a Rolls Royce. I know a lot of ambassadors, Etonians, charming people, and I can't see any of them doing a thing like that. This chap wasn't a fashionable ambassador at all, but that's what he did and I shan't forget it. He was a Carthusian.'

I told T.-R. of George Turner's refusal to allow me to sit for the closed scholarship to Christchurch, and mentioned Robin J., for whom it was held open instead. He remembered R.J. well. His parents had refused to disclose their income, an essential prelude, in those days, to being eligible for a scholarship. They were hostile to R. going to Oxford and chose unsubtle means to prevent it. When Charterhouse advertised R.'s exceptional merits, the House, where Trevor-Roper was Censor, agreed exceptionally, perhaps uniquely, to pay the entire cost of Robin's university career. 'He let me down very badly,' T.-R. said. 'He got into a very odd set and he went to the bad. I'm not sure if they were homosexual, but they were certainly no good at all.' His bitterness suggested that there was a particular moral delinquency in making *him* look a fool. I was quick to denounce George Turner, but T.-R. recalled that Robin's housemaster had been his most fervent referee. That would be my own, Harry March, who was also Robin's form master.

Robin was an admirer of uncomplicated virility. He was quite a good boxer, but admiration for the other, and the desire for his admiration, made him just slightly, fatally, subservient to the force of his opponent's will. He was clever, but not very clever; here again he had a desire to please which made him smile too quickly, keener to be *among* clever people than to lead them. He was also a lover of low life, though he disliked getting dirty. He was a watcher. Was he really a bodyguard in South America? He boasted of it, with a disarmed grin, at the Plaza in New York in 1968, wearing a white mackintosh. He had been supposed to meet us at the airport but failed to show. He offered unlikely excuses.

Trevor-Roper's idea of good and bad need not be a universal standard. What is interesting about Robin, for me, is my wilfully blinkered observation of what yet remains clear. I knew that he was untrustworthy and without an honest heart, yet I wanted to trust him, and have him like me. He was too easy an admirer of strength; that was his weakness. He actually felt other people's muscles. His straight left kept opponents at a distance; he fought to preserve his profile, a narcissist keen to avoid anyone throwing a rock into his pool. Yet I wrote in my first notebook that I would base a novel on his 'goodness' (*A Wild Surmise* was the belated fulfilment of that intention). What did I think was so good about him? A snobbish toady, he did not lavish his servility on everyone, which gave him an air of discrimination. He did not appear to have mundane lusts; he loved himself too much. He drove himself to physical endurance: he boxed, he ran, he played games; and was easily in school second elevens. Yet there was something laborious in his facility. The same applied to his schoolwork: he seemed sophisticated (and recommended Auden's *Age of Anxiety* to me), but he never came top. Without March, he might not have achieved anything much. He ingratiated himself by making it seem that his approval and his company were hard to win. He smiled too much; the smile implied that he knew more dirt than he would disclose. He connived with dissidence, but did not himself dissent. The only other Lockite of my year with intellectual affectations, he was, like Jonathan Miller, a photophobe who went straight for the limelight. I brought him the offer to play Hamlet in the school play like a ploughboy running with the dictatorship to Cincinnatus. He hesitated and he grabbed. He made any act of ambition seem like a reluctant concession to duty. When I found myself in a ghetto of one, he took no part in my persecution, but he also abstained from any hint of blacklegging against my enemies. He was one of the first to prove, with a wink, that the worst was over, but his mild gestures of dissociation from Gladstone and co. were accompanied by genial menace: careful, or I might say something. I put his words in Bill Bourne's mouth in *An Early Life*.

The most honest way of explaining how I misread him, if I did, is to examine my own motives. He appeared in many ways to be what I should have liked to be. He was clean, he bore a faintly Jewish name (Tony Jordan, in the classical sixth, *was* a Jew) and yet he had a straight-nosed profile. He was quite clever (he was in the scholars' form, though not a scholar), but he was not egregiously so. He could insinuate himself in the common herd without losing his air of *sérieux*; he was bright and he was also good at games (spoey, as Carthusians used to say), a good actor, but not theatrical. Good-looking, he was not brazen or effeminate. If he was attracted to handsome males, I imagine it was because he wished to belong *among* them, not because he desired them, though he enjoyed teasing them. I cannot persuade myself that I did not like him. He was a loner who liked company. An aggressive pacificist, he preferred 'estate work' to being in the J.T.C. Did he once tell me that he had a half-brother who was a practising hoodlum and later went to gaol? Was it his timid wish to ingratiate himself with, and disarm, that dangerous older brother that impelled him to admire what he also dreaded, muscular masculinity? He had a sister, with a name of heroic ill-omen, of whose beauty he might have been happy to boast, but she was uncomfortably married to a man (in Bristol) old enough to be her father. Considerably bludgeoned by fortune, Robin had confected a plausible personality; to avoid questions, he became an interested inquisitor of others. Quick with sporting statistics, he supported Hampshire (he lived in *Bourne*mouth) and had a singular passion for a batsman who played for Canford (was his name I.P. Campbell?) and was capable of prodigious hitting. Hitting, that was what he admired. Jessop was another of his heroes. He was enraptured by Joe Louis having split Max Schmeling's kidney with a punch. Schmeling *screamed*. How that worked on his imagination!

I was surprised, years later, to hear that he has a manuscript 'shopping a publisher' and even more so when it failed to find one. Something in him had *almost* intimidated me: I was ready to believe him a genius. He acted as if he knew your secret, but that it was safe with him. Was this the sign of his strength, or of his weakness? If he was pleased to be threatening, a smiling menace, he was happy to be appeased. It rejoiced him to divine weakness in others, just as it did to feel their muscles (he did this literally grinning). He gave an impression of poverty, but at the same time he indicated that his family was – as it may have been – extraordinarily wealthy. Was his half-brother's fortune disreputably gained? His father too had, he hinted, made his money in no very comely style. He excited a sort of suspicious pity (the suspicion being that it was wasted on him). He spoke in an acceptable accent; he aroused no snobbish animosity; yet there was something not quite right about him. When he had half-a-crown it was a surprise, yet for all his ascetic manner he seemed involved in life at a different level, of somehow corrupt knowledge, which made it seem that he was *pretending* to be a public schoolboy, that he had a sense of things – I can see him looking at that half-crown in the palm of his hand – unlike that of the ordinary Carthusian. Money meant something different to him.

Suppose there was in him (and I think it's true) a struggle between decency – whatever that means – and corruption, whatever that does. He longs to escape from the mercenary mess of his family, in which the desire for gold is paramount. His mother has married, for money, a man who 'loves' her, but cannot express love except through the medium of money. The frigid lady/whore corrupts the mercenary man by making money their only 'language': it speaks for him and to her. They have a beautiful daughter whom her mother trains so to distrust men (and their filth) that the daughter too sells herself to an older man. The father's money has been earned through legitimately brutal means, but he has refused to allow his family to enjoy it; it is of his essence, and he keeps it, with corrupt fidelity, to please only his wife.

He has a son by an earlier marriage, or an earlier woman: the criminal of whom Our Hero knows nothing during the first part of his life. The criminal too makes a fetish of money, to prove himself to the father who has rejected him (or perhaps used him) and even – perhaps – to seduce his father's wife. The son's criminality is a kind of vocation, without limits: there is nothing he might not do.

Now imagine the plight of the 'clean' son, his faith in sporting manliness, in never hitting below the belt, in all the proprieties, in honouring the highest standards. And then his horror of acknowledging openly what he 'knows', the pull of money and sex. He has one hope of escape into the light: the University, though he fears that he lacks the intellectual distinction which might gain him a deserved place. He cannot rely on his qualities; the competition is too fierce. His father is against his going to Oxford. He won't pay the bills, he won't even disclose his income so that the state, or the college, might pay the boy's fees. What now? The Closed Scholarship is the only way up and out. But there is one other dangerously strong candidate, who must somehow be disqualified. The only means of escaping corruption is to become corrupt. The strong candidate must be revealed: Our Hero might try to save his rival from a false allegation by revealing it to their common housemaster. He must, of course, protest honourably when the housemaster takes the allegation seriously. 'This is the last thing I wanted to do', etc. There remains the problem of his father's refusal to fill in the form declaring his income. How can such small-minded spite be allowed to remain a crippling obstacle? The only answer is to corrupt the house/form-master in such a way that he is persuaded to advise the college to waive the rules and, in a case of unique merit, undertake the full expense of admitting a remarkable student. Our Hero attains heavenly deliverance from a corrupt world by himself becoming vile. He has had, in the course of seducing (at the least beguiling) his housemaster, to make himself unfit – in his own eyes – for the bliss it has won him.

The boy's knowingness becomes clear only when he meets his housemaster, 'by chance', in Italy during the Long Vac. In languorous contempt and joy, the boy volunteers the kisses which the other's advocacy deserves. The betrayal of the 'faith' his college has had in him becomes the next necessity in order, once again, to free himself from the burden of his own 'sin' in having obtained entrance to it. New, worse sins must be committed. And so he becomes... whatever he becomes. Flight into darkness is a confirmation of something repressed by an ambition which he now sees as malign. What a *relief* to be true, at last, to a character he dreaded for so long! Disappointing H. T.-R. becomes a way of breaking the new, golden chains which he has forged for himself, of quitting the horror that possessed him when he realised that he had sold his soul in order to go to heaven. Of all the charmless characteristics of the damned, what is more disgusting (*and* understandable, finally) than a man's urge to be avenged on his benefactors? They stand between him and himself.

Robin J. was, in fact, taught, very ably, by an old German refugee, Dr Gerstenberg (his initials were E.A., I seem to remember). A scene in which R. goes to tea with the wise, sad old Jew and listens, with temporary sympathy, to the story of his eviction from the little town where he was a happy, respected schoolmaster. Then Our Hero returns to his house and witnesses, with a polluting thrill, the humiliation of his only academic rival, his better. Oh the secret complicity of the observer! What a mystery of gorgeous dread fills his dreams, and stiffens his cock! The thrill of indifference enables him to offer himself, his apparent spiritual fineness (all *agape!*), to his repressed, 'unselfish' housemaster. The latter's purity feeds on dreams of redemption so keenly that he must find, and not realise that he is seeking, the corruption from which he recoils (this is not, of course, merely sexual). For this reason, he, like R., relishes the persecution of the Jew, for it seems to count against his preferred candidate's rival that he is the kind of person (never say Jew) who attracts hostility. The oldest crime of the Jew is that he is persecuted. (Hence, 'People don't like him,' said Jack Lambert of Michael, as if that proved something, and not his genius.) In the actual world of the 1930s, Jews were barred from entry into Great Britain and the USA unless they could produce affidavits of their moral cleanliness signed by the very authorities from whom they were fleeing for their lives.

The housemaster, honouring the rule that the boys were autonomous on their 'side' of the house, allows the sadism of the boys to develop almost to (say) murderous proportions before, with a thrill of regret, he prevents their (metaphorical, *disons*) crucifixion of the Yid. How easy to imagine R. carrying to the lonely old Herr Doktor E.A.G. the sweet and terrible news that the bacillus of anti-Semitism is alive and well in boys of the post-war generation. E.A.G. in his hat and with his silly little dog (which, in the novel, will be 'inadvertently' killed by R., who tries to save it from the traffic on Godalming Hill and frightens it under the wheels of a lorry) always had the air of a man hurrying to catch a train which had already left, of someone served with inadequate notice to quit. 'Vell,' he used to say at the end of a lesson, 'zat's zis.' One could ascribe to him some of the characteristics of the young Wittgenstein: the sadism which expresses sublime impatience with the lazy flesh, a self-scourging visited on those who refuse to think.

Harry March and E.A.G. were colleagues in the Modern Languages department. Imagine the unspoken dialogue between the old man, who had no right to comment on the running of H.A.M.'s house, and the lip-licking sadist who believes that it is right to let savage events take their course (a little God honouring the free will he has granted, that's H.A.M. in a Christian light).

I should need to site this story with precision. The ambitions of Robert Birley ('*Sir* Robert' as H.C. Iredale used sardonically to call him, when he was still Mr) fit neatly into the scheme. The great headmaster, his head turned by the main chance, agrees to go to Germany to arbitrate on the reinstatement, or not, of academics who served under Hitler, and fails to notice what was happening at home. (In fact, 'Bags' Birley proved a gullible censor, and was a poor judge of the moral merit of German professors, whose smoothness counted for more than their actual records under or with the Nazis.) After a brief interregnum under the amiable J.C. 'Tommo' Thomson, George Turner returned from Africa, borne on a fantasy of 'native' gratitude, to accept a headmastership he neither sought nor deserved. The tepid timidity of England could not have acquired a more apt symbol. Turner fell easily for H.A.M.'s (and R.'s) plot; he was almost as much a stranger as poor old Gerstenberg. He had to pretend to scholarship he did not possess, a Galba obliged to give a sovereign impression. Fear was his ermine. He dreaded the post-war world in which the natives threatened to become restless.

R. could well become a mercenary soldier (nice role for the *quondam* estate worker), aping the brother he cannot match and always feared. He is arrested and condemned to die in a fly-blown little ex-colony. How did he ever come to be involved in so igno-minious a role? The narrator might be a Jewish solicitor (the one-time rival for that scholarship) who is amazed to see his 'saintly' (he still believes) old schoolfellow in a news story read casually on an evening train. The Jew travels out to Christ knows where (still theoretically a British protectorate) to see if there is anything he can do. Now *he* is the spectator of a man in genuine danger. How does he feel about it? He makes himself dangerously obtrusive (protected perhaps by some diplomatic warrant from H.M.G.) but cannot secure a reprieve. He stays to see the execution (*because he doesn't want to*). Our Hero has a strange smile on his lips as he faces the firing squad. He seems to be saying, 'At last!'

A further (earlier) ingredient: the beautiful sister is liberated from the vile luxury of her nice husband's tutelage by a strange incident. A burglar breaks into the house and kills her husband when he 'courageously confronts the intruder' (*Western Daily Post*). She remarries a young engineer, with whom she goes (despite her misgivings) to the same African ex-colony to which her brother later goes to find his death.

It is delectable to suggest that the 'intruder' is the rogue half-brother and, by implication, R. himself, since he suggests 'laughingly' that his brother-in-law's rich house could be a soft touch for a practised burglar...

In Africa, the sister's new, happy husband is killed by some drunken clown-soldier in an absurd incident and she is smuggled out by a black doctor who has lost faith in the Revolution which has made him a fugitive from, say, Algeria (a 'fallen' Fanon). Her return to England undoes the marriage of her brother, to whom she confesses that she has been the mistress of the black doctor. Might she and her brother end up in bed, in a rapture of contempt for all 'morality'? His attempt to reconcile himself to propriety (which has resulted in impotence on his honeymoon) is abandoned in a furious passion for his sister. The increasing violence of their passion, and the risks they take to indulge it, amount to a cumulative and prolonged suicide pact. It would be nice if the narrator were to have met them both, by chance, during this orgiastic period, in which, of course, it would be their pleasure to present themselves to him as either a 'nice' brother and sister having tea or (why not?) a married couple doing the same.

The sister commits suicide (or may have done so) and R., in a typical transference, blames not himself but the black doctor, which explains why he goes to Africa. Intent on revenge, and excited by it, he finds himself so fascinated by the man he is literally out to kill that he is mesmerised by him and his disabused (and fearless) intelligence. The doctor tells R. that money is the only thing that will prevent Africa becoming a bloodbath: corruption alone will bring salvation. R. sees that he is superfluous to any moral or immoral scheme and joins the futile rebellion which leads to his arrest and happy execution.

After Jack's goodbye cruise, there was a petty comedy about transport. None of the pundits cared to share a taxi with any of the others. Trevor-Roper was heading for Sotheby's; Piccadilly was not a close enough fit for him. Lacking a Rolls and a driver, he sailed off, with his silk sling as a spinnaker, in the direction of Maida Vale. Jacquetta Hawkes and Raymond Mortimer were uncomfortably pressed into the same conveyance which, to satisfy them, had to drive off in different directions. Desmond Shawe-Taylor, as whitely beardless as a cue ball, had a *Sunday Times* car and driver to rush him to his evening clothes: he was going to Glynebourne. Dilys, staunch as a Greek donkey, set off on neat heels, to prove her spirit.

Wheelchair-bound, Harold Hobson failed to show. Had it been a basement production of *End Game*, he would have been winched aboard, but he cannot endure to be helped into awkward spaces, and cannot help himself. John Peter hopes for his job. The new drama critic is not to be announced until August ('When I am due to go on holiday,' J.P. said), but the rumour is that Bernard Levin is the likely appointment. Jack does not approve (of what did he ever approve?) and says that it is 'the end of the *Sunday Times* as we know it'. Hitherto all the promotions have been from the cadet corps. The arrival of a fully grown General Officer from outside is evidence of the manager's decision to go, expensively, into the transfer market. J.P. seems unlikely to be chosen. Harry Evans refers to him, Jack promised me, as 'that damned refugee'.

The literary department reminded me of a school house from which last year's dreaded monitors had at last departed. Power had passed by default rather than having been wrested from them. The two Johns, Whitley and Peter, are trying on their new footsteps. To prove their edge, they need some blood on their hands. Philip Oakes, with his dated vanity, is the likely victim: he makes too many outside phone calls to women who are 'fucking someone else'. If one is going to ride roughshod, it's unwise to do it in bare feet: no one likes to be trampled by corns. Neither Philip nor Alan Brien is well liked. And with Godfrey Smith in the balloon, someone is clearly to have to be tossed out before buoyancy is achieved.

She has the startling looks of someone who is never quite as plain as one remembers.

I had to face up to my meeting in Red Lion Square to discuss American tax with Bernard and Herbert Alpert (no Tijuana brass about him) and A.N. Other (Alpert's sidekick). I visited my dread on them by assuring them, before they had time to patronise me, that they were my idea of a dull afternoon. Alpert has been thorough, if dilatory: like so many slow coaches, he is prompt with his hooter. The whole business may cost me, he warned, $150,000. Well, the truth is that I have been lavishly paid for *Roses, Roses...* and would scarcely feel a partition from most of it: I would still earn a living wage. But then there is also the English Revenue to deal with. Prometheus had an easy life: only *one* eagle pecked his liver.

My presence was, in truth, superfluous: I had no information to which the others were not privy. I aired my grievances more than my graces. How seriously was I to take them, these three considerate private enterprise tax-collectors, leeches dressed as crutches? Oh, they *were* boring as they narrowed the world to dimensions they could encircle. Alpert looked leaner and less avaricious, a vulture in a lightweight suit, than he had when he called on us at Lagardelle. He was uneasy at the memory: 'Not a good day,' he said.

Afterwards, H.A., Bernard and I went to a wine bar in Lamb's Conduit Street. I glanced up and saw a familiar face: Claire Tomalin. She wore a white shirt and a longish skirt, a scarf over her clever head. She was alone, a yard from the bar, pale in the last of the dusty sunlight, slim, calm, uncertain. I left my legal company – oh, so gladly – and went up to her. 'What the hell are you doing here?'

'Freddie!'

'What're you drinking?'

'I'm not. I'm meeting someone from the office. We arranged to come separately because there's someone we didn't particularly want to come with.'

The *New Statesman* office was just around the corner. Very soon, Claire's 'someone' came in: Martin Amis, a short, pleasant-looking boy of twenty-seven, with innocent gigolo eyes and an air of candid *arrivisme*. I bought them drinks and told M.A. that I had been reading one of his books (I believe there are two), or rather (undue candour) bits of one of them. He was prepared to be silkily wounded, but I said that actually I *had* been reading *The Rachel Papers* and had enjoyed it. 'I only said I'd read bits because I didn't want to spoil you.' He seemed placated, the modest glow-worm, Gary Glitter in mufti.

I left them to hatch their office plot (if that is was it was) and returned to say goodbye to H.A., whose expensive briefcase was more interesting than he was. Boredom rose in my throat like sour soup. If I hurried, I could catch the 7.30 to Colchester. I paused at Claire's table and asked whether she would have some tea if I came by the next morning.

'Coffee,' Martin Amis said.
'Socialists,' I said.

I went to Moss Bros for my tails and boiled shirt for the Mansion House dinner, then to the *New Statesman*, which offers a glossy white and red face to the street. The place seemed understaffed, like a ferry in which one has overslept a call to abandon ship. The only girl on the ground floor said, 'Claire? Three flights up'. I swear that I was seeking neither a book nor a woman, yet there was a certain pumping of adrenalin. Was this a brothel or an examination hall? Claire seemed in more of a tizz than I: the girl had to go and buy some coffee.

New books slouched on the shelves. The desk was thick with letters and open volumes. The top letter was from the drama critic, Benedict Nightingale, whose wordage had been reduced. He cut a very grammatical figure, referring to an imminent 'luncheon' at which the matter would be aired.

I mentioned to Claire that I had a correspondence with Nick's father. 'It's very sad,' she said, 'he's taken up spiritualism.' Stern rationalism, logical pride, forbade C. from indulging in sentimental magic. Her whole life, one feels, is devoted to proving that she is worthy; yet, she is always telling me, she has no faith in her own cleverness. She is such a *wingless* bird. Is she happy at the *Statesman*? She sighs: it's a weekly battle.

She had been thinking about a book for me to review. She had read my account of soliciting a job from Karl Miller, and smiled; she certainly made the room brighter than K. had cared to. She produced *The Freudian Slip*, of which, she said, she could make nothing at all. I paraded my new chains, which forbade me to stray from the *Sunday Times* without the appropriate exeat, but I pouched Sebastiano Timpanaro's (in the end very interesting) study of Freud and his revealing misquotation from the *Aeneid*: Freud omitted *aliquis* from Dido's line '*Exoriare aliquis nostris ex ossibus ultor*', an omission of which Timpanaro makes a Marxist meal. Dido's reference is to Hannibal, who was Freud's avenging Semite, though the Rome on which Freud dreamed of taking vengeance was no doubt that of the Roman Church. Timpanaro suggested that Freudian guilt might as well be about the exploitative role of the bourgeoisie as about Oedipal ambitions.

Claire told me that after our chance meeting in the wine bar, she said to Martin 'Isn't Freddie handsome?'

'Well,' he said, 'he certainly looks very fit.'

Claire and I walked down to the Strand together. She finds comfort in the Cambridge connection; she likes to think that she has known people for a long time. I said that I had no such sensation, but I was not the point. Karl made her cry, she said, but meant no harm. 'You're no longer the same giggling armful,' he said one day, finding her in glum spirits. Claire thinks of me, she said, as 'extremely loyal', a curious quality to ascribe to a writer who, more than once, has sought to render her ridiculous. Yet the target I am attacking is never quite the Claire I meet. She has an almost declared capacity to accept pain; she even seems rapacious for it. Can Karl be being kind in his unkindness?

The writer/producer. He has been at the big table and now, reduced to a modest one, shows no ill humour. Like a reformed convict, retired from the *milieu* but still in touch with old confederates and primed with sly intelligence, he seems to be going straight, in straitened circumstances, but you never know when he will be tempted to join in some *coup*. He is friendly and he is limited; shrewd but not clever. His cynicism alerts one to the vulgarity of the world, and to the actuality of its values and commerce. One is as glad to be with as to be parted from him; he is an ideal but not quite desirable companion; some kind of a gentleman, though not an educated one, he is the good loser who never embarrasses you by seeming to have lost *everything*.

To Ealing to see the rough cut of *Rogue Male*. I arrived untypically late, expecting to watch the film alone, but found Clive Donner and Jocelyn and others afraid to begin without me. Sorry, sorry. The picture was long and needs the screws tightening, but the performances are excellent, especially O'Toole. I never greatly admired him before, but here, whoever else was on the screen, only he was. He plays Hunter with a sense of honour which redeems the dated idea of the gentleman: bugger Hitler, is his attitude, but never fuck him.

Afterwards, I sat with them in a conference room and, although feeling rather ill, and wadded with Kleenex like a baby steatopygous with nappy, analysed the weaknesses of the movie with an orderly skill that would have done credit to, oh, a supermarket manager, or Irving Thalberg: *même combat*, to please the customers. Exophthalmic Jocelyn interrupted with a long irrelevance; having slept with more directors and actors than anyone else in the room gave her rare confidence. I liked her better when it came out that she was a Catullus fan; I promised to send her a few of my versions.

Mainly I was concerned only to put Clive on the right lines for the next three weeks and then get to the Mansion House for the Arts banquet to which B. and I have been convoked.

I raced to Seymour Walk and realised, as I threaded Earl's Court, that I had omitted to bring any cufflinks from Langham. Who sells cufflinks at 6.15 in Earl's Court? If only one could buckle one's cuffs with ready-made Chinese food! I stopped at the top of Seymour Walk and rang the bell of Commander Cresswell's house. Did he still live there? The door was opened by a bearded man, civilly dressed, courteous but hectic-eyed. Was there by any chance a pair of cufflinks in the house I could borrow?

'*Cufflinks?*' He greeted the expression like one he had yet to encounter in his phrase book. He went away and came back with a lower-deck figure, as red in the face as if he had been labouring to get up steam, and with a suspicious scowl. He was a factotum who could not do all that much because he lacked all the top joints of his fingers and thumbs. The stumps stuck out, cruelly pollarded. Frostbite? Burns? A chainsaw? Had he been with Cresswell on some brave convoy? The Commander would be back next day. There were no spare cufflinks in the house.

I rang our neighbours' bell, people whom we had never known and now should never know, since we were selling the house to pay taxes. The lady produced the necessary in no time at all. I seemed fully equipped.

9.6.76. My rented dress shirt was the wrong size and threatened to throttle me. We enlarged the buttonhole to the limit and attached the mooring loop to my trousers and hoped that it would not roll up and make me absurd, but I lacked the white-tied insouciance of a man about to go to town. Should we park in the vicinity and take a cab? There was little about, so we drove to the front door. Was it the right night? A flunkey indicated where guests were entering, by a side door. An amiable policeman promised that the car would be all right in Queen Victoria Street.

Ah privilege! Ah amateur dramatics! By not timing it at all, we had timed it well and joined a decorated, but rarely decorative, queue in order to be announced. Passing between two short rows of Honourable Artillery Company men, we approached the Ruritanian thrones in front of which the Lord Mayor, Sir Lindsay Ring and his lady greeted us: 'Our greetings to you,' I believe he said to me.

Soon we were among the pillars of the vestibule, being offered the red or the white. John and Anne Woolf were nearby and we saluted them as enthusiastically as if we had encountered them in a godawful hotel in Yugoslavia. We were soon into dinner and found ourselves below the salt at a dull table, bracketed by city dignitaries in pie-dish ruffles and decorations. An orchestra played in the high gallery: works of dusty charm to launch our little cruise into the past. My only accessible conversant had, of course, never heard of me. Though *The Glittering Prizes* meant something to him, he watched only – hoho! – 'intellectual programmes like *Cannon*'; my father's kind of joke.

He was about seventy and showed me his hands to prove that he had been a working builder. He had taken over the business from his father, and had sold it, a few years ago, to a large company on whose board he then sat. Tired of board meetings, he started a new little business, for his son, and it was doing rather well. He was genial and tough.

Under the high vaulted roof, sprigged with plaster rosettes, where pretence of historical piety kept other pretentiousnesses out of the way, the society of the successful agreed to find life a game of snakes and ladders in which even the snakes could slither upwards. We ate fish mousse, middle-aged asparagus, chicken escalopes that might have been veal and what had the shape of cassata ice cream, but was plain vanilla. It went down easily enough behind my strained stud.

The speeches were unembarrassing, except for Beryl Grey's prolonged sincerities, but somewhat uneasy. When the English pay tribute to the arts or to scholarship, it is with the eloquence of an Arab toasting Zionism. My little dinner companion, decked with orders like the front entrance of an unpromising AA hotel, was gallant with civility, but how he wished he had been face to face with a real artist such as Frankie Howerd or Eric or Ernie! How I wish I had! His grey hair was brushed straight back and the blue eyes promised a fight if crossed. We did discover that he and Doris (his wife of thirty-nine years, the last thirty of them crippled with polio) were addicted to the Dordogne and familiar with the Hôtel Scholly. Hearing of our house in the region, he said that I must have a good head for business. Was he suggesting that I looked Jewish, or merely recruiting me to a club of which he had long been a scrutineer?

Beetle's neighbour was a Mr Deputy, a magistrate, a prison administrator, a confident, energetic character who thought she should be a JP. He had to be at Wandsworth prison at 10 a.m. He was chairman of the Visiting Committee which decides who shall be put on bread and water, or whatever the punishment diet is these days.

Lord Blake made the best speech. He had a pretty quotation from Disraeli, about a terrible banquet where all the courses were cold. When they brought the champagne, Dizzy said, 'Thank God for something warm at last!'

We trooped back into the foyer, ogling the famous or interesting faces to whom, given a luckier batting order, we might have been adjacent. Was that really Freddie Ayer standing there, with his wife, smiling at the unsmiling void? I had never met him, though we had been promised his company (*en passant*, at Lagardelle, when Clive and accompanying friends, including A.J.A. and Dee, might have needed a bed). I went up to him, unsure whether it was really he. God, how the *enfant terrible* has aged! He looked like an old fool in a college review. We saw him on TV not so long ago and he had been the image (not *very* nice) of middle-aged alacrity. Now he seemed like old clothes from which someone had borrowed the hanger; money-bags under his eyes and a complexion like raspberry mousse. The eminent iconoclast, could it be? It was.

I dropped my earnest compliments in his cup: '*Language, Truth and Logic*,' I burbled, 'is the *De Rerum Natura* of our lifetime.'

'Very nice of you to say so. It still brings me in a thousand a year.'

Beetle mentioned how proud Victor Gollancz had been to publish it.

'And yet, you know, he never really believed in it.' He went on to say that he was writing his autobiography.

'Oh well,' I said, 'there's nothing like a lucid style when one has something to hide.'

Index